The State of Indepen

G000269410

Exploring the most significant challenges facing independent schools today, this book asks leading figures from education, economics, politics, philosophy and the arts to give their views on how independent schools can adapt to rapidly changing markets which see them scrutinised as never before.

Acknowledging the independent sector as a vital and growing part of the global education system, this book explores how schools are to respond to financial, moral, pastoral and academic challenges, and so ensure their own survival, and the futures of the children they educate. Breaking a complex and varied field down into ten clear areas of analysis, essays written by leading education experts tackle the key challenges faced by independent schools around the world. Commentators consider the issues created by the upward trend of educating international students, question the extent to which independent schools have echoed societal movements towards greater access, diversity and gender fluidity, and provide first-hand insight into the experiences of staff, pupils and parents involved in the everyday functioning and longer-term development of the independent sector.

A health check on this most controversial of sectors, this book will enlighten and inform not only those working in independent schools today, but anyone interested in education, and will make an important contribution to a bigger debate about the place of independent schools at a time of political, economic and societal uncertainty.

David James teaches English, and is Deputy Head at Bryanston School, UK. He has worked in independent schools for over 20 years. He is also an editor and author.

Jane Lunnon is Head of Wimbledon High School, London, UK. She has taught in independent schools for over 20 years.

The State of Independence

Key Challenges Facing Private Schools Today

Edited by David James
and Jane Lunnon

LONDON AND NEW YORK

First published 2019
by Routledge
2 Park Square, Milton Park, Abingdon, Oxon OX14 4RN

and by Routledge
52 Vanderbilt Avenue, New York, NY 10017

Routledge is an imprint of the Taylor & Francis Group, an informa business

British Library Cataloguing-in-Publication Data
A catalogue record for this book is available from the British Library

Library of Congress Cataloging-in-Publication Data
Names: James, David (David Arthur), editor. | Lunnon, Jane, editor.
Title: The state of independence : key challenges facing private schools today /
edited by David James and Jane Lunnon.
Description: Abingdon, Oxon : New York, NY : Routledge, 2019. |
Includes bibliographical references and index.
Identifiers: LCCN 2018056688 (print) | LCCN 2019000430 (ebook) |
ISBN 9781351139489 (eb) | ISBN 9780815352402 (hb : alk. paper) |
ISBN 9780815352419 (pb : alk. paper) | ISBN 9781351139489 (ebk)
Subjects: LCSH: Private schools. | School management and organization.
Classification: LCC LC47 (ebook) | LCC LC47 .S75 2019 (print) | DDC 371.02–dc23
LC record available at https://lccn.loc.gov/2018056688

ISBN: 978-0-8153-5240-2 (hbk)
ISBN: 978-0-8153-5241-9 (pbk)
ISBN: 978-1-351-13948-9 (ebk)

Typeset in Bembo
by Newgen Publishing UK

Contents

About the editors   viii
About the contributors   x
Acknowledgements   xx

Introduction   1
David James and Jane Lunnon

1   **The pastoral challenge**   5

Julie Johnson 8
Rachel Kelly 11
Dick Moore 13
Emma Robertson 16
Anthony Seldon 18

2   **The academic challenge**   21

Helen Pike 24
Briony Scott 26
Joseph Spence 29
Kevin Stannard 31
Ian Warwick 33

3   **The junior challenge**   37

Jane Cameron 40
Phillip Evitt 42
Richard Foster 44

Ralph Lucas 46
Ben Thomas 49

4   The financial challenge   **54**

Stephen Crouch 57
John Edward 59
Heather McGregor 61
James Tooley 64
David Woodgate 66

5   The access challenge   **70**

Ian Davenport 72
Patrick Derham 75
David Ejim-McCubbin 77
Nick Hillman 81
Barnaby Lenon 83
Justine Voisin 86

6   The diversity challenge   **90**

Emmanuel Akpan-Inwang 92
Jaideep Barot 95
Jenny Brown 97
Nick Dennis 99
Mary Myatt 102

7   The gender challenge   **107**

Jenny Allum 110
Natasha Devon 112
Richard Hoskins 115
Fionnuala Kennedy 117
Lucy Pearson 119

8   The innovation challenge   **122**

Sean Dagony-Clark 126
Eimer Page 129
Dominic A. A. Randolph 132

Simon Walker 134
Crispin Weston 137
Ian Yorston 139

9 The international challenge   144

Edward Clark and Helen Wright 147
Justin Garrick 149
Virginia Macgregor 152
Jamie Martin 154
Cameron Pyke 157
Russell Speirs 159
Mark Steed 161

10 The political challenge   165

John Blake 169
Ed Dorrell 171
Estelle Morris 173
Tom Richmond 175
Julie Robinson 178
Mark Scott 180
Roger Scruton 182

Conclusion   187
David James and Jane Lunnon

Index   197

About the editors

David James

David James is a Deputy Head at Bryanston School, a coeducational boarding school in Dorset, in the United Kingdom. He has taught English over 20 years.

He is the author and editor of a number of textbooks and study guides, and writes regularly on educational matters in the UK's national press. He is co-editor of *World Class: Tackling the Ten Biggest Challenges Facing Schools Today*, which was published by Routledge in 2017.

David has been a Teacher in Residence at the UK's Department of Education and has also worked as a Senior School Consultant for the International Baccalaureate Organization. He has been a school inspector for over 10 years.

He was the Director of the Sunday Times Education Festival for eight years, is a Google Certified Teacher and in 2016 was selected to be Riverdale Country School's inaugural Zagat Global Fellow, an initiative instigated to foster international partnerships between schools.

Jane Lunnon

Jane Lunnon has been Head of Wimbledon High School since September 2014, having previously been Deputy Head at Wellington College. She has spent 22 years teaching English in UK Independent schools and her career has involved her in pastoral and academic leadership in a variety of co-educational and single-sex schools. She is also a Governor of two prep schools and a senior independent school and a member of the Royal Shakespeare Company Education Committee.

She helped to set up and run The Sunday Times / Wellington College annual Education Festival and she has run (and spoken at) numerous workshops and conferences including twice at the Global Girls Education Forum in the US. She is secretary of the GSA London Region Heads division and sits on the HMC Universities Committee.

Academic researcher

Lana Crowe is a freelance writer and subeditor. She is currently studying for an MA in Modern Literature and Culture at King's College London, specialising in literary jazz scholarship. Having attended state schools in East London before receiving her BA from the University of Cambridge, she is committed to improving access to top universities and careers in the arts.

About the contributors

I The pastoral challenge

Julie Johnson is a Systemic therapist, HGI psychotherapist working in schools, businesses and private practice with children, adolescence and parents. A leading provider of workshops, clinics and seminars for children, adolescents and parents in London. She also teaches mindfulness and mindfulness self-compassion to children, adolescents, teachers, parents in schools and within the charity sector. She is author of several children's books on issues such as bullying, anger and step families and has contributed to Radio 4 productions e.g. 'Bringing up Britain', and a Radio 4 series on Cyber Bullying and so on. Her most recent book (based on HGI principles) is – *Wellbeing the Essential Guide to my Child's Physical and Mental Health*

Rachel Kelly is an author. Her memoir about her experience of life-threatening depression 'Black Rainbow' was a *Sunday Times* bestseller in 2014. She has since written about the holistic approach which helped her recover and runs workshops on wellbeing in schools, universities and companies. She is an official ambassador for Rethink Mental Illness and SANE.

Dick Moore is an English teacher, rugby coach and for nearly 23 years a Head, Dick's greatest challenges have come in his role as the father of four often errant children. Dick has spoken at over 350 schools, colleges, universities, conferences and businesses around the world. What he lacks in clinical or academic pedigree he makes up for in passionate conviction that things must change!

Emma Robertson is the award-winning co-founder of leading digital wellbeing organisation Digital Awareness UK, which works in schools and companies around the world, helping young people to survive and thrive online. Her research explores digital behavioural trends amongst teens and she has written for publications from *The Times* to *Independent Education Today*. Emma can regularly be seen on the news campaigning for more action to be taken to protect young people online.

Anthony Seldon is Vice-Chancellor of the University of Buckingham since 2015, is one of Britain's leading contemporary historians, educationalists, commentators and political authors. He was a transformative Head for 20 years, first of Brighton College and then Wellington College. He is author or editor of over 35 books on contemporary history, including the inside books on the last four Prime Ministers, was the co-founder and first director of the Institute for Contemporary British History, is co-founder of Action for Happiness, honorary historical adviser to 10 Downing Street, UK Special Representative for Saudi Education, a member of the Government's First World War Culture Committee, was chair of the Comment Awards, is a director of the Royal Shakespeare Company, the President of IPEN (International Positive Education Network), Chair of the National Archives Trust, is patron or on the board of several charities, founder of the Via Sacra Western Front Walk, and was executive producer of the film 'Journey's End'. He appeared on Desert Island Discs in 2016. For the last 15 years he has given all his money from writing and lecturing to charity.

Anthony has three children; his wife of 34 years, Joanna, died of cancer in December 2016.

2 The academic challenge

Helen Pike is Master of Magdalen College School, Oxford. Previously she was Head of South Hampstead High School. She began her career teaching History at Westminster School, and then spent many enjoyable years in teaching and leadership at City of London School, St Paul's School and RGS Guildford. She is also a novelist and editor.

Briony Scott is Principal of Wenona, a Kindergarten to Year 12 independent girls' school, Director of the Alliance of Girls' Schools Australasia (AGSA) and a Director on the Board of the Lung Foundation of Australia.

Joseph Spence is Master of Dulwich College. He was previously Head of Oakham School and Master in College at Eton College.

He co-directs the Southwark Schools Learning Partnership and is a trustee of Place2Be.

Kevin Stannard is Director of Innovation & Learning at the Girls' Day School Trust. Previously he was Director of Education for the University of Cambridge International Examinations, and before that taught for over 20 years.

Ian Warwick was a teacher in inner-city London for 20 years. He set up London Gifted and Talented (LG&T) in 2003. Since then LG&T have directly worked with over 3,500 schools and 12,000 teachers internationally. Ian has trained and keynoted worldwide and published extensively about high challenge in education.

3 The junior challenge

Jane Cameron has been involved in education for most of her working life. After a few years in educational publishing, she turned to nursery education and ran the highly successful Acorn Nursery School in West London for over 30 years. In 2003, she was approached by parents to set up a co-educational prep school. Notting Hill Prep, an accredited Thinking School now in its sixteenth year, is celebrated for its rare ability to preserve and promote the special joy of childhood within a rigorous culture of teaching and learning. Its education, with metacognition and well-being at its heart, is summed up in the school's motto: To Think – To Thrive.

Phillip Evitt is currently Head of Highfield School and has been a prep Head for 20 years. Previously he taught at Monmouth School and Dulwich College. He has been a governor at several prep and senior schools and currently governs at two prep schools.

Richard Foster is Head of Windlesham House School. Previously Head of S. Anselm's School, Bakewell, Derbyshire (1993–2007) and Head of Pembroke House, Kenya (1984–1993), he is one of the most experienced Boarding Prep School Heads in the world. He was on the Executive Committee of The BSA and The IAPS) and is passionate about the merits and benefits of a boarding school education.

Ralph Lucas is Editor of *The Good Schools Guide* since 2000, and a member of the House of Lords since 2000.

Ben Thomas was a Head for 22 years and is now a Principal of Thomas's London Day Schools, a family-run group of co-educational schools. Thomas's educates more than 2,000 children, aged from 2 to 13, in four preparatory schools, one primary academy and a kindergarten, in central London. He is also a parent of three teenage children.

4 The financial challenge

Stephen Crouch is Group Finance & Operations Director at Wellington College, Berkshire in a group which comprises senior and primary, independent and state, day and boarding and UK and international schools. He was previously Managing Director of a global transport economics consultancy.

John Edward is Director of the Scottish Council of Independent Schools – representing mainstream and special needs independent education – having previously worked for 15 years on EU and devolution issues.

Heather McGregor is a professor at Heriot-Watt University and Executive Dean of its graduate school of business. She is known for her long-running column in the *Financial Times* under the pseudonym Mrs Moneypenny, and her bestselling book, *Careers Advice for Ambitious Women*, is available in none languages.

James Tooley is professor of education policy at Newcastle University. His ground-breaking research on low-cost private education in developing countries has won numerous awards. Building on his research, Tooley as entrepreneur has co-founded chains and federations of low-cost private schools, in India, Ghana, Nigeria, Honduras and England.

David Woodgate is Chief Executive of the Independent Schools' Bursars Association. A lawyer by training, he is also a Chartered Banker and has been Chief Executive Officer of three membership organisations. He holds an MBA from Warwick University Business School and is Chairman of Governors of an HMC independent school.

5 The access challenge

Ian Davenport is the founding Chief Executive Officer of the Royal National Children's SpringBoard Foundation, which works with over 100 boarding schools and is the largest bursary charity in the UK. Formerly he was the Head of Blundell's School and a housemaster at Radley College. He is currently a governor of four independent schools and is also an advisor to the DfE, ISC and HMC schools. Ian began his career working at Arthur Andersen and Morgan Stanley.

Patrick Derham is Head of Westminster School. Passionate about widening access he has launched a bursary campaign for the school to become entirely needs 'blind'. In 2003 he set up the Arnold Foundation for Rugby School and was instrumental in the setting up of the SpringBoard Bursary Foundation. He is also Deputy Chairman of Trustees of IntoUniversity and a Trustee of the Gladstone Library.

David Ejim-McCubbin is a Private Secretary for a minister of state at the Department for Education. He was awarded a full bursary to attend Rugby School and studied Law at the University of Brighton before completing a masters at University College London. There his research focused on the influences that the fifteenth-century Christian Reformation had on the political landscape of sixteenth-century Europe. He also currently sits on the board of governors at Grange Primary School in East London and is an ambassador for both the Eastside Young Leaders Academy and the Rugby School Arnold Foundation.

Nick Hillman is the Director of the Higher Education Policy Institute and a former Special Adviser to the Minister for Universities and Science. His academic research has focused on educational history, particularly relations between the state and independent school sectors in the post-war era. He was the runner-up in Cambridge at the 2010 general election and, back in the 1990s, he taught history, including for three years at St Paul's School.

Barnaby Lenon was the Head of Harrow and is currently chairman of the Independent Schools Council. He is author of two recent books, *Much Promise* (about schools which achieve outstanding exam results, often in disadvantaged areas) and *Other People's Children* (about vocational education in England).

Justine Voisin is Chair of Governors of Bridewell Royal Hospital/King Edward's School Witley. The foundation and school mission is to provide bursaries for a boarding education for those whose home circumstances mean they would benefit.

6 The diversity challenge

Emmanuel Akpan-Inwang is the founder and chief executive of Lighthouse, a charity committed to improving the lives of looked after children. Emmanuel is a teacher by background and trained on the Teach First programme between 2011 and 2013.

Jaideep Barot is the Head of Bristol Grammar School. He previously worked in leadership roles at Marlborough College, Westminster School and The Godolphin & Latymer School.

Jenny Brown is Head of St Albans High School. Her English teaching career spans 25 years and six schools and includes stints as Head of English at Channing School and senior leadership at St Paul's Girls' School. She frequently gives speeches at educational festivals, conferences and the Cambridge Union on widening access and leadership in education.

Nick Dennis teaches History and Politics at St Francis' College, Letchworth, where he is also the Director of Studies. Nick is a member of the BAMEed Network which supports the development of teaching staff in independent and state schools from a minority ethnic background.

Mary Myatt is an education adviser, writer and speaker. She works in schools talking to pupils, teachers and leaders about learning, leadership and the curriculum.

7 The gender challenge

Jenny Allum is the Head of SCEGGS Darlinghurst, a position she has held since 1996. She is a Fellow of the Australian College of Educators. In 2011, she was awarded an honorary Doctor of Letters from the University of NSW.

Natasha Devon is a writer and activist who tours the UK and beyond working in an average of three schools and colleges per week to deliver talks and conduct research on mental health, body image, gender and equality. Her best selling book *A Beginner's Guide to Being Mental* was shortlisted for the Hearst Big Book Award in 2018.

Richard Hoskins is a *Sunday Times* top ten bestselling author and criminologist. His book *The Boy in the River* (PanMacmillan

2012) was The Crime Writers' Association Gold medal winner for non-fiction. Richard has investigated over 200 serious crimes for police and other agencies. He is currently completing two further books, one of which explores his transgender journey.

Fionnuala Kennedy is Senior Deputy Head at Wimbledon High School. She has 15 years' experience in the independent sector. She has published articles in *The Daily Telegraph*, the *Evening Standard*, *Tatler* and the *TES*.

Lucy Pearson had a 20-year career in co-educational schools, culminating in eight years as Head of Cheadle Hulme School, Cheshire. In August 2018, Lucy became Head of FA Education, overseeing the qualification and development of coaches throughout the game. She is an independent non-executive director of the England and Wales Cricket Board and cites four cornerstones of interest: education, young people, sport and inclusion.

8 The innovation challenge

Sean Dagony-Clark is the Director of Teacher Training for the Flatiron School, an international coding bootcamp. He previously was the Director of Academic Technology and Chair of Computer Science at Riverdale Country School, where he was honored as a Zagat Global Fellow.

Eimer Page is Director of Global Initiatives and Instructor in English at Phillips Exeter Academy. Her areas of interest include postcolonial literature, cultural competencies and issues of diversity, equity and inclusion in student experiential learning.

Dominic A.A. Randolph became the sixth Head of Riverdale Country School in July 2007. He is a co-founder of The Character Lab and has helped develop, with IDEO, a toolkit for educators on design thinking and the Teacher's Guild. Most recently, he has founded, with colleagues at Riverdale Country School, a new learning design studio, Plussed+ that creates products and services for all schools and a new high school program, nXu education. He also serves on the boards of the International Positive Education Network and the Mastery Transcript Consortium.

Simon Walker is co-founder and Director of Research at STEER, Honorary Fellow at Bristol Graduate School of Education. His research demonstrating the role of steering cognition in mental health and learning, has led to the development of pioneering tools reducing mental health risks and improving learning in more than 30,000 children in the UK.

Crispin Weston is an advocate for better data standards for education technology. He has founded a suppliers' group for improving data interoperability; advised the government agency, Becta; and chaired the British Standards Institute's Committee for IT in education. He continues to write on edtech at www.EdTechNow.net, arguing that only digital technology will solve the endemic underperformance of our education system.

Ian Yorston is Director of Digital Strategy at Radley College in the United Kingdom. He has acquired a reputation as something of a 'guru' in the education sector and now lectures around the world. He aims to encourage change in a sector that is often unhelpfully conservative.

9 The international challenge

Edward Clark is Executive Director of LSC Education and has been in education recruitment since 2006, recruiting leaders for international and UK schools. Prior to launching LSC Education he was Recruitment Director for three other leading search agencies and was previously Principal of a coeducational prep school in the South of England.

Helen Wright is a highly experienced international school leader; a former Head and Vice-Chair of the UK Independent School Council, she currently recruits and coaches leaders across the globe, and is an Associate of LSC Education.

Justin Garrick is Head of Canberra Grammar School, a leading day and boarding school in Australia's national capital. In that role, he has implemented full co-education, introduced the International Baccalaureate at Primary and Senior level, and expanded the School's global opportunities. He was previously Deputy (Academic) at Wellington College in the UK.

Virginia Macgregor is writer of both adult (Little, Brown) and young adult (HarperCollins) fiction. She has published five novels which have been translated into over a dozen languages. Before becoming a full time writer, Virginia taught English and was a housemistress for ten years in three major British boarding schools.

Jamie Martin has spent over a decade advising companies and governments on education in the UK, Middle East and Africa. He is Founder & Chief Executive Officer of Injini, Africa's first Education Technology dedicated incubator programme. Previously, he was Special Adviser to UK Secretary of State for Education Michael Gove, and a management consultant focused on Education at Boston Consulting Group and Deloitte. He has also written on education for *The Sunday Times*, *Guardian*, *TES*, *Standpoint* and *Mail.*.

Cameron Pyke is Deputy Master External at Dulwich College and oversees its educational partnerships both locally and internationally. He also teaches Chinese and Russian History and has published on the music of Benjamin Britten.

Russell Speirs is the Chief Executive Officer and Founder of RSAcademics, an international management consultancy which supports over 250 schools around the world every year. A growing aspect of Russell's own work is in the domain of international education, advising international schools and helping UK schools establish a campus overseas.

Mark Steed is an experienced UK independent school leader who is currently Director of JESS, Dubai. He has a particular interest in how new technologies can be used in education and recently completed a Masters degree researching 'Alternative business models for Secondary Schooling'.

10 The political challenge

John Blake is an education policy expert and former teacher.

Ed Dorrell has been a journalist for nearly 20 years He started out in local and then specialist press, joining the TES in 2008 as news editor before being appointed deputy editor and head of content in 2013. He has also regularly contributed to national newspapers and broadcast media.

Estelle Morris served as a Labour MP and was appointed as Education Minister in the government of Tony Blair. Prior to entering parliament, she taught for 18 years in an inner city comprehensive school. She is now a member of the House of Lords and works on a number of education projects, including as Chair of the Birmingham Education Partnership.

Tom Richmond is a Senior Research Fellow at the Policy Exchange think-tank in Westminster. He has spent 15 years in the world of education across different roles, including six years as a teacher and two years as an advisor to ministers at the Department for Education.

Julie Robinson is the general secretary of the Independent Schools Council, serving the interests of ISC constituent associations and member schools. The ISC undertakes research, data collection and analysis to inform campaigning and messaging on behalf of the sector. Julie is a former teacher and Head.

Mark Scott is the Secretary of the NSW Department of Education and has a distinguished record in public service, education and the media. As leader of one of the largest education systems in the world, Mark has a particular interest in preparing today's students for tomorrow's rapidly changing world.

Roger Scruton is a writer and philosopher who has published more than 40 books in philosophy, aesthetics and politics. He is widely translated. He is a fellow of the British Academy and a Fellow of the Royal Society of Literature. He teaches in both England and America and is a Senior Fellow at the Ethics and Public Policy Center, Washington DC. He is currently teaching an MA in Philosophy for the University of Buckingham.

Acknowledgements

David would like to thank his wife, Yvonne, and his children, Chloe, Emily and Ben, for all the suggestions, support and advice given during the writing of this book.

Jane is inordinately grateful to her long-suffering family: Neill, Josie, Jamie (and Tumbleweed), Jenny, Ben, Andrew and Anna for their unfailing encouragement, inspiration and humour, especially when times are tough.

David and Jane would finally like to thank Lana Crowe for her assistance with editing, and Alison Foyle and Elsbeth Wright at Routledge for their support and guidance from commissioning to publication.

Introduction

David James and Jane Lunnon

Looked at from a distance the independent sector is in good health. In many parts of the world – including the United Kingdom – more children are attending fee-paying schools than ever before. Even in a period of political turbulence and economic uncertainty (in Europe, North America, and Asia Pacific) numbers are at best going up and, at worst, staying stable, and this in the face of (in many cases) increases in fees that are above consumer price growth, and average earnings growth.

Furthermore, as Jamie Martin writes in Chapter nine, the popularity of independent schools is not restricted to developed markets: expansion in emerging economies is barely keeping up with demand. New markets are opening up in Africa and the former Soviet Union states, and already-established independent schools, as well as for-profit, commercial providers, are also establishing themselves, helping to transform, and educate, children in these societies.

This is clearly good news for the students in those schools: their parents have exercised a consumer choice (which will often have been at considerable personal sacrifice) and opted to invest significant amounts of money in their children's future. But if we look in more detail we quickly see that such a view is optimistic. Indeed, there is a prevailing sense in many schools that these are dark times for the sector. For many in these schools the next five years will be a defining period, and it is because of this that we feel it an appropriate time to ask what are the main challenges facing the sector today. Some commentators, such as Ralph Lucas, see a gradual decline in numbers; for Lucas, writing in Chapter 3, we will see schools with names as familiar names enter 'a very slow and gentle good night', an anesthesia administered by a fatal combination of dwindling numbers, high fees, and political intent.

These three challenges alone will require all the skills of adaptation that have ensured the survival of independent schools in the past. The difference now though is that in many developed countries, fees are at a record high, and most school leaders can't go much higher without hemorrhaging parents. And (in many case) without losing sight of their founding principles and purposes. Where is the tipping point? In the UK, fees have, on average, risen 100% since 2003. And fees in selective UK schools are roughly similar to fee-paying schools on the other side of the Atlantic. That doesn't seem to be a sustainable strategy for the next ten to 15 years. Of course, markets can change: wealth creation could accelerate ahead of what the boldest economist would currently predict; a sudden (and huge) influx of highly affluent parents could see numbers sustained at current levels, but that seems unlikely, and schools cannot plan on such tenuous possibilities. Indeed, as many of our contributors suggest, they should and must plan for the most pessimistic of economic outcomes; and look at different ways of generating income.

Many of the best schools are already doing this, with UK independent schools leading the way by aggressively expanding into overseas markets. Schools such as Dulwich College and Wellington College dominate this growth industry. One report claims that fee income from Australian, US and UK schools amounts to more than USD $921.7 million, with UK schools accounting for USD $833.5 million.[1] More schools will follow, and they will do so not only because of the obvious financial benefits but because in raising additional funds they will be better equipped to give pupils from disadvantaged backgrounds access to their schools. Despite what critics say of the sector, there remains a strong altruistic strand running through independent schools, many of which were originally founded to help the poor and vulnerable.

Most independent schools are not-for-profit; they are there to educate – as widely as they can and to represent an approach to education which is liberated from policy and bureaucracy and which can, at best, drive pedagogical discourse, lobby for change and draw attention to educational issues which need addressing. This is the case the world over and is at least one powerful reason for the survival of independent education.

But another reason schools could feel tempted to invest overseas is that they increasingly feel more comfortable, politically, in societies which see nothing wrong with parents deciding to spend their money on their children's education. Is it a coincidence that the UK is leading this overseas expansion at the same time that the political debate around the sector is becoming increasingly hostile? And if the gap between the rich and the poor becomes more pronounced, then is it unsurprising if the most egregious symbols of affluence are attacked, even if they are not the cause of that regrettable division?

Of course, there is one 'threat' to the independent sector that nobody working in the sector would see as anything other than progress: namely, that non-fee paying schools improve to such a level that, purely in terms of academic results, there is simply no longer any need for an alternative. Who wouldn't want a school system that meets the needs and ambitions of the whole population? But what levels of government investment would that require? Perhaps more than many taxpayers – even those with children – would be prepared to vote for. That said, for those who support competition, removing a minor 'industry' and a key competitor from the field could drain primary and secondary schools of a valuable source of inspiration, new ideas, and expertise. A school system that has only one model could be weaker precisely because it has nothing to compare and compete against. And you would only get rid of something if you genuinely thought that what was left was better (and not just fairer) than what it had displaced. Even the most ardent supporters of open-access, non-selective state schools would agree that there are many schools who still have room for improvement if they are to meet the demands of all universities and employers. The independent sector plays a significant (and perhaps disproportionate) role in meeting those demands.

There are many more factors to consider when one begins to speculate on the future of independent schools. And clearly the political climate in the United Kingdom is very different from that in Australia, or Canada. That said, there is an anti-elitism surge, powered by social media connection, sweeping across the developed world and in that context, the wealthy margins – the private sectors – whether in education or anywhere else, are being required to justify their approach, attitude, and very existence, like never before.

It is perhaps reductive to claim that there are *only* ten challenges facing the sector today, and that our contributors are completely reflective of the sector. No, it is too diverse a sector for that to be the case and there are not enough pages available to give a fully comprehensive and totally balanced view of where we are now, and where we are likely to be in the future. What we do aim to do is to argue that independent schools have always played a vital part in the education of our young people, and will continue to do so in the future, and for that reason alone they remain important, valuable, and worthy of inclusion in all discussions about schooling today, and if that discussion is free of political bias and financial interference then it is more likely to benefit growing numbers of children from increasingly diverse backgrounds.

There is certainly a diverse range of viewpoints included in this book. We have approached leading figures in the sector, as well as those who have experienced schools from different perspectives and each position taken is valid, constructive, and written with the aim of advising schools about how best to avoid (or navigate) the dark times alluded to earlier. This book is not intended to be an encomium: we recognise that, even individually, no school is perfect, let alone a whole sector. They are essentially human creations, with all the fallibilities that come with that. But because they are human, and filled with young people, they remain places of profound hope, and bursting with potential.

The biggest challenge for all schools, irrespective of whether they are independent or not, is how best to capture that energy and transform it into something which, in turn, can improve the societies in which they are rooted. Being independent is a powerful position to be in, and it is not the same as being autonomous and unaccountable. It comes with responsibility. We hope this book is a small, but useful, contribution to a bigger debate, that is no doubt coming, about how best our schools respond to a rapidly changing world that is asking new, and more searching questions of them. One thing is for sure: our schools have to respond to the challenges ahead – and mapped out in this book – because their futures (and the futures of all the young people educated in them) depend on them doing so.

Note

1   www.tes.com/news/exclusive-record-number-independent-schools-expand-overseas

Chapter 1

The pastoral challenge

Introduction to the pastoral challenge

Anybody working in schools today, whether they are in the maintained or independent sectors, primary or secondary, will surely acknowledge that there has been a significant change in how teachers view children's mental health. If, as an adult, you attended an independent school in the 1980s (or earlier) you would have had little knowledge of what today we may term 'emotional wellbeing'. Indeed, such a phrase would have been effectively meaningless in schools before the 1990s. But, as Anthony Seldon observes in this chapter (with only a modicum of hyperbole) everything changed at the turn of this century. It was at that point in time that schools began to recognise that they had a responsibility not only to the academic success of their pupils, but also to their emotional success. And this change was not limited to schools in the UK: partially fuelled by American authors such as Carol Dweck, Martin Seligman, and Howard Gardiner, trends developed across educational systems that put emotional intelligence at the heart of educational debate.

Prior to this, schools of course engaged with issues that have always been an intrinsic part of dealing with the complexities of growing up. But increasingly, the language used, and also the growing awareness in *all* staff – not just those who were paid to deal with emotional problems – has resulted in pastoral support now typically attracting as much resource as academic teaching.

Of course, many would argue that even to divide a school into the 'pastoral' and 'academic' is in itself a false dichotomy that is, ultimately, reductive and self-defeating. After all, happy pupils tend to be more academically successful, and pupils who are academically successful tend to be happier than those who are not. Of course, creating such a virtuous circle is easier written about than done.

But we have moved very far, very quickly, and although there is, as Dick Moore argues in this chapter, still much to do, it feels as if there is far greater awareness of the pressures our young people suffer today, and they should be supported if they find themselves in difficulty. The surprise is to realise that none of this is really new: Harvard,[1] among other institutions, has been researching the happiness of its students since the early twentieth century. It has taken over 80 years to move from the Ivy League universities to the classrooms and staff rooms of schools, and that protracted process of absorption could be viewed as necessary if time (always a school's most precious intangible commodity) is to be dedicated to addressing the issues such awareness reveals.

Rachel Kelly begins her essay with worrying statistics about the level of depression and anxiety-related issues affecting young people in UK schools today (and it is probably a fair assumption that it would be a similar story in similar schools in similar societies). But in the understandable rush to help our young people, Kelly also introduces a necessary note of caution. She argues that 'the reduction in stigma around mental health now means that more teenagers are talking about their mental health. We must be careful not to be alarmist in this new environment'. In other words, the mental health 'crisis' that we regularly read about in our schools is a result of educational professionals being better trained to spot issues and report them. This must surely be met with muted applause as it clearly indicates some progress is being made, even if the causes underlying the issues remain.

Why is this any different in independent schools? Well, in many cases it isn't: the issues affecting young people today, be they perennial ones for all adolescents, are to be found in as many fee-paying day schools as the nearby comprehensive. The distinction appears when we take into account boarding schools: their duty of care is different in kind, and time, to those that day schools face. Their 24/7 care in term time creates unique questions as well as very considered answers, and it is no doubt true that the work done by professionals in these institutions could be better made use of by all those involved in the safeguarding of children. Boarding schools are now, thankfully, very different places to those that haunt the popular imagination, and legislation and accountability have played significant roles in making them more transparent. That said, there will always be a level of expectation which independent schools cannot always satisfy. Increasingly, fee-paying parents assume that they are paying for their child's happiness as much as their academic success. Neither of these things should be monetised, nor can they be guaranteed by any school, no matter what they say at open days. Growing up can be a messy and turbulent business and no school (no matter how high the fees, nor how insistent the parents) can provide a consistently rose-strewn path through the 14 or so years of formal schooling. Nor should they. The very business of confronting and learning from difficulties, the development of grit and resilience and the adoption of effective coping strategies when challenges arise, are an increasingly critical part of schools' pastoral programmes.

Perhaps, though, we are forgetting something important when it comes to wellbeing in schools. Yes, the focus has to be on the children themselves: they are the reason the schools exist, and they are the bedrock of a society's future. And if schools produce unhappy young people then, eventually, society will have to pay in one way or another for that unfortunate outcome. That said, and Julie Johnson refers to it in her essay, the mental health of staff working in independent schools is too often sidelined. Demands are made by senior management teams and governors, as well as parents who expect a service commensurate with their outlay, that increasingly adds to the pressures of the job. And as fees rise, and the desire for ever-higher grades intensifies, so too will the demands. Schools should be happy places, and let us not forget that our independent schools are, in general, places where our young people enjoy being (the market would soon decide if they were not). But unless the adults who run them are themselves fulfilled, respected, appreciated, and rewarded, then the happiness we seek can only ever be partially met. The smile that the teacher has in front of a class on Friday morning should not be a veneer, a mask that hides the worry and exhaustion of the week, but something sincere: an outward sign of inner health. The pastoral challenges of the future will continue to evolve, and, although it is a truism to say that every child matters, it is no less true to say that every adult does as well.

Julie Johnson

The pace at which many independent schools operate matches that of corporate business. This is exacerbated by expectations from parents who are used to being treated as valued clients: for example, expecting an immediate response to emails and phone calls. It can be stressful dealing with 'helicopter parents' who hover anxiously over their children, or 'curling parents' who want to remove every obstacle in their child's path, acting as though their child is the only child in the world. Added to that, there can be pressure from within the school itself, related to academic outcomes, involvement in extracurricular activities, client satisfaction, and the provision of increasingly broad and diverse programmes. Over the last ten to 15 years, pastoral staff have seen an exponential rise in responsibility related to issues such as: safeguarding, the challenges of the digital world and its impact on education and the mental health issues that affect up to one in ten pupils and also one in four members of staff.

To add to these pressures, staff in independent schools are passionate and committed to excellence in their teaching and care of pupils, which results, more often than not, in self-imposed pressure and long working hours. Though staff in independent schools may have long holidays, research on wellbeing has shown the importance of maintaining a continual work/life balance. If this does not exist, the health benefits following a holiday will disappear within one or two weeks!

Independent schools with packed timetables, homework, testing and exams from an early age face numerous challenges. There's a danger that staff and pupils alike are constantly looking forward to the next school stage rather than flourishing and enjoying, moment by moment, the journey of education.

The key influencers of young people are first parents, then teachers and the communities that they are growing up in, and it is essential that, if meaningful progress is to be made in wellbeing, schools work with pupils *and* parents. But it is interesting to step back and ask: what is being modelled in the fast paced, highly competitive world of independent schools? Is it possible that their culture may be a contributing factor in the deterioration of pupil mental health? With research showing that pupils' wellbeing relates closely to that of staff, maintaining staff wellbeing is an area of vital importance, not simply to the staff, but to the pupils too.

Because of the rise in young people suffering from poor mental health, many schools now employ one or more counsellors or have access to them and refer young people out of school. Though this is a positive development, the approach of the professionals can be problematic. Many counsellors or therapists see the young person with whom they are working as an autonomous individual. This may be a vital part of the therapeutic alliance which meets a core need for teens by giving them a sense of choice and control. However, they are also part of a family and a school community and this can be forgotten or compromised by the therapeutic context.

I recently spoke at a conference for teachers about wellbeing in the twenty-first century. A large number of participants voiced their concerns about just this experience in their own schools. It is a concern often echoed by parents, who recognise that their child or teen needs help, but then feel shut out of the process and end up with a sense of powerlessness at just the point when they might be feeling most vulnerable as a parent.

As human beings, we have a core need to be part of and to be supported by communities: our families, our schools and our peers. Rather than adopting a systemic and holistic approach that recognises this, too often, the child or teen is worked with in isolation. And this is not just about staff or parents being marginalised. This can lead to counsellors being less effective, as they are unaware of something happening at home or at school which the teen may not choose to share and which has not become clear because there is no appropriate system or mechanism for the sharing of information between all parties involved.

Many schools run parenting seminars, seeking to equip parents in nurturing and bringing up their children in the twenty-first century. As we know, it takes a village to raise a child and these seminars, workshops, and courses are of vital importance in addressing not only the predictable issues such as 'the party scene', alcohol, and drugs, or building resilience, but more in-depth topics like developing mindfulness and fostering emotionally intelligent children. One-off seminars can be effective, but they need to be supported by longer parenting courses that address such issues and talk openly with parents about how to avoid the dangers of helicopter and curling parenting.

In my experience, many parents seem to lack confidence in their parenting skills, even though they are respected and confident in their professional arenas. They are uncertain as they seek to parent in an increasingly complex, competitive and digitally-driven world, and feel suddenly out of their depth. The western world is an individualist society; families are no longer bringing up their children in broad communities where they can seek the advice, help, and support of older and wiser parents when difficulties arise. There are many areas in which this seems to have an impact on children's and teens' development. One key area is the already mentioned helicoptering and curling approach to parenting, which can be detrimental to the development of emotional and social intelligence and resilience. Both are vitally important in general wellbeing and can be predictive factors in mental health. Perhaps there is the potential for the school to be the new community, but that would need a change in approach so that pupils, staff, and parents all work together to foster collective and individual wellbeing.

At a recent mindfulness course (in which 50% were fathers), many attendees felt that their lives were simply too busy. They wished to reset them for their own wellbeing and that of their families. They spoke about feeling as if they were on a never-ending treadmill. One mother had been sent by her son who, having recently experienced a mindfulness course at his school, felt she would benefit from it.

In the evaluation at the end of the course, it was notable how many expressed a sense of not being alone, and how they valued knowing that other parents were experiencing similar issues. These parents left feeling better equipped and with a new sense of confidence in their parenting skills, which can only benefit their children and in turn, the schools which their children attend.

In conclusion, it is time to take a long, hard look at the culture we are creating in schools today. Many may already be doing this with wellbeing programmes, school counsellors, parents seminars, courses and pastoral days, staff wellbeing programmes and so on. But are we merely adding these onto already crammed school programmes, thereby simply increasing the pace of life and thus expectations on all? There is a very great risk that this is the case. What is required instead is a whole school review; we must ask ourselves: what are we doing well? What do we need to do differently? And this may mean a radical re-think about the culture, nature, and above all the pace of school life. Are we following a driven, corporate (doing) model, a 'burn out' model or a 'sustainable, flourishing', and caring educational model?

A good question, perhaps, for all schools to contemplate at the start of the school year.

Rachel Kelly

Hardly a week goes by without another worrying headline about the mental health crisis affecting young people.

A few examples make the point. In December 2017 we learned that the number of young children in England seeing psychiatrists rose by nearly a third over a 12-month period.[2]

In 2016, 93 per cent of secondary school teachers in the United Kingdom reported an increase in rates of mental health problems such as anxiety and depression among their pupils over the previous five years. [3]

These statistics are about the child population in general, but are echoed by specific data from independent schools. In 2015, the Headmasters' and Headmistresses' Conference (the organisation that represents many independent schools in the United Kingdom) found that while incidents of intolerance and bullying were down, there were 'unprecedented levels of concern among Heads over pupils' disclosing online threats, depression, self-harm and eating disorders'. [4]

Clearly, both independent and state sectors have a problem. But before we consider some solutions, it is worth putting these figures in context. The reduction in stigma around mental health now means that more teenagers are talking about their mental health. We must be careful not to be alarmist in this new environment. We must also not mistake ordinary human unhappiness, as Sigmund Freud put it, with a diagnosable mental health condition.

In addition, although there are many reports of deteriorating mental health, we should remember that, in many ways, young people are much healthier than they've ever been, according to Professor Andrew Przybylski, an experimental psychologist at the Oxford Internet Institute. Rates of alcohol and drug use among young people are both falling; teen pregnancies are at their lowest level for half a century. [5]

That said, the environment that young people are facing at home and school is more challenging than it has ever been. One problem is that in 2012/13, just 6% of the total National Health Service (NHS) spend on mental health went to services for children and young people.[6]

There's not much teachers can do about NHS services. Equally, they are not responsible for the levels of professional counselling schools provide – which need to increase, given that teachers themselves are not mental health professionals.

But teachers can do something about technology – those slivers of metal, whether laptops or phones, that every teenager is now surgically attached to.

The new pastoral frontline is digital. Messaging online is the new hanging out at the bus stop. The difference, this time, is that teachers do not have their own tried and trusted rules to fall back on. We are in new and unchartered territory. [7]

Some certainties are emerging. The first is that the internet is not a fit place for young children, given the ease with which anyone can access violent or pornographic content. In addition, online bullying is rife.

One answer is to follow the example of some senior staff at Google, Apple and other tech companies. They have chosen digital-free schools for their offspring such as Waldorf School in Silicon Valley. Meanwhile, Jean-Michel Blanquer, President Macron's education minister banned mobile phones from French schools for children between the ages of 3 and 15 in September 2018.

What then of the teenage years when a simple ban on phones may not be possible? Schools that try often find that students outwit them and simply use back up phones.

As professionals, teachers are best placed to explain to pupils the reality of their brains and how they are interacting with technology. They can share the known risks and effects of using technology at different stages of development: that teenagers are becoming short-sighted because they are hunched over tiny screens; that the tech giants deliberately create reward loops to keep them addicted; that time spent on phones means less time to chat and to enjoy emotional experiences in real life; and that late night phone use leads to sleep deprivation.

A second key area in which the curriculum could be expanded is to teach children the kind of life skills, emotional resilience and mindful techniques that positively affect our mental health. In addition, mental health could be woven throughout the curriculum. Keats' poetry could be a trigger for a discussion on suicide for example. A biology class could explain the reality of the stress response and the fear, flight or fight response. An exercise class could include mindful breathing.

Independent schools have the teaching flexibility and resources to make these changes and many are starting to do so.

A third initiative is to encourage peer support by students themselves and mentoring within schools. The Mental Health Foundation's Peer Education Project is one of the first peer-delivered mental health programmes in the UK. Peers are often deemed by young people to be more credible sources of information than adult educators.

And perhaps, more than anything else, this project gives hope for the future. The answer to pastoral care may be not just about asking more of already over-stretched teachers. It reminds us that, though the mental health crisis may be widespread, it may be overcome through the efforts and initiatives of young people themselves. And that is a heartening thought. [8]

Dick Moore

> Education is the most powerful weapon which you can use to change the world.
>
> (Nelson Mandela)

There is a knock on the door. Ashen-faced, the Deputy Head tells the Head that a Year 11 pupil has been found dead, having taken his own life. The Head catches a glimpse of herself in the mirror. Silently, she asks: "Could I have done more to prevent this tragedy?"

Adolescent vulnerability is nothing new, but in recent years adolescent emotional turmoil has assumed epidemic proportions. The fear of suicide is the ultimate unspoken threat, but the huge number of young people who are less content – less productive – than we all need them to be, represents schools' greatest challenge.

British education continues to be admired around the world (witness the remarkable number of schools based on the template of the English public school which are opening in the Middle and Far East). But are schools equipping young people with the academic, emotional and social skills needed for the digital age of the twenty-first century – a high-octane world of incessant pressure? Schools understandably desire success – for their pupils and for themselves – and for many success is judged by the easily measurable: grades, university places and league tables. But in chasing 'success' many schools from both sectors have evolved into pressure-cooker environments. Schools could shape the future; but by conveniently pandering to the wishes of parents – and governments – they abdicate this vital responsibility.

Many parents accept the academic assessment of children as young as three for school entry, and line their children up for weeks of examination preparation at seven, ten and eleven years old. Do we want an education that continues to value knowledge acquisition and retention above creativity, communication, self and social awareness, resilience and other skills necessary for life-long success and contentment? It is heartening that some schools are working to reduce testing and are discouraging the flourishing, toxic tutoring culture. But short term tinkering will lead, at best, to short term solutions.

It is time for radical change: a holistic approach which does not separate pastoral and academic, where the ethos of the school supports the fact that emotional wellbeing and academic performance are directly linked and that developing the former will inevitably enhance the latter. Where every teacher at every level is responsible for managing the emotional *and* academic development of young people through failure to success, and through pressure to preparation for the future.

What might such change look like?

The development of wellbeing policies (not merely generic safeguarding policies) which include ways to identify the most vulnerable children, the early warning signs of common mental health problems, together with protocols for response and referral is one critical approach. And a requirement to include emotional wellbeing within Ofsted's inspection framework would encourage all schools to respond.

Schools require a network of professionals both within the school and outside it, together with specific training for school staff. "Schools are not hospitals," some might observe, and teachers cannot be expected to provide clinical responses. However, they are uniquely placed to offer effective support and early intervention, which would certainly reduce the pressure on Child and Adolescent Mental Health Services in the UK, which currently turn away some 75 per cent of those who seek access.

Social media, demonised as the cause of the new malaise, can entertain, educate and inspire new opportunities for social interaction; it can also isolate, damage self-esteem and create unrealistic expectations.

In many schools, effective work is being done to enhance the benefits and reduce the negative and evolving aspects of the digital age.

Many problems that confront young people are brewed throughout childhood before emerging with the onset of adolescence, when brains are rewired and independence is sought. Neuroscience tells us that adolescence remains in full swing, with all its attendant risks and challenges, until the mid-twenties, or later. That might explain the significant increase in emotional ill-health experienced by many young people on leaving the safety net of school. Schools could facilitate continuity of care during this especially vulnerable time by exerting pressure on further education establishments to match their honeyed words about the care of student emotional and mental health with sustained commitment and financial investment.

When asked what stops teachers being able to support struggling students, the *unanimous* response of over 300 schools was that there is not enough *time*. Investing time and resources, as well as developing the school ethos, will reap huge dividends and positively affect the 'bottom line' – a principle that many of our largest businesses have understood for some time.

The development of the social and emotional skills of our youngest children is often excellent. But once a child reaches the age of five or six, such skills are pushed to the very margins of the curriculum by the demands of subject-based learning and academic assessment. No one is immune from emotional pain; yet what is currently done to help young people understand emotional pain and develop strategies to deal with it? A dynamic, proactive approach across and beyond the curriculum is needed to equip young people with the skills they will need to thrive in the twenty-first century: the ability to withstand pressure, cope with setbacks and relish challenge, all of which require an entirely fresh look at what is taught and how it is taught.

Who will be brave enough to lead the educational revolution that we so need?

In the current climate, it is hard to be optimistic. I worked recently with the governors of a high-achieving school wishing to improve the care of emotionally troubled students and suggested that collaborating with other 'top' schools in presenting a unified front to government and universities would have more impact than each school acting unilaterally. The response was that it would be very difficult to work so closely with their competitors.

Government short-termism and the self-interest of leading schools and universities suggest that leaders will be tempted to continue to tinker rather than change, hoping that the knock on *their* door will never come.

Emma Robertson

'Generation Z', the 'digital natives' – however you wish to label them – are more socially conscious, culturally aware, and economically and politically astute than older generations could ever have imagined. As someone at the forefront of online safety innovation, I believe these attributes are inextricably linked to the access they have to technology, and to social media in particular.

This generation, who are often painted as a group of narcissists too busy sending 'Snaps' to engage in a meaningful conversation, have forced a new and exciting era of online safety education, which moves away from reactive and repetitive messages ("tell someone you trust", "never speak to strangers", etc) to encompass more relevant and context-appropriate solutions. Solutions that account for the fact that it's not always as simple as "telling someone you trust" if you feel embarrassed or humiliated following an online abuse incident. Or that it's not always possible to "never speak to strangers" at a time when modern gaming has such an emphasis on social interaction (as we saw with online video game Fortnite).

Of all the issues currently faced by independent schools, understanding how best to support students through the challenges that a life online presents is perhaps the most pressing. But this is a relatively new and complex area; the legislation that this country has in place to protect us from online threats (i.e. sexting laws) can become irrelevant or outdated overnight. Behaviour that often takes place outside of school hours transcends across neighbouring schools and beyond in minutes. It is behaviour that the vast majority of teachers would never have faced when they were at school, making it harder for staff to draw from first-hand experience when considering how to respond. And these issues can't always be planned for or mitigated against, because of the ever evolving nature of the digital landscape.

Having reached millions of students, parents, carers and teachers through the programmes and resources of Digital Awareness UK, I can confidently say that while the challenge can sometimes seem daunting, great strides are being made to empower young people to enjoy using technology safely and responsibly.

Those schools that we believe are most effective in their quest for safeguarding students online are successful because, at the core of their strategy, they have a clear understanding of just how advanced young people are when it comes to navigating the internet in a way that benefits both themselves and the people around them. However they also appreciate that young minds aren't always developed or experienced enough to independently manage unique and highly complex issues such as data misuse.

These schools recognise that we would be doing our students a huge disservice if we choose to ignore, for example, the fact that they are uniquely positioned to craft powerful, succinct arguments in written and visual formats to campaign about the causes in which they believe. Or that through the immersive and engaging digital learning environments they have access to, they are able to utilise their digital skills to enhance their education (as we've recently seen with artificial intelligence personalised learning platforms).

At a time when issues such as "fake news", digital addiction and online abuse are dominating the headlines, our pupils have acquired a skill-set that allows them to think critically, exercise sound moral judgement and display resilience in the face of adversity. And this is exciting.

My relentless optimism about young people today is not void of an appreciation of the problems they face. I am painfully aware of the pitfalls of technology, not least because I have first-hand experience in managing digital issues such as bullying and grooming in schools on a daily basis. In October 2017 we drew attention to some of these issues in a piece of research we conducted in partnership with the Headmasters' and Headmistresses' Conference (HMC). We surveyed nearly 5,000 students aged 11 to 18 at independent and state schools to explore the emotional impact social media is having on their well-being – 57 per cent stated they had received abusive comments online, 56 per cent felt they were on the edge of addiction; and 52 per cent said social media made them feel less confident about how they looked or how interesting their lives were.

To tackle these issues head-on, we see success in schools that are leveraging the knowledge of older pupils and implementing peer mentoring programmes, have built a bespoke curriculum that is context-appropriate, have an emphasis on 'life skills', involve the whole school community and utilise outside experts to support with strategic planning and delivery. All 'tech bashing' is left at the classroom door; opportunities such as career prospects are spotlighted and students are engaged in positive conversations about their digital world.

The invaluable skill-set young people have often independently developed through their use of technology must not just be acknowledged as part of the education delivered, it must be celebrated.

Anthony Seldon

Independent education offers a beacon of light and civilisation to the world. But it is difficult to do well. No challenge it faces arguably is bigger than the pastoral one.

It used to be so easy. Twenty-five years ago, students did not have problems. Independent schools could get on with doing what they do best, teaching and enriching the life of the young outside the classroom with the arts and sport. Pastoral care was about ensuring that students turned up dressed properly and on time, behaved in a civilised way, and were punished when they failed to do so.

But around the turn of the century, all this began to change. Out of a blue sky, the young started to develop a whole range of emotional, psychological and mental problems.

Take a week in the life of a day independent school. First thing on Monday morning, the Head hears that a child has been kept away with the suspicion of Munchausen Syndrome. At 9:10am an anonymous message is taken in the office, that one of the students is possibly being abused by their parent. In the morning break meeting, staff hear that two new students are self-harming while a third is being watched for the possibility of anorexia nervosa. After lunch, the stressed-out Head receives a delegation of male students to say that they want to be allowed to wear skirts. At 4:30pm a pale Deputy Head arrives in the Head's study to say that a child who is being bullied at school has gone missing and a suicide note has been found. And this is only Monday. The rest of the week is about to get worse.

And if it's a *boarding* independent school, with children present 24/7, the week after Monday could get a whole lot worse still.

As Head of independent schools for 20 years, my biggest single worry always was a student suicide. It never happened, but that was more due to luck than to any clever preventative measures. When it does happen it is utterly devastating.

So what has happened to change the pastoral care scene from the generally balmy twentieth century? Let's coin an acronym, 'SPC' to explain it. The S stands for social media, which is everywhere and relentless. The technology of course can have many benefits, which Facebook, Instagram and the others are anxious to tell us about. But the very real downside is that young people find it hard to live without the technology. It disrupts their sleep, disturbs their quiet time, ruffles their equanimity and intrudes into their privacy, insinuating its way into the very fabric of the life of each student. Yes it connects, but are they real friends online, and what about when these friends bully, undermine and exploit?

P stands for Pressure, which comes from schools, from parents and above all from the young themselves to perform academically and to conform to often impossible expectations. Young men are differently vulnerable to young women. It's an edgy place being young now. Governments and league tables pile on the pressure and make us all think, wrongly, that exam results is what education is all about. Fail to get good grades and you would have failed as a person. This is toxic stuff. C stands for Copycat. Children see others with eating disorders and they follow. Mental illness is now as contagious as physical illness.

What can be done about this, so that independent schools can be on top of the problems and not constantly on the back foot, reacting? There is one figure above all others who shows the way; American psychologist and honorary graduate of the University of Buckingham, Martin Seligman. He tells us that we must not be victims, but need to take control of our lives and our schools. Rather than waiting for problems to emerge, we need to build capacity to prevent them from arising, and cope with them better when they do arise. The analogy of the waterfall explains it best. At present, schools wait for problems to manifest and then try dealing with them at the bottom of the water-fall. But we should be working at the top of the waterfall, preventing people from ever falling over the edge.

Doing this in practice means that we need to put students and staff, not statistics or results, back at the heart of our schools. Children need to feel affirmed, supported and loved. It is the deficit of love that created the problems, because love helps children know who they are and how to negotiate their minds and emotions. Everybody in schools, from governors and Heads down, needs to radiate calm affirmation. Mindfulness is important because it helps children accept themselves and find peace. The charity, Action for Happiness, has a ten-point list for what schools and parents need to do at the top of the waterfall, and how to do pastoral care properly in a way that will reduce unhappiness and mental illness.

So this chapter is optimistic, but also realistic. Do as it says, and there is every chance that Mondays in future will return to being just Mondays.

Notes

1 https://news.harvard.edu/gazette/story/2017/04/over-nearly-80-years-harvard-study-has-been-showing-how-to-live-a-healthy-and-happy-life/
2 Children's Commissioner
3 www.parentzone.org.uk
4 www.hmc.org.uk/blog/first-data-mental-health-trends-independent-schools-shows-pupils-kinder-harder/
5 www.telegraph.co.uk/science/2017/01/13/257-minutes-time-teens-can-spend-computers-day-harming-wellbeing/
6 https://fullfact.org/health/spending-mental-health-services/
7 www.theguardian.com/society/2017/sep/23/mental-health-issues-soar-among-girls-state-school-budget-cuts
8 O'Reilly A., Barry J., Neary M. L., Lane S., O'Keeffe L. (2016) An evalutation of participation in a schools-based youth mental health peer education training programme, *Advances in School Mental Health Promotion*, 9:2, 107–118.

Chapter 2

The academic challenge

Introduction to the academic challenge

The academic challenges facing independent schools today appear, from a distance, relatively unchanged from what they have been for much of the last 50 years. There are two broad objectives, both interlinked: help pupils get the highest grades possible and then try to get them into the best universities. Once those two objectives have been achieved it is, effectively, job done for most schools. But look closer: scrutinise the lettering on those proud notice boards, look at the names in gold next to a recently departed students' illustrious destination that promise success, affluence and, indirectly, a good return on investment. There, between the names, lies untold narratives, of enormous pressures brought to bear (on those pupils, on those teachers, on the schools themselves) to attain those goals. And then there are the absent tales, the missing in action, of the names of pupils who, happily or not, went to lesser-known universities, or did not go on to higher education at all. When will independent schools celebrate *their* outcomes?

Parents will not always notice what isn't there, although many will ruthlessly compare schools. Many will smile, convinced that the fees they are about to spend will, at some point in the future, result in a child going to a university with real status. And why not? Research shows that graduates from highly selective universities earn more money over a lifetime than their peers who study elsewhere. Parents know this. They also know that pupils in the UK from fee-paying schools are twice as likely to attend a Russell Group university, and five times as likely to attend Oxford or Cambridge than their state school peers. Every successful parent who sends their children to university will know the value of the degree that is their next step.

The parents will sit listening to members of senior management teams telling them why there has to be a balance between academic excellence and having 'an all round education'. Buzzwords, like 'holistic', and 'wellbeing', 'work-life balance', 'enrichment', will do what they tend to do: buzz around like flying ants, suddenly there and then, as quickly, gone, as the 4x4s depart down the tree-lined drives. But what drove those parents there in the first place was something else: academic success, a desire to be at the top of the heap, and to give their children that crucial edge when it comes to getting a coveted university place.

The internal contradiction, then, that so many independent schools in the UK have is that, on the one hand, they want to focus on academic success at GCSE and in the Sixth Form, but, on the other hand, they want to reassure the parents that the fees they are paying are worth so much more than nine straight A*s at the end of Year 11. It is a sort of double-think: they know that the subjects they have to teach, and the courses they have to follow are, almost by definition, limiting. That is not to say that teachers should be limited to them; but, because time is always in short supply, and the demand for high grades is relentless, there is little time to teach beyond the curriculum.

For Kevin Stannard, the 'stranglehold of exams' is tightened when pupils go on to study in senior school. The gateway qualification for university has, for him, relegated secondary education to little more than a preparatory role. This is akin to the 'educational grunt work', a process made even less intrinsically meaningful to him because universities tend to be 'detached' from the whole process. The result is that school curricula are shaped not by what is required – and is possible – but by external factors.

Helen Pike argues that this only adds to the teachers' workload because they have to respond to a growing set of demands that are determined by others. This lack of autonomy is a major contributing factor to why teachers leave the profession: they feel they are undervalued, vehicles for government directives, mediums for assessment. For independent schools, the situation should be much better: there should be greater freedom to innovate. Additionally, they are often teaching smaller classes with more resources. And yet, too often, independent schools become restricted by their unwillingness to take risks: they adumbrate state schools in what they teach and how they teach it, even though their colleagues in the maintained sector have far fewer choices. According to Briony Scott, one of the key academic challenges is to 'reclaim the spirit of that independent sacred space'. She calls for independent schools 'to think for [them]selves'. If they are to do so then they must be trusted more by governing bodies, and the parents who scrutinise results.

Joe Spence, in his ten academic commandments, suggests that it is essential to 'encourage a belief in learning for its own sake': we must move away from 'content-heavy and content-prescriptive syllabuses'. For Spence, 'everything else follows from that'. But it takes a school that is very assured of its own position to do so at the risk of some students failing to gain the grades necessary for university. Ian Warwick writes that there is an innate demand from parents to guide what is being taught in the classroom: 'so much money is invested by parents in their children's education that it leads many to believe they have the right to significantly influence the classroom experience of their loved ones'. And, of course, teachers need to be truly subject-specialist if they are to take chances with what they are teaching in a packed weekly schedule. Fixed curricula, although often derided by teachers, act as a necessary safety net for teachers who do not have in-depth knowledge of what they are teaching.

For Warwick, independent schools must have the courage to place their pupils' learning before their parents' expectations and sometimes in the face of their teachers' understanding. In other words, the aspirations they talk to parents about in open days, or on their websites, should be made manifest in their classrooms because 'until independent schools routinely make the... most challenging demands of their students they will never know whether they would have been capable of reaching the highest standards'. Such an approach creates risk, but teaching now has become so regulated, so measured, so assessed, and so focused on academic outcomes, that if independent schools cannot allow themselves to use their independence where it really matters – in the classroom – then it would be understandable if those parents drive away from those open days and never return.

There are no school notice boards of the names not registered, the achievements never reached, the risks not taken. But sometimes they can be the most eloquent stories told about that school's willingness to embody the characteristics they claim they want their pupils to take every day. Unless independent schools make full use of the academic autonomy they have, limited though that is because of accountability measures, they may, in these most turbulent political and economic times, be forfeiting the most compelling reason for maintaining faith in the sector. Although it should be evident in every corner of every independent school, the freedom to take risks, to rise beyond the limitations of a pass grade, should begin and end in the classroom. It is primary, and everything else is secondary.

Helen Pike

I did my PGCE "in service" with the Open University, while I was teaching at City of London School. The course materials suggested that 'there can be no great teaching if there is not great learning'. This was a useful corrective to the idea of the teacher as someone who drones while scrawling gobbets of knowledge on the board – and hard chalk on those pupils who did not benefit from their wisdom. It encouraged teachers to see themselves as the 'guide on the side' rather than the 'sage on the stage'.

I came to question the absolutism of this statement during my placement at an excellent inner London comprehensive. I soon learned to adapt my teaching methods, my classroom management styles, and above all my expectations about how much content I would be able to cover during a lesson. I was working differently: spending comparatively more time on skills-based rather than knowledge-based teaching. My evenings were dominated by devising differentiated worksheets and short focus tasks, rather than reading articles from JStor in preparation for teaching the A-Level Norman Conquest special subject. I was competent enough there, but I knew I was never going to 'fly' in my placement school in the way that I did when teaching bright boys about the Domesday Book.

One of the most significant developments in schools in recent years is research into what actually works in the classroom. Much of this research has been led by teachers themselves and shared via Twitter, blogs and networks such as ResearchEd and WomenEd. The importance of aspiration, feedback and metacognition have become well established. Learning styles have been consigned to the dustbin of educational history.

While expenditure on expensive kit has minimal or uncertain outcomes, the importance of expert teaching in all its nuanced forms has been explored in thousands of studies. High aspirations for pupils and teachers with strong subject knowledge both emerge as being central.[1] This ought to be a cause for celebration in the profession.

We also know what makes for a fulfilled working life. Feeling that we are making a difference and are connected to others gives work meaning and purpose.[2] What could be a more professionally satisfying vocation than inspiring the young? People ought to be joining the teaching profession in droves.

Except they haven't been – and retention of those who have entered the classroom is a growing concern.[3] Only 51 per cent of secondary school physics teachers have a relevant degree or higher qualification,[4] and the retention of STEM teachers remains the biggest challenge. Why has the DfE missed recruitment targets for five consecutive years, when teaching understands itself as a profession better than ever before, and has its very own Chartered College? And why are experienced teachers departing the profession?

The most significant factor cited is workload.[5] As with all burdens, this covers not just the volume of work, but also the way in which the load is imposed and how it is expected to be carried. This gives the independent sector a double advantage over many – but by no means all – schools in the state sector.

Greater autonomy in independent school classrooms means that teachers are more free to teach the content they want in the way they want to present it. This liberty is in part possible because they are usually teaching smaller classes. Perhaps more importantly, they are teaching classes of pupils who are more likely to want to be there. These groups tend to comprise pupils with high aspirations, usually shared by their parents. Faced with fewer classroom management challenges, teachers are more free to teach a knowledge-rich curriculum. These teachers further inspire their already-aspirational pupils with their specialist knowledge, and a virtuous circle continues. Covering lots of content is likely to appeal to more qualified graduates. State school teachers are more likely to have BEd degrees than their counterparts in independent schools, while independent school teachers are more likely to have a master's degree or a PhD.[6]

The higher qualifications of independent school teachers have an impact on aspiration beyond the classroom: the Sutton Trust has reported that more than four in ten state school teachers would rarely or never advise a bright student to apply to Oxford or Cambridge. Approximately 5 per cent of state school teachers with subject degrees were awarded these by either Oxford or Cambridge, while in the independent sector, the figure is almost 17 per cent.[7]

By the time I had secured Qualified Teaching Status, I knew that I had found my niche in top-flight independent day schools. I recognise that might be seen as a narrow vocation. Many regard my choice of career as unnecessary at best, and socially and morally indefensible at worst. Over the years, I have thought of my profession as 'day care for the severely abled', and 'altitude training for intellectual athletes'.

Teaching the very able brings its own challenges – during 20 years in the profession, I have known dozens of teachers who have not been able to win the pupils' academic confidence and who found every working day a struggle. Contrary to the glib cliché, able pupils would not get on just as well if they taught themselves from the textbook, and we would be failing them if we expected them to. Bright pupils are a minority who are as deserving of specialist teaching as statemented pupils – and these categories are of course by no means mutually exclusive.

The challenge for the independent sector, therefore, is not only to continue to attract and retain able teachers, but to ensure that its schools are open to those able to flourish in them, based on their parents' aspirations rather than on their income.

Briony Scott

The world is full of words. Words used to create and to challenge, to inspire and to motivate. Words are particularly used in academia to articulate problems, create meaning or to refine ideas. They are nuanced and powerful and help us to understand where a child is, in terms of their learning. Words show us what young people are thinking, what learning is taking place and where we should next invest. And words, apart from being used to learn, teach us of wisdom and what it means to be fully alive.

With the increased volume and density of words, with the uncensored flow of opinions over expertise, and the weighting that is given to voices online, words that used to mean something are being diluted by overuse. They are thrown around like confetti by those who sit on the sidelines of education, critiquing the role of those 'in the arena'. Labels such as: " twenty-first century skills", "standardised testing", "reforms", "teaching-and-learning". They all roll off the tongue, bounce off the walls of cyberspace, and add more noise and clutter to an already deafening universe.

In contrast, the original academia began in an olive grove, outside of Athens, where Plato taught his students about life and about wisdom and about how to think. Not what to think – how to think. It was a small independent learning community, a space that fostered reflective thought. It was a sacred space, dedicated to the goddess of wisdom, Athena.

This garden became known as *akadēmeia*, an academy, and it was a place to educate, or to 'draw out'. Plato spent hours conversing, challenging and encouraging others to think through the implications of their words, to dwell on life and humanity, and to come to their own conclusions about what it means to live a good life.

Today, one of our major academic challenges is to reclaim the spirit of that independent, sacred space. In the face of relentless pressure to the contrary, it is a challenge to stop, pause and reflect. To think for ourselves. The pressure to wade through the flood of opinions, taking mandates and directives without question, speeding up and making rapid changes, lest we be perceived as old fashioned or out of date, is enormous. It is only human nature to want to be seen as cutting edge and to not be left behind, and we are all falling victim to the urge.

The volume of this noise tends to drown out anything other than binary and dogmatic persuasion. You are either with it or you are not, you are in or you are out, you understand it or you don't, you go to a 'good' school or a 'bad' one, you're outdated or you're contemporary.

But not all change is progress. There is great value in challenging this thinking. There is great wisdom in not following the crowd but determining in your own context what matters and what is important to pass onto the next generation. The ability to be a part of society but to remain independent of group norms and group think is essential for a true education to take place.

When you have those who are not educators, or who, at best, are 'para-educators', sitting on the sidelines, dictating the pace and the terms of educational change, and then demanding what should be taught, and what should not – at the expense of wisdom and relationships and conversations – then we run the very real risk of focusing on elements that create noise but don't necessarily educate. In the immortal words of Mark Twain: "'noise proves nothing. Often a hen who has merely laid an egg, cackles as if she laid an asteroid'". Times are a-changing, of this there is no doubt. We do not want our young people missing out on what they need to live fulfilling, healthy and happy lives, where they can contribute as a thriving adult to the society in which they live.

But life is rarely binary, and young humans rarely flourish in pre-scriptive environments where one person or group of people, believing they know best, dictate the agenda. The role of independent education, in fostering an appreciation of the complex, of the nuanced and of 'first-principle' thinking, is key to developing equally independent and thoughtful young adults.

In some ways, such a position is deliberately anti-minimalist. We must be careful not to focus on skills at the expense of school communities, with all the relational opportunities we have to truly educate young people in the spirit of the original olive grove. And while school communities are such a fundamental building block to these relationships, they must not be at the expense of education. Education is so much more than the school community in which a child is raised. And while education is more nuanced and enriching than skills, and moves well beyond any one school environment, it cannot be at the expense of knowledge.

Education takes place in one context, but knowledge is about life. And even knowledge must bow to wisdom. Wisdom, an old-fashioned word in so many contexts, is what allows our young men and women to make good decisions and to live fulfilled and thriving lives. You can be knowledgeable yet not be kind. You can have all the skills, belong to a great school, be well-educated and even have enormous knowledge – but in the true spirit of academia, it is wisdom we seek to be truly fulfilled, to make good decisions, for the benefit of others.

Independent education allows the development of a culture that actively seeks to bring out the best in young people, that can purpose-fully foster independent thought, looking beyond the status quo to develop wisdom, and to challenge our predisposition towards 'group think'.

Thus, one of our greatest academic challenges is to ensure that, in our desire to equip our young people for a rapidly changing, technologically driven world, we take time in the olive groves of academia, to use our words carefully and thoughtfully, to foster independent thought, and to never lose sight of the importance of wisdom.

Joseph Spence

1. The academic challenge is to promote free learning; that is, to find space – and not just in the crevices of the timetable – for learning that is not constrained by the examined curriculum. For many pupils, it is exposure to free and independent learning opportunities (projects, competitions, trips and expeditions, exchanges, off-syllabus days) that provides the gateway to confident, intellectual engagement, and to the discovery of lifelong hobbies and true vocations.

2. The academic challenge is to encourage a belief in learning for its own sake; to find space for free learning amid a plethora of content-heavy and content-prescriptive syllabuses. Such syllabuses bore the brightest and confound the weak. Everything else follows on from that.

   (This is not to advocate a more skills-oriented approach to learning, which can also be mind-numbing and confusing.)

3. The academic challenge, from the early years to Year 11, is to strive for a curriculum that is broad and balanced, deep and satisfying; the curriculum needs to respond to and stimulate pupils' curiosity and scepticism, not staunch them.

4. The academic challenge is to allow time and space in which teachers and pupils can follow their own enthusiasms.

5. The academic challenge is to think carefully about how children learn rather than to become obsessed with what they learn. The search for the perfect curriculum is the quest for a Holy Grail that will always remain out of reach.

6. The academic challenge is to overcome those who believe there needs to be a league table of disciplines in schools, which will always rank the subjects that are thought to lead directly to well-paid employment above those that encourage debate, doubt and reflection; that will always put science and mathematics before history and art. The independent sector in the 2020s has to be at the forefront of the promotion of the creative arts, languages (ancient and modern) and the humanities; the subjects through

which we reflect on what it is to be human. This does not have to be at the expense of STEM subjects (science, technology, engineering and maths) which are equally important.

We should be celebrating the fact that there are many more jobs, and more good jobs, in what is uncreatively called "the creative industries", than is sometimes imagined.

Asked recently which subject I wish I had been taught at school, I suggested History of Art. It's a subject which encourages empathy and which requires an understanding of the context of one's learning. It affords students an introduction to every aspect of our western cultural heritage. It is creative and analytical, and involves an appreciation of aspects of science, to a greater extent than is generally realised. It is seldom a soft option. I'm delighted that it hasn't been erased from the curriculum completely, as seemed likely at one stage, and I would urge all schools to look for ways to introduce History of Art to their pupils at as early an age as possible.

7. The academic challenge is to ensure that what we need to know about the progress and uses of Information Technology is fed into all subjects rather than IT existing only as a discreet subject for those who have an aptitude for it. When studied as a separate discipline, the IT curriculum needs to go beyond the teaching of digital literacy, and beyond programming and coding, and offer modules in digital citizenship (asking questions about civil liberties and human rights in the internet age), the digital humanities (that is, we need to ensure that teachers of the humanities think about how they can incorporate creative IT into their lessons) and digital entrepreneurship. We might call this enhanced IT discipline Informatics.

When I need to be confirmed in an appreciation of the infinite scope of good teaching and learning I re-read Michael Oakeshott's *Education: The Engagement and Its Frustration* (1972).

Oakeshott knew that good teaching could include "hinting, suggesting, urging, coaxing, encouraging, guiding, pointing out, conversing, instructing, informing, narrating, lecturing, demonstrating, exercising, testing, examining, criticizing, tutoring, drilling and so on – anything which does not belie the engagement to impart an understanding". In essence, this defines the teacher as coach and mentor.

Oakeshott knew that learning came from "looking, listening, overhearing, reading, receiving suggestions, submitting to guidance, committing to memory, asking questions, discussing, experimenting, practicing, taking notes, recording, re-expressing and so on – anything which does not belie the engagement to think and to understand". Neither rote learning nor skill acquisition is enough, but both have their place in the classroom.

8. The academic challenge is to analyse why it is that so many young people who do well at school fail to make the most of their potential thereafter, while many of those who find the hoop-jumping of school difficult, thrive in later life. We need to find ways to ensure that every pupil experiences both success and failure at school.

9. The academic challenge is to convince governments that "five good passes at GCSEs" or any other crude measure of school improvement does not enhance the quality of teaching or learning but simply leads to an over-concentration on the achievement of targets which become meaningless in later life, and in most workplaces.

10. The academic challenge is to find a way to ensure that more vocationally minded children do not have to give up on school but can learn in ways that play to their strengths. That is, I hope Kenneth Baker's life-long drive to encourage good technical education in this country succeeds in the end.

Kevin Stannard

The biggest academic challenge facing independent schools today is to find ways to cast off the educational equivalent of William Blake's 'mind-forg'd manacles'. We find ourselves bound by two related sets of constraints – the exam system and university admissions' requirements.

Secondary education is dominated and distorted by public examinations. The influence of exams reaches down at least to age 14, when programmes of study formally map onto the two-year duration of GCSE specifications. Exam reform has extended this influence, insofar as added content has made it necessary to front-load programmes of study and embark on courses even earlier. As a result, most of the interesting and innovative stuff has to be wedged into the interstices of an over-prescribed curriculum.

Once GCSEs are out of the way, the stranglehold of exams is tightened and the stakes are raised still further. A levels were designed specifically as a gateway to university study – good grades at A level qualified a student to progress to the next stage. This has relegated secondary schooling to a merely preparatory role.

Sir Peter Swinnerton-Dyer, once vice-chancellor of the University of Cambridge, observed that: "each stage of English education is designed for the benefit of those who will go on to the next stage, however unsuitable it will be for the rest". Unfortunately, this 'propaedeutic straitjacket' no longer even serves the purposes of those destined for the elite universities. Hence the undoing of the Curriculum 2000 reforms and the return to linearity.

Schools pay lip-service to the importance of preparing students for work, and developing skills that will equip them for a fulfilling life in social and political, as well as economic terms. But in reality the focus is fixed firmly on imminent outcomes – exam results that will secure places in prestigious universities, and ensure league table success for schools.

The educational grunt work is done in schools. Universities remain largely detached from their own next stage. Alison Wolf asserted that degrees simply confer a 'signalling effect' (as in, *I was clever enough to get a place at university*) rather than any particularly relevant knowledge or skills. David Willetts appears to support this view: "employers are selecting on the basis of A-level grades as transmitted via university admissions decisions". Those admissions decisions dictate an unusual degree of specialisation in the sixth form, and this is largely due to the control of admissions by academic departments. In US universities, decisions are made centrally, using broader assessments, but in English universities departments make the decisions, and their interest is in getting hold of the best students in their subjects. This creates pressure for premature specialisation at A level, and an emphasis on excellence in depth but not breadth.

These strangleholds amount to an over-determination of school curricula by external forces. Even 'independent' schools have very little room for manoeuvre, but it is worth exploring these opportunities. Educational innovation tends to focus on the early secondary school years, before exams kick in. Here is the opportunity for rigorous cross-curricular initiatives, bridging from the primary phase. A holy grail still worth seeking is a joined-up approach to modern languages, avoiding treating the first year of senior school as Year Zero. Ways of breaching the bottleneck at Key Stage 4 include reducing to the bare minimum the number of high-stakes assessments, rejecting not just the EBacc throttling of humanities and creative subjects but providing space for an approach to core subjects that goes beyond preparation for the test. Teaching well beyond the test should be the mantra of any truly independent school.

Many schools have sought to design a sixth form diploma that refuses the conflation of curriculum with qualification *tout court*. Others have sought alternatives to A levels, such as the Cambridge Pre-U. We need to resurrect the idea of the *liberal arts curriculum* – avoiding premature narrowing and pressuring universities to develop four-year degree programmes.

As universities lose faith in public exams as admissions gatekeepers and develop their own tests, schools have an opportunity not just to wiggle around in, but actually to cast off the manacles, and design school-leaving assessments that bring together all desired learning outcomes.

The manacles metaphor understates the difficulty we face, if it implies the removal of a physical restraint. The ties that bind us are as much mental as material, which makes Blake's imagery even more apposite. Freeing ourselves requires a different mind-set. Secondary education should be sufficient unto itself, and not merely a preparation for the next phase of formal education.

Ian Warwick

> It is a wretched taste to be gratified with mediocrity when the excellent lies before us.
>
> (Benjamin Disraeli)

Independent schools aren't subject to the same ill-informed government demands, backed up by the Ofsted scrutiny sledgehammer that state schools face. They are supposed to have the freedom to innovate in the pursuit of educational excellence, not being influenced or controlled by other people, events or things. However, in the independent sector, the stakeholder influence of parents is far greater than in the state sector. So much money is invested by parents in their children's education that it leads many to believe they have the right to significantly influence the classroom experience of their loved ones. They want better results year on year and increased numbers of students going to world class universities. They also want their school to meet their perception of the emotional needs of their children and yet to retain its independence. From the state, from 'the blob', from Ofsted. But not from them: the parents.

Following a three-year project for the (previous) Mayor of London[8] that assessed the conditions needed to achieve excellence and to better understand the teaching and learning approaches that make the difference for achieving top grades across both state and independent schools, it became clear what true academic challenge required. What the balance between support, reassurance, cognitive conflict and high challenge might look like. The requirements are that schools teach to the top and go 'off piste', outside of the exam requirements and explore the core of subjects. By stretching the expectations they have of how much their students will cover in and beyond lessons, teachers can change their perception of what it is possible for their students to achieve. It is important to expose learners to anomalies that undermine comfortable assumptions and that might deliberately threaten their security and self-esteem. To ensure students are routinely given the opportunity to have to defend their viewpoint against rigorous criticism and the occasional intellectual dogfight. To design deliberate disorientation into lessons in order to de-familiarise learning so learners have to cope with and make sense of these experiences. Teachers and students learn best from the moments that jar, not from the moments that gel.

From teachers, it means a commitment to know their subjects extremely well. This expertise is more than the quantity and quality of what they know. It is the specialised ways of thinking with bodies of knowledge and cognition that have become part of the underlying game of any chosen discipline. It is revealing the vast network of connections between ideas and concepts to develop those expert processes in students. It involves keeping students engaged with the threshold ideas in subjects so that they understand why they are engaging with it. Teachers need the courage to expose their students to how difficult and frustrating gaining scholarship can be, and to help them to master challenging academic material to induce long-term cognitive change. From students, it requires a willingness to take on deep content knowledge, the cognitive skills of conceptual understanding and analysis, the ability to make a coherent argument, risk-taking, active questioning of viewpoints and respectfully challenging the arguments of others. It involves genuine struggle in lessons and mistakes being made, because that is when they are required to fully concentrate.

Which leads to a significant series of questions. How many schools are willing to provoke the wrath of their parent body in order to defend an educational belief? If parents don't want 'too much homework/stress/difficulty', what schools will argue for provoking students with highly challenging questions that ripen, via deferral, into genuine interests? If they believe that bite sized/private tutored/scaffolded 'education' is best for results, what schools will push for students to truly take responsibility for their own learning, and expose them to constructive ambiguity and productive frustration? Is subjecting students to deliberate cognitive strain compatible with parental concerns over what they believe to be the preservation of their child's self-esteem?

Until independent schools routinely meet the high level, most challenging demands of their students, they will never know whether they would have been capable of reaching the highest standards. Some aspects of teaching (and parenting) actually make it less likely that learners are able to demonstrate what they are really able to do. By scaffolding work too clearly and for too long, teachers steal the necessary struggle from students. This undermines expectations and restricts the ranges of response that students could develop unaided and off the leash. Despite what parents may want or believe, there is no perfectly paved road to success. Even in the best schools.

Notes

1 See, for example, John Hattie, *Visible Learning for Teachers* (Routledge, 2012); Coe et al., *What Makes Great Teaching?* (Sutton Trust, published online 2014).

2 For a summary of research on this, see William McAskill, *Doing Good Better: Effective Altruism and a Radical New Way to Make a Difference* (Guardian Faber, 2016) Chapter 5.

3 See, for example, House of Commons Education Committee, *Recruitment and Retention of Teachers* (House of Commons, published online 2017).

4 Philip Kirby, *Teaching by Degrees* (Sutton Trust, published online, 2015)

5   This is recognised by the House of Commons Education Committee in its *Recruitment and Retention of Teachers*.

6   Kirby, *Teaching by Degrees*, p.4

7   ibid., pp. 3–4.

8   www.london.gov.uk/what-we-do/education-and-youth/education-and-youth-publications/lsef-teaching-resources/christ-king

Chapter 3

The junior challenge

Introduction to the junior challenge

It is the best of times, and the worst of times, to be working in junior education today. For some, such as our first contributor to this chapter, Jane Cameron, those working with young children 'are the custodians of childhood', and surely there can be fewer jobs that have more innate joy, but also responsibility, than this. This period of 'play and exploration' has always been short lived, but for Cameron it is critical that it retains its essential innocence. For her, schools that educate our youngest pupils must ensure that 'a child is not defined by the exams he or she passes'. In these formative times, schools must be spaces where children can find out about themselves and the wonders of the world around them.

Such a view, although admirable, is under threat. Prep school Headteacher Phillip Evitt writes that, increasingly, parents 'want their child... "optimised" and if they feel this isn't happening, they will look elsewhere'. It is difficult to imagine that this 'optimisation' will be defined in how many goals a little girl can score, or how many trees a little boy can climb. No, as Richard Foster writes, 'the "return on investment" is now characterised by [the pupils'] academic results and the senior school their child is accepted by'. To get to that point, an expensive school is not enough, and parents are increasingly turning to private tutors to further prepare children from as young as five or six to pass entrance examinations.

Those of us who work in the independent sector will no doubt regret such developments: it is a sign that the trend towards utilitarian methods of education are winning. But before we accept that this is true, we should answer two questions. Firstly, when does learning about mathematics, literature, science and other disciplines become, necessarily, A Bad Thing? Aged 5? 7? 11? Where is the cut-off point between play and study, and who decides it? Those who wring their hands about the end of innocence, tend to characterise formal learning as anathema to enjoyment, only to adopt an opposite vocabulary when they feel it is not doing any 'damage'. For educationalists to subscribe to this view seems at best inconsistent, and at worst hypocritical. The second question for those working in the sector is: what are we doing to challenge this trend that places test scores above anything else? Are we designing different methods of measurement? Do we refer to a happiness index rather than a spreadsheet when we are considering whether to offer a place to a pupil? If not, then we are a part of the Gradgrindian machine that many of us actively speak out against: independent schools' websites echo each other in their claims for 'all rounded' and 'holistic' education, but the KPI is always academic, whether we like it or not (and we clearly do not dislike it enough to do anything about it).

A quick look at a highly successful inner city prep school's website will highlight how the very youngest children are being primed for adulthood from the start: here the talk is of the 'competitive nature of the workplace', of 'leadership positions', of the need to inculcate 'resilience' and 'responsibility'; it is a place of 'innovative application', for 'working in teams', developing 'synergy', and, of course, of 'working hard' to 'meet the demands of modern life'. This is the language of the boardroom, not the playground. But it no doubt meets the expectations of parents. And there is no suggestion anywhere that those pupils are anything less than happy and fulfilled. If they go on to form companies employing lots of people, who is going to complain?

But the blue remembered hills of youth are, perhaps more than ever, seeing dark clouds gathering above them. If there is hope it is dappled, shining on the 'land of lost content'. The pressures on our youngest children to succeed in our most selective schools are serious – and endorsed by the termly cheques. The reality is that most children flourish. But some do not, and perhaps the issues discussed in Chapter 1 are an indirect result of hothousing in the early years. There are too many variables to find clear links. And the relative lack of 'joined-up thinking' between junior and senior schools is well known for those who work in both sectors, but it nevertheless persists. For

Ben Thomas, this emphasis on academic outcomes is an approach which, when 'taken to extremes', could result in 'the very purpose of prep schools' coming under threat. Worse, writes Thomas, it is 'a system entirely self-imposed by the independent sector'. We only have ourselves to blame. Only those schools who are oversubscribed, or have a unique ethos, will resist the demands from parents to achieve ever-better results at the cost of less measurable targets.

But those looming clouds hold other threats that are even more challenging than those self-imposed. The most obvious is cost. This is looked at in more detail in Chapter 4, but any discussion about the future of fee-paying schools will soon return to it. Fees in the UK have become 'horrendous', according to Ralph Lucas. Despite what might be written in the media, this is not as a result of greed; indeed, many prep schools are barely covering costs. No, all schools are seeing rising costs, and most have just two very blunt tools to meet them: raise fees and cut expenditure. Lucas gives other, very pragmatic advice, but there are no easy solutions to this deepest of issues. Dig deeper, though, and it becomes more complex. Again, we come back to 'parental demands', which is a motif that runs through this chapter. For Evitt, there has been an unavoidable increase in staffing to 'compensate for the reduction in the teaching done by staff to allow them to manage parents' daily academic and pastoral concerns'. Such a development seems difficult to sustain, but equally difficult to cut back once a certain level of service is provided.

Richard Foster describes another threat to prep schools: namely, the senior schools themselves. For him, a growing number are becoming 'competitors rather than allies', with some offering ever-younger provision in order to secure established markets. In addition, schools opening branches overseas could threaten the 'increase in numbers' that Foster refers to in his essay. But there are more existential threats that loom large over all independent schools. Political uncertainty has been a perennial issue, especially in the United Kingdom, for as long as anyone can remember. If our most vulnerable schools are our prep schools, then they will be most at risk if a government that is overtly hostile to the sector is elected. Such events might be replicated in other societies, where politicians' desire to do something about anything perceived to be unfair grows each year, and deepens in intensity as the electoral cycle turns.

There are no easy solutions offered by our authors in this chapter. They all believe, rightly, that at their best, prep schools can offer a wonderful foundational education for our youngest children. They can light those fires to which Jane Cameron refers. Every year they produce happy and balanced young people ready to go on to senior schools full of hope and eager to learn and contribute. But if they are not planning for the next 20 years now, they risk seeing that future put at significant risk. Planning for the future is, for many prep schools, planning for survival. It is in the interests of the whole sector, even though this means working directly with competitor schools, to come together to agree on shared strategies that will minimise the threats that our authors explore in this chapter.

Jane Cameron

'*Next the whining schoolboy with his satchel and shining morning face creeping like snail unwillingly to school…*' The second of Shakespeare's stages of man is spent, almost in its entirety, at junior/prep school. As the whining schoolboy approaches adolescence, he will move on to his senior school.

Unlike most of Shakespeare's themes, which have stood the test of time, I don't think the 'whining schoolboy' accurately reflects the joy with which most young children run into school every day.

A family I know, off on holiday with their reception-age child, travelled to the Outer Hebrides by train, car and ferry, arrived very late and all tumbled into bed. In the morning, the exhausted parents were greeted with the cry from their child: 'hurry up, I want to go to my school'. Joy at home, on holiday or at school was indistinguishable for that little boy.

As educators in junior schools, we are, to a considerable extent, the custodians of the joy of childhood.

Of course, reception is very much a time of play and exploration, of learning through experiences, the 'I do and I understand' philosophy of curriculum development introduced by the Nuffield Foundation over 50 years ago. But what happens beyond reception? Can the joy of childhood continue to flourish as the looming cloud of fiercely competitive exams grows ever closer, ever more competitive and ever more unsuccessful in celebrating the qualities that will ultimately lead to fulfilment and a purposeful life?

A preparatory school is defined by its name, and the curriculum dictated by the requirements of the schools it feeds. Places in London day schools, in particular, are fiercely contested and tutors may be taken on board by parents as early as Year 1. Wide-eyed innocence, communing with nature, dream-catching and star-gazing can drown in the pursuit of exam readiness.

In these circumstances, can academic rigour sit comfortably with the joy of childhood?

I believe it can. Learning is part of a joyous, fulfilling childhood, a time for experiencing awe and wonder. We have the opportunity to light a fire, not just fill a bucket, to challenge children to take risks, to embrace making mistakes as a means of becoming independent learners, to develop a growth mindset where perseverance and resilience bring self-esteem and the knowledge that 'I can't do that' must always be accompanied by 'yet'.

When taking visitors around school, children will often declare that what they like about their school is the 'fun lessons' or the 'fun teachers'. Whilst the modern use of 'fun' jars, the sentiment is spot on. The neurologist Judy Willis has written:

> The truth is that when we scrub joy and comfort from the class-room, we distance our students from effective information processing and long-term memory storage. Instead of taking pleasure from learning, students become bored, anxious, and anything but engaged.[1]

A child is not defined by the exams he or she passes; exams are only part of the process of a good education, not the end in itself. As our digital world becomes ever more sophisticated, it is the qualities and attitudes that artificial intelligence cannot master that we need to develop in our pupils: empathy, kindness, collaboration, sensitivity and effective communication. And passion: there must always be space for allowing and encouraging passions to develop. A child's passion, if nurtured, may develop into action that will bring change and true innovation.

No longer can teenage mental health be a concern of senior schools alone. Exam stress, increasing numbers of family breakdowns and the pressure of social media present a toxic cocktail of challenges for pre-teenagers to navigate. And in our efforts to preserve the 'joy of childhood', we try to support and shield, but we must also educate and provide strategies for self protection.

In this time of fracturing of communities, one of the most important roles of a school is to create a sense of belonging where all the stakeholders (children, parents, staff) take ownership of their community and enjoy shared experiences and opportunities to work collaboratively, young and old together, for the greater good and happiness of all.

The idealised picture of childhood would very likely include scenes of laughter, singing and dancing. We sing to our babies from earliest days and we delight in seeing their first smile. These instinctive interactions with a new baby are powerful promoters of a sense of well-being and we would be well advised to learn from what nature has instilled in us. Laughter and singing together should be integral parts of the well-being curriculum of any school. What better way to start the school day than with a gathering of all members of the school community singing joyfully with a collective sense of empathy and purpose.

Tomorrow's movers and shakers, tomorrow's artists and innovators, tomorrow's scientists and politicians will emerge with integrity if children are given the opportunity to be just children and are equipped with the skills to navigate the pressures of our modern, digital world whilst being allowed time to grow into themselves – that is our challenge.

Phillip Evitt

Like it or not, private education is a commodity to be bought, and a very expensive one at that. Inevitably, there is greater focus on what is on offer and the quality of the 'after sales care' than ever before. Parents who can afford the fees, those who are still in the game, are, by definition, successful and affluent. They carry great responsibilities, lead demanding lives in roles where high expectations and efficiency are the norm; to put it crudely, they know what good looks like and expect it from others. They understand the dangers of complacency, mediocrity and poor customer service and they don't want this from their child's school. The relationship between the school and parents has moved from one where respect for and trust in the school was a given, to one where trust and respect must be earned.

Parents expect a level of individualised care and knowledge of their child that goes far beyond what was demanded in the past. Most parents do not have unreasonable or unrealistic perceptions of their children, they accept they are not A★ pupils, they are soon reconciled to them not making the A teams, or staring in the year group production, but they won't accept their child being failed by the school, either academically or pastorally. They want their child to become the very best and happiest they can be, given their abilities and character and they expect the school to deliver on this. They want their child, to use Mungo Dunnett's phrase, 'optimised', and if they feel this isn't happening, they will look elsewhere. Given we are dealing with the single most important thing in parents' lives, their children, and that private education costs serious money, such expectations are not unreasonable. Today, parents want a far more 'hands on' and collaborative role in their child's education. They want to be a part of 'the journey', not necessarily to tell us how to do it, unless they feel we are getting it badly wrong, but because they care deeply about their children. Schools are seen as service providers, held accountable when that service falls short. Email and smartphones make contacting schools easier and even boarding prep schools, once largely immune to regular parental visits, now deal with parents living much closer to their child's school, so face to face discussion is another expectation.

The challenge for schools is how to deliver on such expectations. And how to do this without putting their staff under unreasonable pressure. Schools have explored a number of ways of doing this, but the most common has been increasing staffing levels to compensate for the reduction in the teaching time needed to allow them to manage parents' daily academic and pastoral concerns. This shift in time commitments has had a profound impact on fee levels. I have no evidence, but I would be surprised if private junior schools in other countries have not seen a similar change in staff/parent interactions. But in addition, schools in England have had to cope with rises in the costs of employment, particularly in pensions, where employee contributions have risen from 8 per cent to 24 per cent, along with increased National Insurance contributions.

How can schools best respond? The levers on cost that are likely to have the biggest long-term impact are class sizes and staffing levels. Yet increasing class sizes presents major challenges to a sector where smaller classes are another expectation. Reducing staffing levels requires great courage and resilience on the part of any Head. However, courage to tackle both, however unpalatable, will have to be found if fees are to be kept in check. The slow unwinding of the 2008 financial crash and the impact of Brexit, coupled with the increased quality of many state primary schools, has seen numbers in pre-preps and preps, even across the affluent South East of England fall sharply, as many parents looking at affordability are choosing to take the 'State till 8' route. The outlook for boarding and Saturday school is even more challenging. Prep Heads are now looking at smaller intakes at Year 3 and 4 from their own feeders, driving the need to make up numbers from elsewhere. Things are not getting any easier.

Prep Heads must identify how they and their colleagues can deliver the very best all-round education that genuinely *and evidentially* fulfils their promises to their parents, while offering the highest levels of customer service, without allowing fees to continue their giddy ascent. We offer sensationally good education, but if we fail to balance the challenges of aspiration and expectation with affordability, that education and our schools will be, as Ralph Lucas suggests, *going very slowly and gently into that goodnight.*

Richard Foster

The pupil landscape is evolving.

Ten years ago, pupils would predominantly be from the UK, with parents and grandparents who had more often than not attended an independent school. Mostly driven by affordability, the landscape is changing, especially in the prep school arena. There is an increase in overseas pupils and a decrease in the more local 'traditional' children. Parents are increasingly judging schools on the outcome of their child. However, 'returns' are not those that could be broadly categorised as creating a 'rounded' or 'broadly educated' child; no, the 'return on investment' is now characterised by their academic results and the senior school their child is accepted by.

We have a number of good state schools in our local area (West Sussex) and there is a growing number of parents choosing to send their children to these schools for the first part of their schooling. This is driven by affordability. Some then come on to Windlesham, especially if they are looking to go to an independent senior school, but also to take advantage of the breadth of education and activities on offer.

Boarding is also changing to meet the requirements of parents. The trend for UK-based parents is for schools to provide more accessibility and flexibility to them, especially at prep school age. However, this isn't an attractive model for overseas parents who want a good number of children in at the weekends and activities to keep them busy and interested.

My school has strong relationships with all the senior schools we send to them at 13 although there are still a small number of girls who leave at 11 to go on to single sex schools, who suggest it is more competitive to gain a place for them at 13+. Until recently, I was confident that these schools would always encourage parents to keep their children at their boarding prep school.

Whilst the day of the eight-year-old boarder is becoming very rare, those of us with a majority of boarders are still attracting parents where circumstances necessitate placing their child in a safe and caring environment. In the main, I would suggest that parents are willing to consider boarding at Year 5 and certainly Year 6.

Safeguarding has in the last few years become the most important factor in any schools' make up and nowhere more so in a prep school where children are looked after 24 hours a day. Safeguarding is at the top of any agenda whether it be a departmental meeting, a whole school staff meeting or Governors' meeting.

The secret of being not just a good school but a great school is the quality of one's staff and I include non-teaching appointments as well as teaching appointments in this. Recruiting staff is an art as well as a lottery. Retaining good staff is a key element to school management. At the same time, a reasonable turnover of teaching staff is important in creating a new outlook and good practice.

I am concerned that there is a distinct trend in teachers not wanting to be so involved and committed to working at weekends and I would suggest boarding schools will have to be more creative in their boarding provision at weekends.

There does seem to be a growing number of senior schools that are becoming competitors rather than allies to prep schools. More and more senior girls schools are taking children at 11+ and there is a growing trend in London and the Home Counties to convert to 11+ schools so as to boost their numbers.

There is little doubt that the scene is changing and lots of strategic planning is very much on the agenda within governing bodies. We must continue to be agile and adapt to ongoing changes whether they be about affordability, the political arena or parent demand, but the primary focus will always be putting the child and their 'whole' education and wellbeing at the heart of everything we do.

Ralph Lucas

In 1896, there were 76 independent schools in Eastbourne. Now there are four (or, if you were being scrupulous, you'd say that there was just one, plus bits of two others). Putting money on the decline of the prep school has been a one-way bet for more than a century – is there any sign of their luck changing?

No. But the decline is slow, and within that trend, some parts of the system are growing, and others are undiminished in their strength.

So let us begin with all the reasons why prep schools will continue to flourish.

In London, there are a large number of foreign nationals for whom the state does not cater, and will probably never cater. They want schools that are, like themselves, high-achieving and highly ambitious schools, where they can drop in whenever their career takes them to London, wherever they are living and whatever the ages of their children. State school admission rules are a long way away from offering this, and there is no sign of change. While London flourishes, so will its preparatory schools, and such schools will attract natives as well as foreigners.

There are families for whom getting their child into a top-brand senior school is a must, and who will therefore patronise prep schools with a track record.

There seems very little chance that there will ever be more than a couple of good state primary schools that a child living at a particular address will have a decent chance of getting into, given state admission rules (rediscovering religion can add an option or two). This is not just a matter of parents caring about academic results: pedagogy, discipline, religion, hours, ambition and attitudes all count. I remember being told by a London state primary: "We don't teach children here, we give them the opportunity to learn"; it appeared from observation and enquiry that what they were actually doing was letting them mess about and fight. No way was I having that. Private schools will continue to do well where the state refuses to provide what parents want: it is remarkable how much parents will sacrifice for the sake of a good education for their children.

And what about grammar schools? Because grammar schools exist, offering a prestigious, well-behaved, aspirational education for free if only you can pass the test, there will be a role for prep schools that specialise in doing just that.

Some parents' lifestyles – long hours, the likelihood of an overseas posting for relatively short periods at short notice, problems at home – make the parent-focused practices of a prep school (particularly the availability of boarding) very attractive.

Many prep schools are, for a host of reasons, superb places to be educated, and their virtues will attract parents from the UK and overseas. They come in a wide range of styles and specialisms, so you have an excellent chance of finding one where your child's particular talents will be nurtured, particular challenges be accepted, and particular parents be put up with. There is something very special about a good boarding prep in the sheer breadth and depth of education.

Nonetheless...

Fees in the UK sector have become horrendous, and there seems no easy way down. What surplus becomes available is directed to bursaries, with one eye on the Charity Commission and the other on the prospect of a Labour government that is more left wing than previous administrations. Sections of society that, in my youth, thought independent education well within reach, now give it no more than a passing thought.

State schools, taken as a whole, are improving. And all those fees, or a part of them, can be redirected into tutoring (much more available and much better than it used to be) and home-produced educational experiences (such as holidays in Rome).

The independent senior schools have cast aside their loyalty to the prep system. Time was, the registrars of even the grandest schools would take a prep Head's word on the quality of a pupil. Not these days: they rely on a tiered system of exams (pre-tests and Common Entrance), for which prep schools have to spend their final three years cramming instead of educating (depriving prep schools of a chunk of their attractiveness to parents), and open their doors wide to state school pupils (especially if their parents have hired tutors). If parents are cutting back on the money they spend on schooling, the senior schools are determined it should not be on their bit of it.

International schools are multiplying in many countries, and are often good (often offshoots of British schools as Chapter 9 explores). So now you can take your children on that overseas posting and have the benefits of their company and of an education that will transfer seamlessly into the UK – or another overseas posting. This makes it much easier not to send your children away to UK prep schools.

What can be done?

Not much to cut costs – other than joining a chain (good chains reap large financial efficiencies, compared to the corner-shop economy of an independent prep). If you are the first in your patch to let the paint peel and the staff grow seedy in order to cut fees, what chance is there that enough parents will choose you over the glossy establishment down the road? At the core of the parent body are the ones who can afford the fees and want the quality. All local preps would have to move at the same time.

Swallow a charitable school. Cannibalism is usually followed by a great fat property sale that the cannibal can live off for years. Finding that the backing for your dartboard is an Assyrian frieze (as Canford School did) is also recommended!

I cannot think of much that can be done to defeat the other challenges either, and there may be some rapid changes if, as I say, a politically hostile government that takes an active interest in private schools is elected.

Balancing these forces out, the future looks safe enough for London, for the best boarding preps, and for the specialists – schools that cater superbly well to children with particular gifts or challenges.

Preps will also survive as the junior parts of senior schools because the senior schools would be undermining their own defences if they tried to survive without secure feeders.

Beyond that? Some entrepreneurs with charisma, a few chains that really believe in education and know how to cut costs will ensure survival but for the rest there could be a very slow and gentle good night.

Ben Thomas

In many respects, this could be seen as a golden age of junior education in the UK's private sector. The national total of privately educated pupils remains buoyant. The quality of teaching and learning is better than ever before. The best prep schools, unfettered by accountability for national examinations, are able to offer an astonishing breadth of curriculum, which bursts with innovation, imagination and creativity. Above all, commitment to pastoral care has never been stronger. Most junior schools recognise the extraordinary opportunity they have to be nothing less than guardians of childhood; places of kindness and care, whose young charges have time and space to grow and to flourish, to put down roots for their adult lives that are deep and strong; to develop a strong moral code and a set of values which will equip them superbly for the fast-moving world and complex lives that lie ahead of them.

Small wonder that a British independent education – particularly in the younger years – is widely considered to be setting a gold standard, which is admired, and increasingly replicated, in countries throughout the world.

So far, so good. And yet. Whilst we might bask serenely in these sunny uplands, anyone who takes more than a short term view of education, anyone who is looking ten or 20 years ahead (and there is nothing like being a second generation family firm to encourage a generational perspective) may well survey the darkening clouds that are gathering on the horizon and tap the falling barometer with a growing sense of anxiety and foreboding.

For some daunting large-scale and structural challenges lie not very far into the future, for the independent education sector in general and for junior schools in particular. In summary, these are affordability, relevance, parental expectation – and nothing less than a threat to childhood itself.

Affordability

The financial challenge facing all independent schools is addressed in detail elsewhere in this book. Briefly, then, private schools are already almost entirely reliant on the nation's top 1 per cent of earners, in order to maintain their existence. Where resources are stretched at home, parents in the independent sector are already turning to day schools over boarding schools and in many cases, if they must choose, to senior independent education over junior.

The buoyant national picture therefore masks some stark regional differences, with (broadly speaking) growth in London and the South East compensating for a significant decline in the number of pupils in private schools in the North East. Running a boys' boarding prep school near Newcastle is already a profoundly different (and more challenging) proposition than running a coeducational day school in the middle of central London.

The most established senior schools have seen this challenge approaching for some time. As well as looking to international families to maintain their pupil numbers (in boarding schools), the best connected senior schools have long since undertaken huge projects – such as mobilising their alumni network, or starting franchised schools abroad – to raise funds that will safeguard bursaries and protect (to some extent) the social and economic breadth of their intake. Few junior schools, however, have alumni organisations that are extensive or loyal enough to be able to raise significant bursary funds (how many readers of this essay have kept in close contact with their junior schools, I wonder?); few have the governance resources or a sufficiently recognisable 'brand' to start schools abroad. For the average, stand-alone prep school in the UK, school leaders are at full stretch simply trying to keep the lights on at home.

As a result, merely to keep pace with the average increase in teachers' pay (and no one is yet claiming that teachers are overpaid), many prep schools have no option other than to raise their fees, year on year, by some 3 to 5 per cent – even in a zero inflation environment – simply in order to stand still. It is a case of pressing on, hoping for the best and praying that enough prospective pupils will come through the door.

This is not a sustainable strategy. The difference between survival and failure can be paper thin. In cases where those vital pupils do not materialise, decline can be swift and terminal. A steady trickle of private prep schools across the nation have already, quietly, closed their doors. Others will surely follow.

(Ir)relevance

Those private junior schools that *are* still fishing successfully in the diminishing pool of the uber-wealthy nevertheless face a different problem. The first is that, in national terms, they could before long become simply irrelevant. Seven per cent of children in the UK currently attend private schools, the vast majority coming from families who are, as I have said, amongst the top 1 per cent of earners. It follows that 93 per cent of children and 99 per cent of families in the UK simply have no engagement with private schools at all. Private schooling is, for the vast majority, an unaffordable luxury, not even worth contemplating. In fact, in some cases, the sense of unreality of private schools is so great that a proportion of families who *could* afford it choose not to, shunning the privileged 'bubble' of independent education in favour of outstanding schools in the maintained sector, where they believe their children will more likely encounter 'the real world', which they will enter as adults.

It is for this reason that Thomas's shouldered responsibility for a primary academy in Fulham, now in its third year as Thomas's Academy. This is no cynical move to demonstrate public benefit: as a proprietorial organisation, we have no charitable status to defend. It has been, however, a vital lesson in community, in living out our values in the 'real world' and in the mainstream challenges of running a school on a central government budget. It has kept us firmly relevant, authentic and engaged in the national educational debate.

Parental expectation

The affordability issue also drives a second, significant challenge, which – at risk of generalising – is the changing nature of independent school parents. With school fees in England up by nearly 100 per cent since 2003, parents' expectations are, not unreasonably, sky high. The days of the laid-back, hands-off middle class parent (if they ever existed) are long gone. Parents choosing private schools now are highly educated, highly discerning and very often buying into such an expensive product for a very specific purpose: the educational advancement of their child and a firm foot in the door for the next stage of their education. "I pay therefore I expect" has fast become a mantra that is hard for any but the most confident (and secure) of schools to dare to contradict.

In London, this has been compounded by a subtle but discernible shift in admissions amongst a small but significant number of senior day schools from entry at the age of 13 to entry at the age of 11. The effect of this has been to shine a spotlight on the fiercely competitive admissions process to 'the best' senior schools (with ten applicants to every place not unknown, or even unusual). A growing number of these highly-informed, highly competitive parents (themselves employed in highly competitive industries) now engage tutors for their children at an early age, in order to secure a perceived advantage in the race to gain admission for their child to the best senior schools, to secure a place in the best universities, to secure the best possible prospects in the job market.

Despite the stated values of many prep schools and parents' instinctive understanding of the benefit of a broad curriculum in childhood, when push comes to shove, such parents are more concerned about exam practice over art and interview practice over independent study. "A broad education is all very well", the modern parent might say, "but getting my child into the senior school of my choice is your responsibility – and trumps all".

The threat to childhood

As a result, taken to extremes, the very purpose of prep schools is under threat. Increasingly reliant on highly affluent, highly focused parents who expect results, all but the strongest schools are having to bow to demand. From Year 5 to Year 8 (the ages of ten to thirteen), in precisely the years when children's young minds should be free to imagine, explore and create, the prep school curriculum is in danger of being reduced to preparation for competitive entrance examinations in English and Maths – in a system entirely self-imposed by the independent sector. Senior schools cry out, on the one hand, that they do not want to encourage the recruitment of over-anxious, over-prepared young robots. At the same time, the same schools are quite happy to let slip the number of applicants per place, by way of illustrating their popularity – hence feeding the anxiety of junior school parents.

There are exceptions. In a flight to excellence, the best will always survive. Some schools do an excellent job of standing up for childhood, of promoting music and drama, sports and the climbing of trees – and command a loyal following for doing so. On the whole, though, these are the schools that are confident enough in their popularity – and their future – to take the risk of putting off a number of parents in order to stand by their principles. Many – perhaps most – are not in such a luxurious position, and cannot afford to take the risk of putting off any prospective parents at all.

Looking ahead

Such are some of the challenges facing independent junior schools today. Some may choose to stand firm by their principles, refusing to adapt or change. Whilst one can admire such a heroic stance, one cannot help feeling that, Light Brigade-like, "*c'est magnifique, mais ce n'est pas la guerre*". Surely no independent school can afford to ignore the seismic shifts of the tectonic plates on which it currently stands?

Independent junior schools must be thinking in terms of the next 20 years and considering how to tackle these issues of affordability, relevance, managing parental expectations and safeguarding the kind of childhood which they were founded to promote.

These are deep-rooted and fundamental challenges, to which there are no simple solutions. But junior schools that are not already actively engaged in a search for answers have good reason to fear for their very survival.

Note

1   Willis, J. (2007). Educational Leadership, *Journal of the Department of Supervision and Curriculum Development*, N.E.A. 64 January 2007 *with* 187 Reads.

Chapter 4

The financial challenge

Introduction to the financial challenge

Almost everyone associated with independent schools – be they parents, teachers or governors – agrees on one thing: the fees are too high. Additionally, many would also state that the current rate of increase is unsustainable. This is not an issue limited to the United Kingdom, but is true of all developed markets in industrialised economies. The exception is in the developing world where, as James Tooley writes, low-cost independent schools are opening at a fast rate to keep up with demand. As these markets stabilise, no doubt some schools will begin to charge more than their competitors because they are getting consistently better results or offering superior facilities. A hierarchy of cost and status will establish itself, as it inevitably does in any free market as it matures.

There are many people, mostly on the left of politics, who oppose fee-paying schools. For them, such schools deepen social divisions, exacerbating the growing gap between rich and poor. This is where the economic merges with the political. It seems to be the case, however, that most societies that adhere to broadly free market economics do not outlaw independent schools, or place restrictions on families wishing to send their children to such institutions, either in their home country or abroad. No doubt such constraints would be seen as a slippery slope: if you stop someone spending their money on education, why not on private health care? Or pensions? If you start doing that, the rich will simply go elsewhere. And in those countries that charge university fees, how would it be possible to charge a fee for going on to higher education, but claim it is immoral to do the same when the students are younger? In a free society people should be entitled to spend their money on what they want, as long as it does not explicitly cause other people harm.

Most people would agree that today's independent schools do not harm the pupils they teach. And if we accept James Tooley's snapshot poll of people on a Newcastle street corner, it seems that a majority of ordinary people (rather than millionaires) would like to send their children to a private school. The reason they don't, of course, is that they can't afford to. The reality in England is that school fees have risen nearly 100 per cent since 2003. As Heather MacGregor writes in this chapter, 'at this rate, the only people able to afford an independent education for their children will be the very wealthy, and the teachers who work at those schools and get fee discounts. That doesn't sound like a very balanced set of students to me'. Few would disagree. MacGregor has sacrificed much to send her children to independent schools, and in her essay she explores initiatives that could broaden the intake for pupils. She believes innovation is necessary if the financial challenges are to be met. It is essential that schools explore every possibility, or they risk becoming increasingly removed from the societies that allow them to operate. Independent schools, so good at developing and sustaining networks, should perhaps look instead at the communities they are in.

And independent schools should consider, even more carefully, what they spend their fees on. The 'facilities arms race' that Stephen Crouch refers to has probably run its course in all but the more heavily over-subscribed schools. But even they must be questioning whether any profits they generate would be better spent on increasing the number of bursaries. For Crouch, 'money belongs to the world of actions rather than words. Actions often *reveal* where words *conceal*...Money lays bare what we really *value*'. It would be interesting to discover how much some independent schools invest in the further professionalisation of their staff compared to the new sports centre, or tennis courts. Or how many 110 per cent bursaries they have awarded in the last five years. Any such imbalances between facilities and results can be explored by an inspection, and they can easily turn out to be a false economy because, as we have read in Chapter 2, parents increasingly place a premium on academic outcomes, not the number of squash courts a school has.

Money and education are uneasy bedfellows. For some, learning has an innate purity which is sullied if it comes into contact with finance. Teachers are not business people, and they didn't go into the profession to worry about profit and loss. That said, in independent schools, now there is greater awareness of the value of each pupil's place, and the days when a headteacher could airily allocate money worries to his or her bursar are (not so ancient) history. For David Woodgate 'the strongest schools in the future will be ones which operate like businesses, with robust short-term operating plans and budgets, which underpin longer term strategic objectives, which support in turn rolling ten-year aspirational plans'. This may be the language of the boardroom, not the classroom, but there is undeniably a strong element of truth in the claim. And it could mean, as the market adjusts to economic and political turbulence, that some schools will see their common rooms shrink, and other schools will go out of business altogether.

If things are bad in England, then they seem to be worse in Scotland. The drive for independence in that country has seen greater powers ceded from Westminster to Edinburgh. The result is that the Scottish Nationalist government has begun to bring in measures that will see schools lose charitable relief on business rates. For John Edward, this is 'quixotic' and incoherent, and looks suspiciously like 'a proxy for their own opposition to the independent sector'. He remains defiant, however, believing that the sector is robust enough to fend off politically motivated financial constraints.

Others are not so bullish. How, governors will ask, can we keep putting fees up year-on-year? Where is the breaking point for parents? But the fees keep climbing and the pupils keep coming, for now at least. And other threats may be developing. Jame Tooley is in the process of establishing a low-cost independent school that those aspirational parents on average incomes can afford. If he succeeds then others will follow. And who is to say that companies like GEMS, or Bridge International Academies – who have expanded in clearly identified target markets – may not expand into more established markets, such as the United States, the United Kingdom and Australia? Indeed, perhaps such markets need to be disrupted.

The bottom line has never mattered more for independent schools; the margins have never been so narrow, the market never more competitive. And yet demand is still there. Although the fees are too high, customer satisfaction remains, for the most part, good. And those who oppose fee-paying schools, but who are broadly in favour of market forces improving standards, should keep in mind Stephen Crouch's direct statement that our schools' value 'lies in the state not having a monopoly on educating children'. That role, seldom discussed openly in political circles, should not be underestimated. Competition, and independence, are valuable commodities. If we lose them because of short-termist goals, we run the very real risk of making the major provider of education less effective and open to change because service benefits from becoming a monopoly, especially if it is underfunded and has difficulties of its own to contend with. If independent schools do not meet the financial challenge, thus making them increasingly unaffordable, they will have to face the consequences. But nobody will benefit from this and it will undoubtedly be a price too high to pay.

Stephen Crouch

There is an honesty in cold hard cash.

Money belongs to the world of actions rather than words. Actions often *reveal* where words *conceal*. In schools, where founding myths and drab mission statements can divert attention, the willingness to pay exposes our motivations, fears and hopes. Money lays bare what we really *value*.

For me, the value of independent schools lies in the state not having a monopoly on educating children. Whole community state provision can be wondrous, but it can also be dire. The liberty to choose an alternative to the state outweighs the potential for minimising inequality of opportunity through standardising access. Schools should defend this independence at almost any cost – even, god forbid, by paying tax. When we give up our independence at a government's bidding to save a few pounds, we undermine our very best reason for existing.

Fine sentiments on liberty in education these may be, but none of it really tells you why I give up a substantial part of my income to send my child to your school rather than the free one nearby. Financial pessimism is fashionable and fee-paying schools everywhere are nervous about their future. The sources of potential systematic woes are manifold: the end of the late twentieth-century boom in professional jobs, housing and financial asset price bubbles that transfer wealth to older generations and away from new parents, increased regulatory burdens. The growth in income inequality and the increase in competition for top university places maintain demand, but government intervention looms. In the UK, pessimism deepens with the prospect of a 20 per cent sales tax being applied to private school fees by a Labour government.

A free(ish) market in education means that all price points will be served – from local day schools with budgets that may not far outstrip state provision to the grandest of boarding schools with acres of manicured lawns, golf courses, riding stables and performing arts centres. For schools at lower price points, financial challenges are the stuff of everyday trade-offs and decisions; parents, often both working, may be at the margins of affordability. Families may be escaping a local state provision beset by behavioural challenges or just a persistent lack of aspiration. In fee paying schools, often the most important choice being made is the attitude of the families whose educational journey your children will share; that determines outcomes at least as much as the smart tartan uniform, the playing fields, the drama shows and the exotic trips.

At the top end, schools are a positional good – it is their exclusivity both in terms of the wealth of the parents as well as the school's capacity to be academically selective, that makes them so desired. Access to such a school shows not only that you are part of the social elite, but that you have produced a child who is able; this heady mix of privilege, in the positive sense of the word, and meritocracy is irresistible.

Choice in fee-paying schools is always and everywhere about relative status rather than an absolute level of provision. Prices can go up and down, cost structures and provision can change without any existential threat, as long as the relativity that drives your customers' choices endures. Independent schools in the UK at both ends of the spectrum were as much in demand 15 or 20 years ago, when their prices were 20 per cent lower in real terms. If the dreaded sales tax comes, the adjustment will be painful, but the sector can survive largely intact. The main impact in the long run, apart from a pause in the facilities arms race, would actually be to reverse the teacher pupil ratio gains of recent decades, releasing thousands of teachers back into the market. This will be a boon for a state sector, where a lack of high quality applicants for teaching posts has been a persistent challenge. This could threaten the cheaper end of the fee paying market more than a return to the fee levels of the early 2000s.

So, my advice to fee-paying schools is to stay calm as the economy and government chip away at prices or add to costs. Focus on your "value add" – not so much in grades for the pupils as in the perceptions of the parents. Take a cold, hard look at why parents pay you; ignore vested interests who will defend their territory, whether it is set sizes, obscure minority sports or long-dead ancient languages. There are many possible versions of your school. The books can be balanced in any version parents will buy.

John Edward

> I was born in London, and went to school in Scotland – I used to be dead tired when I got home at night.
>
> (Sir Norman Wisdom)

Any venture north (or south) of the border is a long journey in terms of education. That much is nothing new. While challenges, choices and charges of schools are the same, there have been many years of divergence in structure and approach, increased by recent debates over Scottish independence. It is more than an adherence to Harry Lauder-esque clichés about parsimony to recognise that the financial challenges are different too.

Education has always been a Scotland-specific matter, from long before parliamentary devolution caught up with the administrative variety. The Education (Scotland) Act took over the running of schools from the Church of Scotland's Board of Education in 1872. In the independent sector, some schools became independent following the changes of the 1970s while others pre-date the Treaty of Union itself.

Devolution to the Scottish Parliament in 1999 kicked off a game of educational reorganisation and accentuates the extent to which the financial environment for the sector is discrete from other parts of the United Kingdom.

The key funding difference between Scotland (and Wales) and England is that there is no halfway house, financially or academically, between the two sectors. The end of selective education in the 1970s leaves 'grammar' schools in name only, and the move towards free schools or academies is limited to current tentative proposals to increase some of the autonomy of comprehensive school heads. As a result, there are only two funding models[1] – local authority or fee-paying independent. Some independent schools for complex additional support needs operate under wider bodies such as the National Autistic Society, the Priory Group or Capability Scotland, but there is no mainstream presence of Multi-Academy Trusts or external private funding.

The proportion of parents employed by the public sector in cities such as Dundee and Glasgow is likely to be higher than the South-East of England, which in turn leaves their prosperity at the mercy of national budgets. In the same way, schools in cities like Aberdeen and Edinburgh, strongly reliant on key industries like oil or financial services respectively, will feel any chill wind that blows through those sectors. Independent research shows that day and boarding fees in Scotland are generally below the average in England, while the recent rate of annual fee increases has been shallower as well.

Of course, the sector in Scotland has faced unique challenges, which others elsewhere may have watched with doleful sympathy, but should probably be savoured as a taste of things to come. The Charities and Trustee Investment (Scotland) Act 2005 has left independent schools the most tested and scrutinised of all the 24,400 registered charities in Scotland, 180,000 in England and Wales and, arguably, across the English-speaking education world.

A public benefit test for each individual school was designed in the Holyrood Parliament's 2005 Charities Act, and schools then spent 12 years meeting that test – tripling the annual provision of means-tested fee assistance to pupils as a result. School staff help design the curriculum and National Qualifications, work as Assessors for school inspections (which remain uniform across Scottish schools), share staff and teaching resources with hundreds of local authority schools, and open facilities for free or at non-commercial rates across the country. It is not fanciful to imagine that a future administration in London might also consider a similar, tailored, test of public benefit for schools in England and Wales. Such a test would surely be a more palatable and practical contribution than recent suggestions of a substantial tax levied on school fees.

Progress in Scotland has been thrown into question by the Scottish Government's recent decision to accept the conclusions of the Barclay Review of Business Rates. The Review concluded, despite evidence to the contrary, that independent schools were uniquely remiss in not paying 100 per cent rates, despite their status along hundreds of other educational charities, including universities, that restrict admissions and charge fees, just as schools do. (The Welsh Government has announced the intention to consult on a similar move). The sector's simple view of the Barclay Review was that it raised issues the Scottish Parliament had already worked long and hard to tackle, and awaits with curiosity the draft legislation that will put these changes into law.

Those who have used business rates or charitable status as a proxy for their own opposition to the independent sector will receive no satisfaction. There is not the slightest chance it will diminish the dedication, energy, expertise and prudence that independent schools have shown over decades, if not centuries. Scottish schools will, as ever, continue to define independence in Scotland in their own terms.

Heather McGregor

Independent schools, as we know, educate only 7 per cent of the children in the UK. I was once one of those 7 per cent, my husband had also been independently educated, and we aspired to provide that education for our children. We wrote our first cheque for independent school fees in 1991, when our eldest was not yet three (£500 for a term at a nursery school in central London) and have just written the last one, in 2018 (£12,500 for a term at a boarding school in Oxford). During that time, we have done everything (legal) you could think of to pay the fees. Paid them in advance to get a discount, used installment payments when times were tougher, borrowed the money through remortgaging, taken on second jobs, you name it.

Since we started paying, independent school fees in the UK have risen by more than twice the amount that wages have. Is this sustainable? I doubt it. At this rate, the only people able to afford an independent education for their children will be the very wealthy, and the teachers who work at those schools and get fee discounts. That doesn't sound like a very balanced set of students to me.

The solution? I am not sure that there is any one solution. I believe that a whole range of initiatives needs to be considered if independent schools are to continue to be viable (and available) to parents in the UK. Here I set out four ideas that I believe are worthy of debate and development.

New models of loan for parents

Parents often have assets (home equity, future inheritance), or future expectations of income (bonuses, increased pay), that would suggest that they could pay for school fees through borrowing. But the current options for doing so are very limited. The most easily available model for installments sees the annual school fees, plus an interest charge, divided by 12 and taken monthly by direct debit. This only spreads the repayment over one calendar year, which, while more manageable for many than three major cash demands, doesn't really extend the time horizon meaningfully over the parents' earning expectancy. The only current proxy is to take out extensions to their mortgages, which is not really a sensible way of matching assets to liabilities. Long-term (10+) year loans secured on property or other tangible assets, specifically for school fees, could see grandparents act as guarantors where necessary. Will someone out there please develop this product?

New models of school

I have watched with interest the continued expansion of low-cost private schools in developing nations. In India and Africa there has been an explosion of provision since 2005. Just as there is demand in the UK for the stripped-down service of budget airlines, so there may well be for a school that doesn't offer the most well equipped language labs, swimming pools etc, but just focuses on getting five GCSEs at grades A–C (or 9–4 using the new currency). These could be free schools (for those outside the UK these are – confusingly – state-sponsored schools that are 'free' of local authority management) or even private, but cutting extras to the bone to make them affordable. I suspect there is a whole market for people who would not be concerned about the absence of a polo field. I am particularly struck by the King's School for Mathematics, a state school sixth form founded by King's College London to address the pipeline of talented pupils in STEM subjects. It's third intake completed their studies in 2018. Fifty-nine per cent of all A levels achieved were A★ grades, 88 per cent were A★/A and 97 per cent were A★/A/B, which – when the league tables are published – are likely to place them top of all UK state schools, the rank that they also enjoyed in 2017. Even more critically, each student on average did more than one whole grade better than the GCSE grades predicted.

True, there is a restricted range of A levels, and purists would argue that they are missing out not rubbing shoulders with people studying Latin or dance, but their curriculum includes personal development and a whole range of extension activity. I predict more schools where this came from, and not just in the state sector.

New models of bursary provision

Well capitalised schools with access to substantial endowments (e.g. Eton) run extensive bursary schemes to ensure that they are not just educating the children of the wealthy, and those of their own staff. Even King's School for Mathematics gives travel bursaries – and other financial support – to all who need it. Christ's Hospital runs, in effect, a means-tested fee scheme – it provides more bursarial support to its pupils than any other school in the independent boarding sector and has done for over 460 years. Bursaries are granted to 75 per cent of students, who receive between 5 per cent and 100 per cent assistance with their boarding fees according to their household income, and families on very low incomes may also be assisted with the cost of extras including pocket money. But how can a school achieve the endowment funds needed to provide such access? Here I would look to the US, where every private university works assiduously with its alumni to raise the money for future funding. The time to start doing that is before they have even left school – every leaving class could raise a class gift, and compete with the previous year to better it. My alma mater the London Business School does this to great effect. Students could undertake sponsored activities and events to raise the funds, and if that interferes too much with A level revision (or Netflix viewing) then I am sure the odd parent would write a cheque.

New models of capital provision

One of the fascinating facts for anyone logging onto the Charity Commission's beta site[2] is that you can obtain the most recent accounts from any of the UK's independent schools operating as a charity (i.e. most of them). The 'financials' analysis shows how much of the fee income is being spent on educating your children and how much on servicing debt. I suspect that parents would prefer schools to spend most of their current income on their children. Given the debt burden of many, indeed most, independent schools, I would encourage those of sufficient size and asset base to investigate the long term bond market – here at Heriot-Watt University we issued a very long-dated bond in December 2016, raising £112m to retire all existing debt and secure our capital investment programme for the foreseeable future. The terms of such an instrument are much more conducive for longer-term capital planning than a standard bank loan, and could reduce the servicing costs that are being covered by parents in their fees. I would also suggest that schools add onto the bill each term a small contribution for capital expenditure and then invite parents to remove the item if they wish. All UK tax-paying parents should sign gift aid forms when the child starts in the school. I introduced this when I was a parent governor at a prep school over a decade ago and I believe the school has used it ever since to service capital borrowing.

I hope that these ideas have been food for thought. None of them alone will solve the affordability question overnight, and even all four put together will not provide the complete answer. But radical thinking is needed if independent education is going to be accessible, even for the 7 per cent.

James Tooley

Private education in the UK is too expensive for all but the elite. But low-cost private schools, affordable even to the poor, are ubiquitous across the developing world. Could we not see the same here?

Private (day) school fees reportedly average £15,500 per annum,[3] or £298.08 per week (dividing £15,500 by 52). Data on UK family *discretionary* income[4] shows that this is only affordable to the richest quintile (columns 3&4, Table 4.1). Discretionary income takes gross family income, subtracts (or adds) taxes (or tax credits), and further subtracts the amount required for necessities such as food, clothing and housing, as well as costs such as school uniform and books. The richest quintile has on average £688 per week – so if two children are in school, even these families will use up *all* their discretionary income on fees. (Regional data doesn't give a better outcome: e.g. average school fees in the North East are 69 per cent of fees in London, but average discretionary income is only 49 per cent, so school fees are *more* unaffordable in the North East than in London[5]).

Table 4.1 UK family income, gross and discretionary, and school fees (average and low cost)

Quintile	Discretionary income (per week)	Average weekly school fees (£298)		Low cost weekly school fees (£52)	
		Discretionary income as proportion of school fees (one child)	Discretionary income as proportion of school fees (two children)	Discretionary income as proportion of school fees (one child)	Discretionary income as proportion of school fees (two children)
Poorest income quintile	−£23	−0.08	−0.04	−0.44	−0.22
2nd quintile	£56	0.19	0.09	1.08	0.54
3rd quintile	£111	0.37	0.19	2.13	1.07
4th quintile	£264	0.89	0.44	5.08	2.54
Riches income quintile	£688	2.31	1.15	13.23	6.62

Source: Data on discretionary income from Centre for Economics and Business Research (2017), pp. 5–7.

Clearly, private education in the UK is only for the elite. Does it have to be that way?

In the developing world, there is an extraordinary burgeoning of low-cost private schools. In urban areas, 70 per cent or more of children uses private education, while in rural areas the figure is 30 per cent. This education is affordable – schools can be found where fees for all the children make up 10 per cent of income for a family on the poverty line.[6]

Now there are chains of low-cost private schools emerging. One, Bridge International Academies, founded in 2008, is the largest chain in the world, with over 100,000 children in Kenya, Uganda, Nigeria, Liberia and India. A more modest chain, which I co-founded in the same year, Omega Schools, has 60 schools in Ghana and Liberia.

Could the same emerge in the UK? A couple of years ago, I interviewed parents on street corners in Newcastle-upon-Tyne; 62 per cent said they would be interested in an affordable private school. Around one-fifth thought they could afford a school costing around £50 per week.

So I developed an outline business plan, got an experienced private headmaster enthused, and we began to develop the model and get a school registered. The figure we've come up with is £2,700 per annum, or £52 per week (over 52 weeks), which we believe will create a viable business, giving a reasonable return to investors. The schools will be 'no-frills', but this doesn't mean low quality. We can bring costs down by renting premises rather than tying up capital in purchasing; rents in low-income parts of town are cheaper than we expected. We won't be able to employ expensive teachers, but believe that we can create a great school with energetic new teachers, or those who are retired but eager to contribute more, or with those who are no longer enthused about working in the public sector who may be willing to work for less if greater satisfaction was guaranteed.

In the United Kingdom, the media liked the idea: the *Telegraph, Mail, Sun* and *Times* all somehow picked up on the development. Before we knew it we had expressions of interest from over 100 families, without any marketing. Many parents, it turns out, think that state schools are not good enough for their children, or simply want more control and accountability than is found in the public sector.

Table 4.1 (columns 5&6) shows that £52 per week is affordable even for parents in the second poorest quintile – for one child at least (their discretionary income is £56 per week). Parents in the third quintile can now afford to send two children to private school (discretionary income £111 per week). With fees as low as we are offering, private education need no longer be the preserve of only the richest. For such families, this may mean cutting back on 'holidays, cinema, eating out, national lottery and other gambling' (but not alcohol, as this is included in necessities). In developing countries, it is reported how families scrimp and save to afford private education. Perhaps aspirational families in the UK will also favour this kind of prioritising of their needs.

David Woodgate

Independent schools' fees have been rising for some time at rates well above inflation. For many schools, this is not sustainable. Parents cannot afford annual rises of 3 per cent or more. Schools therefore need to challenge their cost bases and become financially 'future-proof'. If fees cannot go up, schools must control costs even more tightly. The average day fee in an ISC school in 2018 is nearly £14,000pa, compared to a cost per pupil in similar-sized state schools of around £5000pa, even though a typical state school may have many more disadvantaged or special needs pupils: this suggests that there's ample room for making independent schools more affordable for their traditional parent base.

Inexorable external factors are pushing up costs: apart from wage, food and energy price inflation, there are political uncertainties around VAT on school fees, levies on schools and abolishing mandatory business rate relief. Financial viability, and the need for cost savings, has been thrown into sharp focus by the proposed increase of 43 per cent in employer contributions to the Teachers' Pension Scheme. Cost savings flow from challenging sacred cows and thinking the unthinkable. Accepted wisdom is being challenged – for example, with pupil/staff ratios[7], the curriculum, means testing staff fee remission and removing sibling discounts. But there are other options.

The Independent Schools' Bursars Association (ISBA) supports schools in difficulties; it identifies common factors. Some financial problems originate within school leadership. A breakdown in the relationship between the head, bursar, chairs of governors/finance committees can be very damaging. A lack of engagement with ISBA, the relevant Head's Association or the Association of Governing Bodies of Independent Schools to address weaknesses, is a common factor. There is often a lack of understanding of key performance indicators, such as how many pupils are needed to break even. Dysfunctional boards have a short-term focus, considering the narrow outlook for the year, or even just the current term, rather than three to five years ahead. There is a general unwillingness to address the cost base, market the school, overhaul governance and decision-making, fill skills gaps and to act commercially. There may be ideological barriers to change. Some single-sex schools – particularly girls-only – will not countenance coeducation as a strategic option. Charitable status and religious underpinning can cloud rational business decision making (including in areas such as fee debt collection). Boards cannot remain in denial about the problems they face and must be activist in facing up to current and future threats.

Financial forecasts need to cover the short, medium and long term – with budgets constantly monitored and updated to reflect performance. Schools under financial pressure may be inclined to sell off the family silver – particularly land – without any long-term plan, which buys a few more years of operation but is not financially sustainable without other robust remedial action. Similarly, ambitious building projects are pursued without pause for thought, which can prove problematic if finances tighten in the future. Schools can be guilty of 'buying pupils' with unaffordable levels of fee remission, and waste money on scholarships that are larger than needed – whereas non-means-tested awards should be given for their prestige, not their monetary value. There is a lax culture of cost control in some schools, exemplified for instance by supplier contracts not being continually reviewed, and a failure to consider counter-intuitive options, such as declining in size (but improving profitability) or reducing fees as a precursor to growth. Support staff growth needs to be watched – more schools are employing more non-teaching staff, such as sports coaches or compliance managers, which may not be sustainable. Teachers are allowed generous timetable remissions, and pay may reflect length of service, rather than contribution.

Many schools are exemplars of best practice in facing up to the future. Schools can address financial challenges by careful financial and business planning and challenging the status quo, by mergers or acquiring feeder schools, by specialising (e.g. in elite sports), by joining an established schools' group, possibly by applying to become a state school, or by attracting international investors. In some locations where there are many independent schools, the more forward-looking will realise, strategically, that there is not the room. It is important for proactive discussions around mergers to take place from a position of relative strength, rather than when the cash has run out. Two schools of 500 pupils could come together as a strong future-proofed school of 1000, with the option to sell one site to fund future bursaries and capital development. They can develop new income streams through international expansion or by more proactive marketing to international boarders. Most schools with heritage assets – or modern facilities – are learning how to 'sweat' those assets to generate additional income and to build foundations.

The strongest schools in the future will be ones which operate like businesses, with robust short-term operating plans and budgets, which underpin longer term strategic objectives, which support in turn rolling ten-year aspirational plans. They will be far-sighted and, whilst respecting heritage, will not be hide bound by the past in making decisions; they will change their business models to reflect the environment in which they operate. Critically, they will realise it is possible to run a successful school of virtually any size as long as costs and income are managed within a clear strategic blueprint. The aim should be increasingly for 'affordable quality' and every business assumption must be challenged to achieve this.

Notes

1 The one exception being Jordanhill School, an unique mainstream Grant Aided school funded by a grant from the Scottish Government. www.jordanhill.glasgow.sch.uk/history/.

2 http://beta.charitycommission.gov.uk

3 www.independent.co.uk/news/uk/home-news/the-charts-that-shows-how-private-school-fees-have-exploded-a7023056.html, accessed 06/04/2018

4 Centre for Economics and Business Research (2017) Asda Income Tracker, Report: February 2017, Released: March 2017, London

5 For regional fees see www.telegraph.co.uk/investing/funds/five-ways-to-meet-the-156653-cost-of-private-school/. For regional discretionary income see Centre for Economics and Business Research (2018) Asda Income Tracker, Report: February 2018, Released: March 2018, London, p. 5.

6 See Tooley, J. (2009), *The Beautiful Tree: A personal journey into how the world's poorest people are educating themselves*. Cato Institute, Washington DC; Tooley, J. and Longfield, D. (2016) Affordability of Private Schools: Exploration of a conundrum and towards a definition of "Low-cost", *Oxford Review of Education*, 42(4), 444–459.

7 The pupil-teacher ratio at ISC schools is 8.6: 1. This compares to an average of 17.7: 1 across all state-funded schools in 2017 with the average PTR in senior and all-age day schools being 9.4: 1, and 9.8: 1 in day junior/preps. Parents like the idea of small class sizes but there is little research evidence that small class sizes improve pupil outcomes (this is a matter which has been extensively studied in all advanced nations). Teacher quality matters much more than class size.

Chapter 5

The access challenge

Introduction to the access challenge

Independent schools have become less accessible to ordinary people with average incomes. As we have already read, this often comes down to money: they are simply too expensive for even the comfortable middle classes. But it is goes beyond this. Some schools (and this is not restricted to the United Kingdom, as anyone who has visited leading schools in Asia Pacific and the United States will confirm) have been caught up in an 'arms race' to not only expand and improve their facilities so that they are truly world class, but to also maintain small class sizes. They do the former in order to outdo their nearest competitors; they do the latter because they believe that parents want this. Mostly, they're probably correct, although as John Hattie argued in 2015, smaller classes do not have a clear and beneficial impact on the quality of learning.[1]

Costs are often maintained or increased by independent schools so that they can deliver not just a quality education in the classroom, but also in every other area as well: visitors to some of our schools are often astonished at the number of support staff employed, but it does take this level of investment to ensure that those expensive playing fields, the excellent food, the sports centres and concert halls are maintained. Additionally, many independent schools often see themselves as something more than employers: they sell themselves as benign institutions, places where staff live on campus and send their own children; they are places which have often seen several generations from the same families pass through; and many independent schools have on their payroll old boys and girls who have formed a special bond that is difficult to break.

Ensuring all this continues – and improves – is costly. But the cost reaches beyond the sector's collective bank balance. We have become not only irrelevant to most people but, as Barnaby Lenon writes in this chapter, 'the average independent school has lost a group of doctors, solicitors, university academics and… upper middle class parents… Independent schools have not only lost pupils but also the goodwill of this influential demographic of parents'. Furthermore, he warns that 'the tide of both public and political opinion is turning against us'. The supportive articles in broadly sympathetic newspapers are drying up, and it may well be that the editors commissioning those pieces no longer have any vested interest. Despite those who claim that independent schools are disproportionately influential, we may become more marginal, and less listened to, because we are educating an increasingly exclusive intake. That will have ramifications for the whole sector in the future.

How, then, can that tide be turned back in our favour? How can our independent schools become more accessible to more people? We clearly have to change the conversation around them to start with, and ask ourselves where, as a sector, we want to be in the future. For Patrick Derham, the terrible fire that engulfed Grenfell Tower in 2017 illuminated the gulf in opportunity between the classes in the United Kingdom: 'It made me feel even more uncomfortable about the job I do and made me feel even more passionate about the fact that the opportunity gap between rich and poor in this country, and across the world, is morally unacceptable. It is wrong that the doors of opportunity are open far wider for the wealthy and the privileged few'. We have to have that moral drive – which still characterises some of our schools – to do everything we can to change society for the better.

According to Barnaby Lenon and Nick Hillman, schools have to identify wealthy individuals and persuade them to donate significant sums of money to fund bursaries. But vast sums of money must be involved to have a real and lasting impact on society: to fund 100 places at a boarding school would require an endowment of approximately £200 million. Very few schools, or individuals, could afford such sums. That said, the response in the face of such cold mathematics should not be to give up altogether: that will just ensure that our schools move further away from the people they should seek to serve.

The only way such sums could come into the sector is through government involvement. But as Hillman points out, 'independent schools have been lukewarm about taking public cash as a route to expansion. They have worried about the strings that would be attached – and, rightly so'. Nevertheless, new relationships have to be established between independent schools and government so that we can become accessible to more families. The bursaries that currently exist are selective, and usually awarded by ability. But the sector could explore new awards, using different criteria. Ian Davenport writes in this chapter that in the United Kingdom the sector 'is playing a less than impressive role in addressing the educational causes of social inequality and immobility'. Such criticisms can be heard in other educational systems. SpringBoard's excellent work should be scaled up with the mutual support of independent schools and government. The 1000 looked-after children that the organisation will have helped place in the near future shows that, with leadership and a sense of moral duty, schools can achieve a lot. But they have to be more tactical and transparent in what they are doing, and why. As Davenport writes, 'if these children were either looked after children or children eligible for free school meals then the package starts to drill more effectively into the social mobility debate'.

There are persuasive arguments that could compel them to do so. Some have argued that if independent schools had to show a level of support to low-income families in inspection it would soon speed up their desire to change. It is surely only a matter of time before schools not only show their public benefit, and their income and outgoings, but also how they have decreased costs every year. That will mean that the level of service, and the numbers employed, will have to go down, but they will still surely meet the expectations of parents, especially if the money saved could be reinvested in providing transformative opportunities to young people. The trend in most developed societies is for greater openness and increased social equality. For the sector to isolate itself from such currents would be myopic in the extreme.

And if there was any doubt about how important such programmes are then we need to look no further than David Ejim-McCubbin's essay.

Ian Davenport

As I write, we have just heard that one of our founding SpringBoard students, now a medical student, has been awarded a first class honours degree. Yesterday, we heard that a student placed more recently is to become head girl of her prestigious boarding school; she will join the roll of honour that includes, among other students, Yuriel, who was featured on BBC's The One Show when he became Head Boy of Millfield School. Three examples of success, three examples of remarkable children forging a powerful relationship with impressive schools. In each case, their success has had a profound effect on their community groups in Croxteth and Tottenham; through their commitment to galvanise aspiration in their communities, they are playing their part in the social mobility debate.

The biggest challenge for the independent sector is to maintain its relevance to a rapidly changing society, though one which exhibits a curious paradox: on one hand, society is advancing technologically at a frightening speed (one only has to think AI and robotics to see how fast things are developing). But on the other hand, society has become increasingly immobile, with a growing gap between those who can succeed and those who can't through no fault of their own. There are great challenges ahead for the sector, among them a perceived irrelevance, a view that it is playing a less than impressive role in addressing the educational causes of social inequality and immobility. There is a growing clamour from some influential quarters that compulsion is the best way forward. Access lies at the heart of many of these initiatives; that is, access to the resources of the schools, most obviously in partnerships, and access to independent schools by children whose family income precludes them considering an independent education. Ironically, most of the schools they can't afford access to were founded on just these principles.

Once upon a time, the cry from the independent sector was, "we are not social engineers". They felt that effecting social change was not their responsibility. But I think there is now a realization from the schools themselves that they do not sit outside the social mobility debate. Our experience is that almost all independent schools take this challenge seriously or, more accurately, increasingly seriously. What schools do best is influence those who attend them and so it makes sense to me that one of the most effective ways for independent schools to maintain relevance in the complex debates concerning education and social mobility is to encourage greater access. By this I mean offering fully-funded life-transforming bursaries. The Royal

SpringBoard model draws together both the benefit to the individual child and the benefit for the wider community. Independent schools charge fees, and typically fees that exclude the vast majority of children, and certainly they are way beyond the means of those children who find themselves eligible for free school meals, a metric which drives many social reformers.

What are the main issues? Our experience at SpringBoard shows that the schools are willing and positive about offering life-transforming experiences; there is an abundance of evidence that the schools are quite exceptional at working with the children, their families and their communities, not least the independent impact assessment of Royal SpringBoard's work by the National Foundation for Educational Research. But it would be a naïve reader who thought that the process was without complications. Transposing someone from urban Forest Gate to rural Norfolk requires thought and care. The period before the pupil begins at the school is, in our opinion, almost as important as the time spent at school. It is essential that the pupil feels supported, able to develop academic confidence, and that all connected with this journey are also prepared for the experience that lies ahead. For us, this means building close links between the school, the parents, the community and the pupil. We know that the children we have placed report a multitude of positive outcomes, not only academic but social, personal, emotional and aspirational. In addition, we know that the bursary children in the schools have a powerful effect on those around them, both staff and children alike, as well as exerting a strong influence of their community group at home. We know, through our STEER mental well-being tracking process, that these are remarkable children who are determined to make the most of their opportunities, and who might face personal challenges along the way. This is why schools are trying to understand the difficulties that bursary children could experience.

There are just over half a million children in independent schools,[2] representing about 7 per cent of all school age children in England and Wales. The challenge is how to make an impact on wider society despite being proportionally small. I don't mean by providing a disproportionate number of judges or senior civil servants, I mean having a considerable effect on society by influencing a greater number of children. If these children were either looked after children or children eligible for free school meals, then the package starts to drill more effectively into the social mobility debate. The challenge for independent schools is to use what they do best: educate children, to the greater benefit of society, and prepare their pupils and staff for the great challenges ahead. Our experience is that the bursary pupils are willing, able an enthusiastic participants in this endeavour.

Patrick Derham

Grenfell Tower was an event that changed everything for me. That tragedy, more than anything I have lived through in my 22 years of Headship, highlighted the issues of inequality in this country like nothing else. It showcased the chasm between the haves and the have-nots. It made me feel even more uncomfortable about the job I do and made me feel even more passionate about the fact that the opportunity gap between rich and poor in this country, and across the world, is morally unacceptable. It is wrong that the doors of opportunity are open far wider for the wealthy and the privileged few. The lack of educational opportunity is without doubt the biggest social challenge of our time. Something has to be done: to ignore these issues and see so many young people fail violates our deepest moral values. As a sector, we have a role to play – we can be catalysts for change. But it cannot be tokenism to meet a political end; it has to be heartfelt and genuine and, although we shall continue to be friendless in the eyes of the politicians and the media, we should recognise our responsibilities and help address the social mobility challenge.

There is no one more passionate about the transformational nature of bursaries than me. My life was transformed by such an opportunity and I demonstrate the powerful ripple effect of bursaries done well. Throughout my life, I have worked hard to repay my debt by trying to make a difference. A criticism of bursaries is that they only benefit the beneficiary, but, if the model is done well, this does not have to be the case. The shift in emphasis to means-tested bursaries has been one of the significant changes in the sector in recent years – but are we really reaching out in all cases to the most deserving? The groundbreaking work of The Arnold Foundation at Rugby, which led to the creation of SpringBoard in 2012, which has now become The Royal National Children's SpringBoard Foundation, is leading the way by working with partner charities and schools who are dealing with issues of social exclusion and underachievement on a daily basis, and help identify young people who will benefit from the stability that a boarding education can bring. There are some excellent examples in the day sector, too: Manchester Grammar School and King Edward's School Birmingham prove what can be done. But there is *more* that can be done, of that I am quite sure. I have a vision that, in my dotage, I will look at a sector where some schools are genuinely needs-blind, providing a superb education to those who would benefit from it irrespective of parental means and I hope to see Westminster as one of these.

Bursaries are not the only answer, of course, and there are some fantastic examples of partnership work that are making a difference to young people's lives. Here too it is important that schools are doing this because they believe in it and they have to approach this work in a genuine spirit of partnership. I have learnt a huge amount from my maintained school colleagues in the partnership work I have been involved with in the three schools I have had the privilege to run. These partnerships can take many forms, but as long as they start from the premise of closing the opportunity gap then they are worth doing and celebrating. There are so many examples of innovation in the sector that should be recognised and celebrated – but again, we must do more.

Reading Robert Putnam's book *Our Kids: The American Dream in Crisis* was another game changer for me. It is a book that anyone with an interest in education and inequality should read. There is so much in this book that is thought-provoking and challenging, wherever you are in the world: the recognition that schools cannot fix all of society's problems, the importance of the pre-school years, the value of extra-curricular activity and a longer school day, the myth of Higher Education for all, the recognition of the importance of vocational education, apprenticeships and workforce training and above all the need to broaden the debate and to look at the vexed issues of parenting, community and economic inequality. Putnam highlights the importance of high-quality teaching in poor schools as being the key, although he argues that it has to be under conditions in which they can teach and not worry about classroom order. What we take for granted is sadly denied to too many. It is another form of partnership that more of us can be involved with.

So, as I am very much in the twilight of my educational career, I am more concerned than ever about these issues. What has given me great heart is that so many of my colleagues share these views and individually and collectively we can make a difference. In that way, we will not only be returning to the historic roots of so many of our schools but we will be demonstrating that we recognise our role in helping address the issue of inequality in this country and enabling all young people to become authors of their own life stories, regardless of where they start in life.

David Ejim-McCubbin

I attended a state secondary school before gaining a full bursary to study A Levels at Rugby School, an independent boarding school in England.

Within the state school sector there remains various demographic sub-groups that stand to benefit tremendously from exposure to the form of education that independent schools can provide. Let me assure you that this essay is not going to be a diatribe against the UK state school system, nor is it my aim to pit state schools against their private sector counterparts. My intention is to highlight the need for independent schools to become more accessible, and also to argue that disadvantaged student groups within the state school system would benefit beyond academic performance – which is, of course, simply the surface measurement of success – if they were able to attend schools like Rugby. Whilst exam grades remain the key indicator of both a student's and school's success, the benefits conferred by attending an independent school referred to in this chapter stretch further than academic attainment and include the softer, less obvious by-products of attending such establishments. Benefits that students such as myself profited from.

I was born into a single-parent home, in an inner-city London borough that ranked as the second most deprived local authority in England and attended a secondary school where less than one in four pupils achieved a 'good pass (C grade)' or above in five or more of their end of senior school exams (including Maths and English). Evidently, I wasn't born into privilege. The structure of my family was neither uncommon nor unusual, with one in five Black-African families in the UK consisting of one lone parent (usually the mother) with a dependent child. Outside the front door of my block of flats I was accustomed to witnessing hostile interactions between local residents and the police. From my bedroom I had heard a shotgun fire twice at my childhood friend. And on three separate occasions I passed through the police-cordoned murder scenes that were now tragically marked as the settings for the fatal shootings and stabbings of neighbours and friends, one of whom lived in the flat below mine. Three different head teachers during my five-year stay at a failing secondary school sets the scene for this real-life drama. As a young black boy, it seemed as though a life of chaos, criminality and substandard grades were inexorably mapped out for my friends and I.

What I have described above is not borrowed from a Dickensian novel set in poverty-stricken London. It is an honest depiction of the environment and social context I endured during my most formative years. It is a reality that tens of thousands of gifted, intelligent and ambitious young people navigate each day. More tragic is that the young people who exist in the most undesirable boroughs and estates often forget or never get the chance to realise that they are just that – gifted, intelligent and ambitious. The suffocating nature of their compounded, multi-layered disadvantage holds them back from realising their potential; their efforts are focused desperately on gasping for survival in their stifling concrete jungles. Wings are clipped. Dreams deferred. Ambition absconded. These young people lose before they have a chance to try. In an attempt to advance the power of individual human agency, some demand that such young people simply work hard to escape their pitiful communities. Some commentators declare (in a misguided attempt to be sympathetic) that such groups are helpless and inherently unfortunate, and therefore need state support. But the first view disregards the essence of the problem and the latter disregards the potential of the people. Unsurprisingly, many of the young people they refer to can be found in local underperforming state schools where classes are rife with behavioural management issues. Students reflecting chaos of their home life into the classroom; their schools planted on the intersections of gang turf and territory. This is where you'll find these young people. This is where I was found.

Whilst working at just an above average level during my third year of senior school (UK Year 9), I was identified as a repeatedly distracted student failing to fulfil my academic potential. If I had a pound for the number of inner city state school black boys that fell within this category... The reason for this? A failure to take school seriously enough to care about how the decisions I took then would affect my future. Sadly, for my friends and I, school largely functioned as an escape from our dire realities outside its gates. We didn't run to school to enjoy its merits, we ran to school to forget for a moment our hostile living environments.

Thankfully, my lax approach to my academic progress didn't go unaddressed. My secondary school at the time began working with the Eastside Young Leaders Academy (EYLA), an East London based education charity aimed at supporting the academic development and leadership qualities of young, black boys. I soon started to attend the charity's after-school and Saturday morning programmes, progressing under the Academy's core academic subject support and developing through the leadership traits taught and examined. The acute intervention that EYLA targeted for me and so many other black inner city boys equipped me not only with an improved attitude towards school but (unbeknown to me at the time) it also prepared me for an education at an independent school. Soon after joining EYLA, the charity formed a relationship with Rugby School. Together they sought to provide full bursary places into their senior school (aged 13) and Sixth Form (aged 16) for the boys who would most benefit from it. Propelled by their pioneering headmaster at the time, Patrick Derham, Rugby opened up a world of untapped opportunity.

Rugby School is ranked in the top 100 schools in the United Kingdom. It wouldn't surprise the reader to learn that while at Rugby, I received a rigour to my education unparalleled with what I'd experienced before. The high-quality teaching had a lasting impression on my ability to think critically and logically whilst recognising the importance of evidence. Class sizes at Rugby were less than half those at my previous school. Managing behaviour in a classroom was never an issue for teachers. Many of the staff were experts in their fields; a considerable number had doctorates. But of even greater significance was my attitude to school and learning. I had a greater self-belief that my aspiration for the life that I wanted to live was matched by teachers and encouraged within the school campus. Students at Rugby generally achieved excellent exam results, partly because of the quality of the education they received in the classroom. But it was the acquisition of these other skills, through a kind of osmosis in the corridors, boarding houses and around the school environment that had the most profound effect on me. I believe that the most compelling argument to make in support of independent schools becoming more accessible to state schools lies here.

Students at Rugby had an air of audacity. In a more positive sense, they acted in a manner that suggested that they deserved to receive the best education, with the expectation of a good life ahead. Even the younger boys and girls were confident in who they were. Observing the way in which they communicated their ideas and thoughts to adults with self-assurance was impressive. They expected to meet their aspirations because the school provided the resources and support to do so. Added to this was a growing number of international students, which also helped in forming well-rounded, culturally aware individuals. Of course, private school students are not perfect individuals, but it is no exaggeration to say that the privately educated leave school at 18 years old with a readiness for higher education and the workplace that students from my community are simply not equipped with, nor privileged with the foundation that provides them with the greater chance of success in the next stage of their education or career.

I did not possess a special inner gift or sacred talent that afforded me my place at Rugby School. I immediately became saddened at the apparent material difference between the students at Rugby and the students at my previous state school: the difference didn't lie in natural cognitive ability or innate intellectual capabilities, the difference was and remains money and opportunity. Rugby provided me with an opportunity to be freed from circumstantial obstacles, including an unstable neighbourhood and a classroom environment entirely unconducive to learning. Of course not all state schools are like this, but mine was, and many remain in such schools in some of the most deprived areas in the country. Independent schools need to improve access to such groups of students who, if given the chance, can begin to fulfil their potential and have a more promising future. Visibility here is key. Students need to see an environment they can succeed in before they will believe in it and themselves. I have no doubt that many of my secondary school peers would have excelled beyond what I achieved at Rugby had they been given the chance.

Fundamentally, we need to give these students more opportunities to have a better chance in life. This is not the only way to achieve social mobility, but for many it may be the only and best way for them. Essential to making this work is finding more EYLAs and Patrick Derhams who passionately seek to draw out the potential within students who are victims of their neighbourhoods. It should be the shared duty of the education sector to provide all with the best possible start in life. Independent schools, I call you to rise to the challenge and do your part.

Nick Hillman

The post-war school system in England and Wales was established by the 1944 Education Act. Section 81 of the Act that enabled Local Education Authorities to pay for people to attend independent schools also enabled them to pay the costs for people to attend university. This made sense as leading independent schools and leading universities have a great deal in common. Both are elite, academic, selective, autonomous, expensive and offer an all-round education, and they both have a long tradition of providing residential education.

In the decades afterwards, university students gradually received more and more public money – the state effectively bought hundreds of thousands of university places and the financial barriers blocking access to higher education were removed. For a while, it seemed the same would happen at independent schools. A 1944 report commissioned by Winston Churchill's wartime Coalition Government recommended one-quarter of places at leading independent boarding schools should be funded by the state.[3] Two decades later, a report commissioned by Harold Wilson's Government recommended taxpayers should sponsor half the places at leading independent boarding schools.[4] That never happened, but Margaret Thatcher responded to the abolition of direct-grant status by Shirley Williams – still probably the UK's worst-ever education policy – by introducing the Assisted Places Scheme. This took up 75,000 independent day school places before its demise in 1998.

State-funded independent school places have come and gone (exceptional circumstances aside), and it is unlikely they will come back soon. Even the Conservative Party has not backed the policy for 20 years.[5] Yet, we continue to subsidise hundreds of thousands of undergraduates at our universities, which have many of the same features as our leading independent schools. Why?

First, school bursaries seem very expensive to ministers. The fees for a day place at an independent school for just a single term are often broadly the same as the annual amount spent on each child in a state school. Taxpayer-funded bursaries fail every official cost-benefit test as the money can always secure more bang-for-buck elsewhere. In contrast, the subsidised loans that university students receive do not count as current public spending. It is sometimes said that state-funded bursaries can be made affordable by clever tweaks.[6] Perhaps that is so, but it does not tackle the second problem.

Bursaries are, by definition, selective. They have to be rationed because they are not available to all. So there has to be a mechanism for deciding who is to benefit. Yet it is 50 years since the UK had a government that was firmly committed to secondary-school selection. When it comes to deciding who should receive state-funded independent school bursaries, as a Minister for Education said over 50 years ago, 'nobody knows what would be just or why'. A good teacher deals with each pupil as an individual, but governments feel that tackling social mobility through boosting the life chances of a few individuals is, in David Cameron's memorable phrase, 'splashing around in the shallow end of the educational debate'.[7]

The third factor explaining why our universities are full of state-sponsored students but our independent schools are not is that our university sector, with the notable exception of Oxbridge, has displayed a voracious appetite for expansion. In contrast, except when suffering particularly torrid times (as in the early years of the Second World War) independent schools have been lukewarm about taking public cash as a route to expansion. They have worried about the strings that would be attached – and, rightly so, for they are less able to defend themselves than universities.

State-sponsored places are not the only way for independent schools to boost social mobility. Another route that has found support in the past is to fund bursaries by charging more for full-fee pupils – in other words, introducing as much means-testing as possible by ensuring rich families cross-subsidise poor ones. The university system in the United States is instructive here. At private not-for-profit colleges in the

United States, nine-out-of-ten new students do not pay the 'sticker price' and the average discount is half the full fee. But this is a recipe for confusion because people are unsure how much they will pay.[8]

Yet robust analysis shows bursaries can work well for individuals when donors are willing to pay for them.[9] Take the very talented Professor Sir David Watson, who understood the potential for education to transform lives better than anyone else I have ever met. Before he died in 2015, he was the Vice-Chancellor of the University of Brighton, Principal of an Oxford college and the UK's foremost Professor of Higher Education. I wonder if that would have happened if an Eton housemaster had not decided he needed someone who could sight-read on the piano when deciding who deserved a funded place.[10]

Or take Sir Michael Moritz, a venture capitalist who felt he owed so much to his time at the University of Oxford, that he donated over $100 million for student bursaries.[11] That is the sort of money that can make a huge difference to individuals and society. So if there is a lesson from my own educational research for independent schools today, it is this: look less for support from government and invest even more in finding support from individual and corporate donors.

Barnaby Lenon

The access challenge is twofold: improving access for children from low-income households and maintaining access for children from middle-income households. When considering the first half of this challenge – encouraging independent schools to take more low-income students – several motivations come to mind. A diverse intake makes for a more socially balanced pupil population. Many larger ISC schools used to be Direct Grant schools – that is, their less well-off pupils were funded by the taxpayer. Before the scheme's abolition in 1976, the *majority* of pupils in schools such as Manchester Grammar and King Edward's Birmingham came from low-income households. These schools have found that former pupils who benefitted from the Direct Grant are keen to give money back to the school in order to fund bursaries and see the school become less socially selective. All independent schools that are charities are *required* to make their schools accessible, in some way, to low-income families. Some may use bursaries to attract able pupils.

Finally, there is also significant pressure on independent schools from the public and the government to improve their accessibility. Many people, including politicians from across the spectrum, regard the academic and career success of ISC pupils as problematic. Social mobility has become a priority for all political parties, and one response is to increase the number of pupils from low-income households.

But government policies seem to change year on year, and if a school is worried about losing charitable benefits or incurring additional taxes there is no evidence that simply offering bursaries will save them. In 2017, 14 per cent of pupils in England's state schools were eligible for free school meals. Some politicians argue, therefore, that independent schools should have 14 per cent of their pupils on full bursaries. A few schools are already meeting this target: Manchester Grammar has 220 pupils on bursaries, at an average level of 93 per cent of school fees, and King Edward's Birmingham gives bursaries to 20–25 per cent of pupils, half of whom are on free places. Independent schools would be in a stronger position politically if they were to means test *all* fee reductions and fund more pupils from very low income households.

One significant example of improving access is the Royal National Children's SpringBoard Foundation: it has placed 650 children, who were previously on free school meals, in state and independent boarding schools, all on bursaries. Local authorities part-fund the places, often for Looked After Children. The scheme is not academically selective – unlike scholarships, it does not cherry pick the best and brightest out of the state sector. Within a few years, they hope to have at least 1000 children in boarding schools.

For schools that lack an endowment, there are four main ways of funding these bursaries. If a school has many wealthy parents – which can be discovered by employing someone to undertake a parental wealth survey – it may be sensible to increase fees to generate a surplus and fund bursaries with fee income. However, if a school has few wealthy parents, it would be better to keep fees down and offer fewer bursaries; there is no point raising fees to fund bursaries if that means that many prospective parents find the school unaffordable. Most schools have raised some funding for bursaries by making significant cuts on scholarship spending. Fundraising is another lucrative source: some wealthy donors are attracted to bursaries for philanthropic reasons.

Finally, other non-fee income can be raised through projects such as franchise schools abroad. The second half of this challenge is maintaining access for children from upper middle-income households. According to the Institute of Fiscal Studies, the median disposable income of a household in the UK for the financial year ending in 2017 was £27,200; the average ISC day school fee in the same year was £13,419. In 2016, average earnings increased by 1.9 per cent, whereas average fees went up 3.3 per cent. In 1996, the proportion of household earnings for the top 55 per cent of earners that would be required to send two children to a junior day school was 50 per cent; the same figure for 2016 was 80 per cent. As a result, the average independent school has lost a group of doctors, solicitors, university academics and other second quartile, upper middle class parents who can no longer afford these fees. Independent schools have not only lost pupils but also the goodwill of this influential demographic of parents. The tide of both public and political opinion is turning against us.

This problem has two potential solutions. Schools could consider offering bursaries for middle-income parents: the group is large and the cost per child is much less than that for low-income pupils, making them a natural source of pupils. But another important way to maintain access for middle-income students is to cut costs. Top state schools, some of which achieve results as good as some independent schools, manage on £5000 a year (about a third of the income of independent schools). The extra cost incurred by independent schools is largely down to small class sizes and generous timetable remissions for staff. A small number of private schools have successfully sought to increase access for middle-income students by reducing costs and consequently cutting fees. It can be done.

There is a difference between what may be in the short-term economic interest of an individual school (e.g. lots of small bursaries for middle-income parents) and what is in the medium-term political interest of all independent schools (more full bursaries). However, having lots of full bursaries may still not be enough to reduce the political pressure on independent schools to improve access in the United Kingdom. Both the current Conservative government and some Labour politicians in England have expressed more of an interest in independent schools sponsoring academies than offering bursaries. This is why Brighton College, for example, decided to set up a Free

School in East London rather than spend the money on bursaries. While bursaries increase access to independent schools, they do little to improve the quality of education in the country as a whole.

Justine Voisin

Most of the country's leading schools that produce the perceived "best" results are highly academically selective. This selection criterion continues to apply for means-tested bursary pupils in the majority of the independent senior schools that take such pupils. The opportunity given to such pupils through this access is of undoubted benefit both to them and society as whole. It is rightly celebrated and praised for helping to address the current lack of social equality and mobility in society.

However, why should the "best" education and social opportunity be the preserve of the most academically gifted, whatever their background? A bigger challenge, and arguably greater achievement, is to take pupils with a broad range of academic skills and social backgrounds, mitigate their disadvantage and raise their performance and life/work outcome through an outstanding education.

King Edward's School, Witley has been pursuing its mission to provide a boarding education for students from disadvantaged and/ or vulnerable homes since it was established by royal charter as Bridewell Royal Hospital in 1553. Although the nature of the institution has evolved significantly over the intervening centuries, the broad founding mission has remained the same. This "mission" is at the heart of King Edward's and informs and underlies all that it does. Today, 20–25 per cent of the school's pupils are supported by the foundation and other charities with financial contributions up to the full annual boarding fees.

Once it is established that the child would benefit from an academic schooling, pupils are selected in relation to this criterion of need, not academic ability. As a result, the school has a uniquely diverse pupil body – culturally, socially and economically. This in turn produces a tolerant, diverse and integrated school community that has a strong shared purpose. The school is about value added for all and not just the transformational social opportunity and mobility experience for foundation pupils. All pupils benefit from an excellent academic and pastoral education, steeped in a social and cultural mission that produces pupils equipped to participate successfully in a modern globalised society. There are significant benefits for the privileged and less privileged in the school community alike.

At a time of perceived increased inequality of opportunity and lack of social mobility in the United Kingdom, the "social" mission of Bridewell is more relevant and important than ever. Society is made up of increasingly less porous socio-economic silos. People living within such silos (which are not just the preserve of the privileged) often fear, or fail to understand, people who are different and consequently seek to reinforce their "silo" position, resulting in further inequality and division. Hopefully, children educated within the King Edward's environment are more inclined to embrace people who are different or who come from diverse backgrounds. As well as a social benefit, it gives pupils an advantage in their future work lives due to their enhanced ability to integrate with diverse people and their understanding of others' priorities and needs.

The school continues to be at the heart of the assisted boarding movement in promoting this message, mission and pupil outcomes. We have more children placed with us by the Royal National Children's SpringBoard Foundation than any other school in the country. We also provide places to many other pupils, part funded by partner charities such as Buttle UK, Reedham Children's Trust, Sir John Cass's Foundation and The City of London Corporation.

Before the 1980s, local authorities supported 100,000 assisted places nationally. Today just 26 local authorities are funding 120 places in total. As a result, they have less knowledge and experience concerning assisted boarding. There is increasing pressure for authorities to show "quick" results from intervention rather than demonstrate the long-term nature of the "investment" in realising beneficial outcomes for pupils.

In July 2017, the Department for Education launched Boarding School Partnerships, a new information service designed to make it easier for local authorities to access information and expertise concerning boarding school placements. King Edward's is one of the initiative's co-founders together with other leading children's charities.

Throughout its long history and particularly since the early 1800s, King Edward's has been at the forefront of providing social opportunity and mobility through a boarding education to those who are vulnerable and less advantaged. The school continues passionately to pursue this mission and leverage its considerable expertise and experience for the benefit of the school community. There are considerable challenges in fulfilling this mission in the current political and economic environment. However, the overall opportunity and benefit achieved means that it is essential that King Edward's continues to deliver its founding mission.

Other schools understandably may question how they can move towards a 'needs'-based bursary provision from their current base point, especially so in the current climate. An answer is that we must all collaborate and engage in a national dialogue to raise awareness of the need and significant educational benefit leading to better work and life outcomes for all. By shouting more loudly and proudly about all that we do – and could do – through a national network of partner schools, charities and local and national agencies much more could be achieved in terms of engagement as well as fundraising and development. Schools such as King Edward's Witley can be at the forefront of providing, at the very least, practical advice and support in best practice needs based selection processes and outreach programmes to other partner institutions, tailored to help those children most likely to benefit. We are adopting such an approach more actively with partner institutions such as SpringBoard and Sir John Cass's and with more national engagement hope to develop this more extensively for the benefit of others. There is a wealth of experience already in the sector: the next stage is to debate, share and learn.

Notes

1   www.pearson.com/content/dam/corporate/global/pearson-dot-com/files/hattie/150602_DistractionWEB_V2.pdf
2   ISC 2018 Census: www.isc.co.uk/media/4890/isc_census_2018_report.pdf
3   Nicholas Hillman, 'Public schools and the Fleming report of 1944: Shunting the first-class carriage on to an immense siding?', *History of Education*, 41(2), 2012, pp. 235–255
4   Nicholas Hillman, 'The Public Schools Commission: "Impractical, Expensive and Harmful to Children"?', *Contemporary British History*, 24(4), 2010, pp. 511–531

5 BBC News online, 'No return to assisted places', 15 October 1998
6 Independent Schools Council, 'Joint funding could see 10,000 free new independent school places every year', 9 December 2016
7 BBC News online, 'Cameron steps up grammars attack', 22 May 2007
8 College Board, Trends in College Pricing 2017, October 2017
9 National Foundation for Educational Research, *The SpringBoard Bursary Foundation Impact Assessment: Year 3*, November 2016
10 Nick Hillman, 'History proves private school bursaries will fail', *Times Educational Supplement*, 28 October 2016
11 Jeevan Vasagar, 'Venture capitalist gives £75m for Oxford's poorest students', *Guardian*, 11 July 2012

Chapter 6

The diversity challenge

Introduction to the diversity challenge

There is a danger that not only will independent schools become too expensive for all but the super wealthy, but that they will become increasingly unrepresentative of the societies they seek to serve. They will become irrelevant 'bubbles of privilege' (as Jenny Brown calls them) in an increasingly meritocratic, ethnically fluent world. Should this happen, they risk producing young men and women who are not fully prepared for the universities they will apply for, or the workforce they will have to enter after they have graduated. It wouldn't be surprising if parents, taking a long-term view of their children's prospects, felt that this is not worth investing in.

This relative lack of diversity is not limited to the pupils. Go in to most staff rooms in any fee-paying school in any developed society and ask yourself this: how representative of that society is this group of teachers? As several contributors in this section point out, independent schools have a slightly higher proportion of ethnic minorities in the UK than state schools (33.4% to 31%) but this could possibly be because of pupils from China and Russia. No data exists for the diversity of their teachers, but it is unlikely to reflect the student intake. Making our independent schools more diverse should be a priority for our governing bodies, and, as Nick Dennis points out, 'everyone already has enough motivation to change. The real question, when thinking about diversity in the independent sector, is whether the people installed in positions to make substantive change really want to'. But they should not be compelled to do so because various voices in the media are telling them to: tokenism does few favours for those it seeks to promote, or for the credibility of the existing recruitment and retention programmes the institution has in place. They should do so because more diverse organisations tend to be more innovative and successful and – importantly – because it will benefit the pupils.

This last point is seldom discussed in enough depth, but as Jaideep Barot writes in this chapter, 'as long as it remains the case that BME (Black and Minority Ethnic) pupils are more likely to see such adults in cleaning and catering jobs than they are in teaching and leadership, we are failing not just them, but *all* of our pupils'. Diversity, then, should go well beyond the recruitment of teachers, and schools should look very carefully at their whole workforce to see what stereotypes are unthinkingly reinforced in every key area. Are all the cleaners women? Do those women come from one ethnic group? What about the school's senior leadership team? Is this made up predominantly of middle-aged white men? Is the recruitment process indirectly working against bringing in a more diverse group of applicants? The questions get more interesting, and more difficult to answer, when you look at single sex schools: what models do those young men and women see around the school? How representative is that of the lives they will live in the near future?

Ironically, diversity is sometimes understood to refer only to ethnic diversity, but that is a limitation in itself, and Emmanuel Akpan-Inwang takes it further in his essay. In a series of probing questions, he asks the sector to reach beyond simply bringing in bright pupils from relatively disadvantaged backgrounds because 'for diversity to encompass real diversity of thought, opinion and experience, the word needs to encompass diversity beyond mere skin-colour'. For Akpan-Inwang this could mean recruiting from refugee and asylum seeking families, as well as from families who have never seen a child to university, and from families who have to use food banks to get through the week. Headteacher Jenny Brown shares this desire: for her, it is time 'for the independent sector to commit more adventurously to this mission and work with partners who share the aims of minimising social inequality and increasing social diversity in schools'.

Of course, there are many partnerships between independent and state schools (according to the ISC they number 1137)[1] of which around 900 can be defined as focusing on academic links (including the sharing of teaching staff, classrooms and workshops). And a growing number of schools work with third parties such as IntoUniversity and

SpringBoard to ensure that the right families are brought into contact with the right schools. But there is a problem of scale: admirable though each of these initiatives are, to what extent do they make schools more diverse? Many would agree with Akpan-Inwang, who suggests a fixed number of places to children from low-income families: 'no entrance exams, no tests, just a simple lottery system'. But just as those who want to abolish independent schools to make society fairer, forcing the same schools to adopt diversity-increasing quotas is likely to have only limited impact if those schools do not see tangible benefits, including the 'increased performance' that Nick Dennis refers to. For him, it makes sense for diversity to become a 'strategic intent' because it actually improves the schools who prioritise it. And he is surely right in saying that a school committed to lessening inequality (as all schools should be) should live its values at every level. Those values, for Mary Myatt, should be delivered through the curriculum as well, in programmes of study that focus on understanding the world beyond subject-specific content or curricula that is assessed. Schools need to find time on the timetable to ensure this happens, rather than squeezing it into unwanted times and delivered by teachers either unenthusiastic or unqualified to do the issues involved justice.

But the sector, and the profession, should and could do more to bring teachers from more diverse backgrounds into our schools. In doing so, they will tap into skills, perspectives and experiences that will enrich their colleagues and the pupils they teach. As Barot writes, 'a workforce short of BME teachers and leaders – just as would be the case in a workforce low on, say, women – must necessarily be missing out on large swathes of the talent pool, too'. It makes no sense to continue with this approach. Of course, there will be cultural barriers in some communities, but the sector has to learn from the minority of schools who are recruiting more widely and making a concerted effort to increase diversity in a long-lasting, coherent way. In this area we can learn from ourselves, and come up with solutions that reflect an image of society now, and how it wants to be in the future.

Emmanuel Akpan-Inwang

I feel I should show my cards from the outset: I'm not a great believer in private education.

We live in a stubbornly and increasingly divided society where your opportunities in life are too often defined by the accident of your birth, and our private education system only compounds this.[2] Private school students dominate the highest echelons of our society: politics, journalism, the judiciary…so, to ask how private schools can be more diverse is to consider how to extend undue privilege to a slightly wider group of people. Whatever my thoughts, private schools have been around since 597, and are likely to remain part of the education fabric, so with this in mind I'll attempt to tackle the issue.

What is diversity?

On the surface, it may appear that private schools are already quite diverse. A peek into one of their classrooms will often reveal a suitably broad range of ethnicities. In fact, according to research by the Independent Schools Council, about a third of students at their schools are from an ethnic minority background,[3] about the same as it is in the state sector.[4]

But ethnic diversity is only one factor among many and has multiple facets. A growing proportion of this figure is made up of the children of wealthy Russian and Chinese oligarchs. In some boarding schools, up to a third of students come from Russia and China,[5] yet British pupils from Afro-Caribbean backgrounds continue to be underrepresented.[6]

I believe that private schools need to carefully consider what they mean by 'diverse'. They have always been interested in taking wealthy pupils regardless of ability, but only interested in poor pupils who happen to be very bright. This needs to change. For diversity to mean real diversity of thought, opinion and experience, it needs to go beyond mere skin colour. How many children in private schools came to the UK through a dangerous migration route? How many have relatives who have never gone to university? How many private school pupils even know second or third hand what it has felt like – in your pockets or on the family dinner table – for wages to stagnate since the financial crash, or to suffer the effects of rising food prices? By making private schools more diverse, we increase the opportunity to interact with people who have different experiences and perspectives which, in turn, makes for more thoughtful, critical, empathetic and potentially more active citizens. This is particularly important in a time when politics is becoming more polarised and divided between the more and less educated; the metropolitan and economically-declining regions; and between older and younger generations.

Why bother with diversity?

The arguments in favour of diversity are well established, and we have moved far beyond it being seen as simply 'a nice thing to do'. Take a look at the *Financial Times* markets page and you'll see that diverse companies have higher than average returns on equity, scientific research is of a higher quality when research teams are diverse, and diversity is increasingly seen as an important factor in innovation.[7] Diversity offers higher productivity, broadens perspectives, diminishes discrimination and enriches life experiences[8] and these benefits extend to education: schools with a diverse intake are well placed to benefit from the advantages bestowed by diversity.

So, the narrow intake of private schools is not just a detriment to the rest of society, it is arguably detrimental to the experiences of the children that attend them.

Are private schools open-minded?

It seems private schools are increasingly in pursuit of shiny state of the art facilities designed to satiate China and Russia's growing appetite for elite British education. This has resulted in a substantial increase in fees. Average day fees have risen above £17,000 for the first time in 20 years, and continue to rise above inflation, meaning that the top 5 per cent of earners in the UK would have to spend a fifth of their income to educate one child privately.

So far, these fee rises have been offset by substantial bursaries, financial support and the rise in the wealth of the country's top earners. In future, mounting financial pressures, competition among schools and the weaker post-Brexit pound may mean that schools continue to mount an 'arms race' of providing ever more opulent and ostentatious facilities to lure in wealth, and as a result have less and do less to provide for the less well-off.

A suggestion that I agree with is to allocate a fixed number of places to children from low-income families. No entrance exams, no tests, just a simple lottery system. This would mean that private schools will be able to support children from low-income backgrounds.

There are pupils for whom a private education may be a saving grace. Particularly children in need, those on the edge of care and those who are in local authority care, the vast majority of whom fail to achieve anywhere near their academic potential. These children often have a very difficult and challenging start in life and this disadvantage follows them into adulthood. They are more likely to have to change schools, more likely to attend an underperforming school and few go on to university.[9] Attending a private school as a boarder may provide the family experience and lifelong relationships which are built there, and go some way towards rebalancing a scale that is weighted against them.

Do I actually think that this is going to happen? In the long term probably not. But in the short term, taking on looked-after children and offering places to children on low incomes regardless of ability and those in the care system would go some way towards increasing their diversity.

Jaideep Barot

I was honoured to receive the email asking me to write a piece for this publication. It was recognition, surely, of my time at several top UK independent schools, and of my elevation to a first headship at another. "We'd like your advice about diversity…" continued the email. Clang. Pride instantly giving way to doubt and a depressing inevitability. Was I only being asked because of the colour of my skin? Because I was one of the very few senior leaders in the sector from a minority ethnic background? Was I basically being used to lend this publication more credibility?

It makes perfect sense, of course, to ask for my thoughts on diversity in the independent sector – I am of Indian heritage, and I have worked in its schools for 20 years. Where did that initial doubt and disquiet come from, then? Simply from this: *that even as we approach 2020, my promotion to the leadership of an independent school is so very unusual.*

Let's put this into context: the 2018 annual census[10] by the UK's Independent Schools Commission states that within its member schools (which contain over 80% of the UK's independent school children), 33.4 per cent of pupils come from minority ethnic backgrounds (compared with 31.0% in state-funded schools). This figure rises in the most ethnically diverse regions of the UK, and even in the South West – the least ethnically diverse area – the figure is close to 25 per cent. So, on the face of it, independent schools have no diversity problem.

Except for this: around a third of pupils across all UK schools are from black and minority ethnic (BME) backgrounds, but fewer than one in ten teachers are from such backgrounds;[11] only 3 per cent are Heads, and just 6 per cent are Deputy Heads or Assistant Heads.[12] Such information is not currently collected for the independent schools, but the corresponding proportions will certainly be lower still. As I move on to my fourth HMC school (HMC being the Headmasters' and Headmistresses' Conference, a professional association of Heads of some of the world's best-known independent schools), not a single current Head amongst its 289-strong UK membership, is of obvious BME heritage. (HMC, it must be said, recognise this issue and have set aside manpower and funds to tackle it).

The problem, therefore, is the profound lack of diversity in the teaching bodies of our schools – particularly in senior roles – and it is one that cannot be overstated. All pupils need positive role models – adults with similar backgrounds, upbringing and experiences to theirs – and as long as it remains the case that BME pupils are more likely to see such adults in cleaning and catering jobs than they are in teaching and leadership, we are failing not just them, but *all* of our pupils. In a world that is building up walls rather than tearing them down, we need pupils of *every background* to understand that aspiration is open to all, and to reject lazy stereotypes. A workforce short of BME teachers and leaders – just as would be the case in a workforce low on, say, women – must necessarily be missing out on large swathes of the talent pool, too. The best teachers and leaders cannot all look the same.

So, what to do? To start, the conversation has to become much louder. To stand any chance of meaningful redress, the diversity problem in our schools' staffing has to become one of our top priorities. Recruitment needs an overhaul – everything from our job advertisements, which often appeal only to those similar to us, to the places we advertise, to our longlisting and shortlisting, to the very interviews themselves, which research shows are next to no use in filtering out the best candidate (we'd apparently do just as well flipping a coin).[13] We have to be better at seeing beyond those who simply look and sound like us. The best person must get the job, of course, but we have to prioritise getting more ethnically diverse shortlists than at present. That, in itself, will not be easy, given that BME communities have traditionally placed higher value on the professions such as medicine, engineering, law and finance – certainly it took years for my mother to understand why I would leave a job at a global investment bank to become *just a teacher*. Initiatives such as the UK government's Leadership, Equality and Diversity Fund, and the National Education Union's Equal Access to Promotion, are steps in the right direction, but they merely scratch the surface. We need greater celebration where this diversity already exists, and more coaching opportunities for candidates from *all* minorities (not just BME). Above all, we need our schools, our governing bodies and our associations to take a long, hard, and – most importantly – honest look at what we should really value in our teachers and leaders, and then to commit time, energy and resource to finding the right people. Until that happens, and on a large scale, this will remain just another article on diversity, penned by someone who was only asked because of the colour of his skin.

Jenny Brown

A recent taxi drive from Luton airport in grey English drizzle proved inspirational because of the open-hearted confidences of my taxi driver. A Kurdish refugee who had arrived in England in the back of a lorry a quarter of a century ago, shortly after the political murder of his father, he shared his joy in his 16-year-old son's life-changing 100+ per cent scholarship to Harrow School. The proud father regaled me with tales of his son's difficult first few weeks but how his brains, bravery and boxing had got him through to the point of happy assimilation and success by the end of the first term, with an Oxbridge application now in train.

Such instances are powerful, as transformations always are. The magic of such dizzying social and academic alteration and revolutionised prospects excites. This school had the vision and means to offer transformation, this family the ambition to accept it and the boy had all the talent and tenacity to make it work. But such stories are rare.

Fee-paying schools across the world struggle to achieve fully diverse pupil bodies. Most fee-paying schools remain affluent, white and upper middle class and are regrettably not seen as realistic or comfortable destinations for minorities or socially disadvantaged pupils. There are a range of diversity issues that warrant attention in the independent sector, but I will here focus on the challenge of social diversity.

Bursaries can be powerful, as they were indeed for me and my siblings: they lift individuals from disadvantage like a benevolent arcade claw machine dangling the prize of 100+ per cent funded education, but they rely on robust fundraising beyond the means and culture of many schools. The answer must lie in better affordability so that affluent (by most measures) middle classes are not priced into the bursary market and resources can be allocated more broadly.

Independent schools with means owe it to their pupils to make sure that they do not grow up in a bubble of privilege, so they all have to think differently about creating access. Fundraising is engrained in many, but far from all, independent schools, and it needs to go hand in hand with cutting costs. There is a terrible irony in the fee increases that help to resource fundraising departments but simultaneously push independent education further and further away from lower income families.

In part, too, we have an image problem. There is a deeply-felt perception that 'elite' private schools across the globe do not speak the language of the pupils they hope to attract from disadvantaged backgrounds. The belief of education, in the words of Indira Ghandi, as a 'liberating force', remains elusive in practice. Education should be able to lead people out of the position they were born in, but can get stuck in the very 'barriers of class' it is designed to overcome.

Leadership is therefore critical. The increase of ethnic minority pupils in the UK is encouraging (nearly 30% of independent school pupils are from Black, Asian and minority ethnic backgrounds, as against 14% of BAME citizens in Britain as a whole). This in part results from wealthier overseas students taking up places in boarding schools, but it offers something, at least, to build upon. We must now aim to increase the role models for these pupils amongst teachers and school leaders, where minority ethnicities remain woefully under-represented.

This may feel like a tough ask in times when recruiting teachers at all in some hard to fill subjects is difficult, so we must sell what is one of the best jobs in the world more convincingly to create the wide social and ethnic mix that creates fully rounded and powerful learning.

A recent effort to take an honest look at the lack of diversity in school leadership among one of the independent school's heads' associations reminds us of the problems of tackling this. It foundered at the first hurdle: deciding which diversity problem was most pressing – social, ethnic or gender. Still, at least the issue was 'on the table'.

Identifying and discussing the matter is one thing. Finding practical solutions quite another. The initiatives established to widen university access are worth considering to see if the sector can learn from them or emulate them. Oxford University's Lady Margaret Hall, for instance, offers a foundational year for students who show potential, but are not yet at the level of attainment required for degree-level entry to the university. This seems a powerful and practical way to increase diversity. Could schools adopt similar practices and provide tailored and targeted prep for their entry points on Saturdays or in after school sessions within the communities they want to attract; or establish more flexible entry criteria and a foundation year for disadvantaged students with potential?

We could work more systematically with social mobility charities, like IntoUniversity, which has established an inspirational and successful model for widening access to university. By setting up centres in some of the UK's most deprived communities it replicates, as one of its founders puts it, 'what happens across the middle class kitchen table' – offering the aspiration and support to keep socially disadvantaged pupils in education. It's time for the independent sector to commit more adventurously to this mission and work with partners who share the aims of minimising social inequality and increasing social diversity in schools.

There's no easy solution, but we have to grasp the exciting opportunity of this challenge and provide the funding, the leadership and the partnership to provide education that truly liberates pupils, whatever their background.

Nick Dennis

Increasing diversity in the independent sector is not a matter of motivation. The incentive to change is clear. The real question is whether the people installed in positions to make a substantive change really want to.

The latest survey from the Independent School Council (ISC) reveals that 33.4 per cent of students come from a minority ethnic background, a considerable rise from 22.8 per cent in 2009 when the figures were first reported. There is no statistical information on the diversity of teaching staff, senior leaders or governing bodies from ISC, the Headmasters' and Headmistresses' Conference (HMC) or the Association of Governing Bodies in Independent Schools (AGBIS). It is worth thinking about why there is a dearth of data collected or published on this metric. The experience that the Universities of Oxford and Cambridge have had recently over their reluctance to share information on the diversity of their undergraduate student bodies should offer salutary lessons to the sector. Despite the progress both institutions have made regarding the constitution of their student bodies, their reticence to tackle this issue head on has seen a number of missteps. Sir John Parker's 2017 review into the ethnic diversity of UK FTSE 100 boards has set the target for at least one ethnic minority director by 2020. It also recommends that Human Resources or executive search firms should produce at least one candidate from a minority ethnic background for consideration. Lloyds Bank in February 2018 has set a target of 8 per cent of its senior managers to come from minority ethnic backgrounds by 2020. The current government has set a target of 14 per cent from a minority background to be appointed to public bodies. Independent schools are, in this regard, out of step with the society that they reflect and help shape.

The easy method when highlighting an issue to be addressed within the independent sector is to lay as much blame as possible, in the hope that shame will act as a motivator. This is not as productive as people think. Instead, I want to think about what it might mean for the sector if it did change and why it would be good for them and the communities they serve locally and internationally.

One outcome linked with diversity is increased performance. Management consultancy firm McKinsey estimate that companies with diverse leadership outperform other organisations by 35 per cent when financial performance is taken into account. We should always be mindful that figures such as this are correlations and not causes, but it is reasonable to suggest that diversity, in people, ideas and an open organisational culture, drive improved performance. If the discussion was limited to the financial health of schools, a 35 per cent increase would be a significant boost for redevelopment projects or bursary funds. If this broadened out to include academic performance, the implications would be huge. Diversity of leadership would then be viewed as a strategic decision, and not simply a Human Resources or executive search one. Diversity becomes strategic intent, not a 'nice to have'.

Another example might be improved decision making. In the great leadership teams that I have worked in, divergent voices focused on a single issue has always led to better outcomes. This is also reinforced by the research published in the *Harvard Business Review* and work in academic fields such as Behavioural Economics and Psychology. One example about why diverse teams improve decision making is that there is a greater focus on the facts, issues are considered more carefully and more innovative solutions are generated. Avoiding 'group think' is essential in a world where different experiences, approaches and cultural backgrounds are part of the parental and student body and demand an enhanced understanding of pedagogy and pastoral care to meet their needs.

Finally, there is an example of living the values of the school. Former prep school Head Peter Tait wrote earlier this year about the importance of living a school's values in its marketing. This is important, but not as important as actually realising the values through every element of the school before crafting a narrative for external consumption. Every single independent school is distinctive − it's what makes them independent − yet there is a unifying theme that can be traced either to their original founding or recent formulations of the school's aims: to make a difference. In living its values, independent schools can seek to make a difference to the individual student who comes from a minority background and can see themselves, as they look at the staff and governors, as being part of the community. Independent schools can make a difference to local communities by possessing a level of understanding before projects and partnerships are suggested with local schools or groups. Independent schools can make a difference to wider society by expressing openly, but not forcefully, that excellence truly knows no boundary regarding skin colour and that established institutions can change when they are motivated by doing the right thing.

The independent sector would gain a great deal by being more diverse, but I don't need to convince the governors, associations and senior leaders to change. They already possess enough motivation to change themselves, and the world beyond the school gates, for the better.

Mary Myatt

Look at situations from all angles, and you will become more open.
(Dalai Lama)

If a school is to become more diverse then this has to happen in the classroom and through the curriculum. Spiritual, moral, social and cultural education (SMSC) can play a key part of this, and independent schools, with their freedom to innovate and resources to deliver on those initiatives, are important for ensuring the programme remains relevant and central to how our young people develop into responsible citizens. SMSC has been part of education in England since the 1944 Education Act. However, the principles of spiritual, moral, social and cultural education also apply to high-quality education worldwide. Education is more than the subjects taught: it is also about the way they are enacted and the opportunities that emerge for pupils to develop the characteristics of well-rounded and principled active citizens.

It sums up how good schools prepare pupils to live full, active lives as part of their community and into adulthood. Many schools express aspirations to be safe, happy places where pupils can fulfill their potential and appreciate others. But it is a slippery element, until we pay attention to what it might encompass. It is possible to consider SMSC through three lenses. The first is in terms of 'how we do business here': in other words, what are the ways in which we approach our work? How are our values lived and not just laminated? This aspect is highly qualitative but it is possible to gather evidence, nonetheless. The second concerns what this looks like in specific subject areas and the wider curriculum. And finally, the third considers how SMSC has an aspect of pedagogy within it.

The elements of spiritual, moral, social and cultural describe those aspects of the curriculum and school life that should be threaded throughout the daily practice. They are not an add-on and they should not entail additional work. It is very important to note that the 'spiritual' aspect, which is often hardest to talk about, has nothing to do with making pupils, or anyone else, religious. The spiritual element refers to the ability of pupils to be reflective about their own beliefs, religious or otherwise, which inform their perspective on life and their interest in and respect for different people's faiths, feelings and values: whether they have a sense of enjoyment and fascination in learning about themselves, others and the world around them; whether they are able to use imagination and creativity in their learning and a willingness to reflect on their experiences. So it is clear from this that there is no expectation for anyone to be religious. Rather, it is about the capacity to take an interest in others and the wider world.

Pupils' moral development is characterised by the ability to recognise the difference between right and wrong and to readily apply this understanding in their own lives, recognise legal boundaries and, in so doing, respect the civil and criminal law of England. It concerns the extent to which they understand the consequences of their behaviour and actions, their interest in investigating and offering reasoned views about moral and ethical issues, and their ability to understand and appreciate the viewpoints of others on these issues.

The social development of pupils is shown by their capacity to use a range of social skills in different contexts: for example working and socialising with other pupils, including those from different religious, ethnic and socio-economic backgrounds; their willingness to participate in a variety of communities and social settings, including by volunteering, cooperating well with others and being able to resolve conflicts effectively; acceptance and engagement with the fundamental British values of democracy, the rule of law, individual liberty and mutual respect and tolerance of those with different faiths and beliefs. They develop and demonstrate skills and attitudes that will allow them to participate fully in and contribute positively to life in modern Britain.

The cultural development of pupils is shown by their understanding and appreciation of the wide range of cultural influences that have shaped their own heritage and those of others; their understanding and appreciation of the range of different cultures within school and further afield as an essential element of their preparation for life in modern

Britain; knowledge of Britain's democratic parliamentary system and its central role in shaping our history and values, and in continuing to develop Britain; willingness to participate in and respond positively to artistic, musical, sporting and cultural opportunities; interest in exploring, improving understanding of and showing respect for different faiths and cultural diversity and the extent to which they understand, accept, respect and celebrate diversity, as shown by their tolerance and attitudes towards different religious, ethnic and socio-economic groups in the local, national and global communities.

When considering the 'how we do business' aspect, the sorts of questions we need to be asking are: does everyone feel part of this community and does everyone have a voice (this is different from having a vote), and how do we know? Are we thinking carefully about inclusion, about how we set pupils, about ensuring wider curriculum opportunities are available for everyone, for instance? Is there a sense of hospitality? That everyone is welcome? Does our school have rules for behaviour which are clear for everyone to understand? Do our pupils have opportunities to make a contribution to school life and the community? Are our values, rules, sanctions and rewards clear and understood by everyone, are we providing plenty of opportunities for pupils to work with those who have different backgrounds, prior attainment and interests from themselves, and are we taking advantage of the myriad of cultural opportunities in our local area and nationally.

Then to consider specific subject areas. The one subject area which seems to produce more concern than any other when considering SMSC is maths. How, people ask, can I get SMSC out of maths? So, if we are asking pupils to share their ideas, respond respectfully to one another, do some research on an aspect of the history of maths, or consider the impact of globalisation on wages, then we might reasonably say that SMSC is being included. This type of work is going on in many classrooms anyway, it is just a matter of seeing how current practice has deeper links with the SMSC plank.

And of course, there are some subjects in which the SMSC is easier to discern: religious education, history, geography all have content which supports the SMSC agenda. However, it is important that the humanities in general and RE in particular are not expected to carry the whole of the SMSC agenda. It is a thread which should be running through the whole provision.

Some schools such as Rugby School take community contribution very seriously. They understand that students need opportunities to translate good intentions into action and so encourage projects such as visiting local primary schools, where students offer classroom support; visiting elderly members of the community either in their own homes or in nursing or care homes; assisting local families who have disabled children; supporting local cub packs; working at a local youth club; assisting in local charity shops and supporting local school children in maths, Latin, music and art. And the important thing to note is that this is not a one-way street. Students as well as the local community benefit from these relationships.

Similarly, at Wellington College, all students are expected to engage with community projects as soon as they arrive at the College. The aim of the school's community action programme is to ensure that all Wellingtonians have the opportunity to follow their individual passions, to see the impact they can have on society both now and into the future, and to be inspired to help others at all life stages. Pupils engage through a sense of individual wellbeing and inclusivity within different communities, and the benefits this can bring can be life changing. Knowledge gained through these direct interactions with other communities can help with intellectual pursuits both in college and beyond as pupils' understanding of our world and the difference they can make becomes more apparent.

Placements take many different forms and connect with various communities, from working with the young, vulnerable or elderly (such as sport coaching, music to help dementia, craft activities, teaching language skills, foodbank) to working with animals or environmental projects (for example dog rescue, bird and bat boxes for the local community), or simply charity related projects such as Dukes Coffee, all proceeds from which go to good causes.

When we map provision across the school curriculum, this should not involve more work. The mapping should just highlight those areas where we are doing well, which we might have known about, those areas which we now realise support SMSC, and then, when opportunities occur, to build in additional links if needed. The point is to bring it more to consciousness, rather than an additional scheme of work. The Diocese of Norwich has produced an SMSC mapping tool, which is useful for all schools.[14]

Often, schools are doing more than they realise in terms of SMSC, but they are unconsciously competent – and when they think and talk about it, realise that they are doing more than they thought. This thinking and talking shifts from unconscious competence to conscious competence. When we bring things to the fore we are likely to do more of them and embed them, than if they languish as part of our forgotten practice.

Notes

1 www.isc.co.uk/media/4890/isc_census_2018_report.pdf
2 https://assets.publishing.service.gov.uk/government/uploads/system/uploads/attachment_data/file/569410/Social_Mobility_Commission_2016_REPORT_WEB__1__.pdf
3 www.isc.co.uk/media/4890/isc_census_2018_report.pdf
4 www.gov.uk/government/statistics/schools-pupils-and-their-characteristics-january-2017
5 www.theguardian.com/education/2016/sep/01/third-of-students-at-many-british-boarding-schools-come-from-overseas
6 www.telegraph.co.uk/education/educationnews/12186770/Private-schools-move-to-accept-more-black-students-as-pupils-living-in-wealthy-cocoon.html
7 www.mckinsey.com/~/media/mckinsey/business%20functions/organization/our%20insights/why%20diversity%20matters/diversity%20matters.ashx
8 Harold Patrick, ,and Vincent Raj Kumar (2012), *Managing Workplace Diversity: Issues and Challenges*. Sage Open
9 http://reescentre.education.ox.ac.uk/wordpress/wp-content/uploads/2015/11/EducationalProgressLookedAfterChildrenOverviewReport_Nov2015.pdf
10 www.isc.co.uk/media/4890/isc_census_2018_report.pdf
11 www.ethnicity-facts-figures.service.gov.uk/work-pay-and-benefits/public-sector-workforce/school-teacher-workforce/latest
12 www.gov.uk/government/statistics/school-workforce-in-england-november-2016
13 www.inc.com/jessica-stillman/yale-researcher-to-bosses-science-proves-job-interviews-are-useless.html
14 http://marymyatt.com/resources

Chapter 7

The gender challenge

Introduction to the gender challenge

It was in the 1980s that literary criticism really took hold in our universities. Old certainties about language began to crumble, and it was increasingly seen as something slippery, unreliable and driven by seemingly endless (and previously) unrecognised political, cultural and social assumptions. Words ostensibly conveyed meaning, but what did meaning actually mean? It was just another construct. The notion of any kind of fixed truth or inherent, definitive reality behind the relativism of words, was being challenged and rejected by academics and the undergraduates they taught. For those who experienced it first hand this process could be viewed as either deeply unsettling, or profoundly liberating. Now, those undergraduates are in positions of power: they are leading politicians, op-ed writers for our newspapers and even headteachers in our schools.

It feels like we are in a similarly protean moment as we consider the question of gender identity in our schools. As educators, our job is to help children navigate the tricky, often confusing and disconcerting process of growing up, and to help them find the fixed, solid ground from which they will embark on adult life. The best independent schools do this with considerable success, born as it is from a long history of pastoral care. And yet, so many of the certainties we previously took for granted are now under scrutiny, perhaps none so strikingly and so radically in the last few years, as the issue of gender.

For most of the twentieth century, the gender debate centred around whether or not girls were getting as many opportunities to succeed as boys, and whether schools were doing enough to reflect the different needs of both sexes in the classroom and beyond. How well curricula reflect the varying interests of our young people and the different ways girls and boys learnt (at every level of school) have also been perennial elements of the discussion around gender in education.

How dated this now seems. Today, the very notion of gender is being challenged to its core. As Natasha Devon explains in her essay, our physical sex (a feature of biology) is increasingly being seen as entirely distinct from our gender (a feature of cultural conditioning and our own emotional and psychological development). Gender (just like meaning for the post-structuralists) is now fluid, relative and, crucially, non-binary. There is a spectrum and there are at least 72 recognised gender manifestations on it. Approaching a pupil's gender identity in this way means that no matter what the biological sex of the child in front of us, teachers can no longer confidently say: "this is a girl (or a boy), I know what that means in the classroom… this is the kind of thing you like, this is the approach that will work … off we go".

In some ways, this is liberating. As Devon points out (and as the strikingly higher percentages of girls opting for STEM subjects in single-sex rather than co-ed schools seems to suggest), if you take away the gender conditioning and all the "oppressive gender expectations" that go with it, children are more likely to make choices to study what they love and are good at, rather than what they (generally unconsciously) think they should be doing.

Equally, this new way of talking about gender feels like it should be empowering for children. They have the freedom to place themselves on the gender spectrum wherever they feel comfortable and surely that has got to be a good thing. And yet, as Hoskins suggests in his moving and personal essay, no amount of positive, supportive comment from those in authority, can make these decisions straightforward or easy. Far from it. For children whose gender identity feels wildly out of kilter with their biological sex (potentially up to 10% of pupils), the decision to transition can be difficult and traumatic. And it is never one to take lightly. Meanwhile, schools, anxious to support children who are transitioning, feel increasingly out of their depth. They are on unfamiliar and uncertain ground. And whilst parents of transitioning pupils are desperately seeking reassurance and support from schools, most teachers lack specific expertise in this area and the professional support groups (referenced by Kennedy in her piece) are reeling under the exponential increase in referrals over the last three years.

And it's not just about the psychological and emotional support which transitioning teens might need. The practical questions arising for schools in re-thinking gender boundaries are clear and are referenced by a number of our contributors here. Whilst co-educational schools might wrestle with uniform, sports and bathroom facilities, as well as (in the case of boarding schools) sleeping arrangements, single sex institutions have even more existential concerns. The very heart and identity of some schools are intimately connected with gender. What does Wimbledon High School for Girls mean, for example, if 'girls' is a discredited notion which no longer means anything very much? And how can schools support the minority of individuals in their pupil body who no longer identify as a girl or a boy, whilst at the same time, educating and empowering those who have opted to be in the school precisely because it celebrates and empowers girls or boys in all their variety, richness and possibility?

Fionnuala Kennedy and Jenny Allum both argue the case for gender equality. Whether in Australia or the UK, it seems there are injustices still to be addressed and there is work still to be done to enable girls and young women to own their voices and find their places in the world with confidence and authority. How can schools continue that fight whilst at the same time being open to the non-binary gender position? A similar problem arises for boys. How can we help our boys become effective, assured young men in a world which on the one hand seems to provide unrestricted access to explicit porn and on the other hand, requires them to seek consent at every stage of a first date?

There are no easy answers to these questions. But one thing is clear: the world has changed and schools will simply have to change with it. Lucy Pearson's rallying cry is particularly apposite when she asks: what about approaching the whole issue not as a problem to be solved but an unprecedented opportunity for independent schools to truly lead? A chance to be innovative, imaginative and flexible in our thinking, to throw out the old assumptions and start again with a blank sheet of paper. In a world where we saw children as children, rather than boys and girls, what would we do differently? Reinventing what education and schools look like for twenty-first-century children. Isn't that just what independence is for?

Jenny Allum

Fewer large Australian companies were run by women in 2017 than were run by men named John. There were also fewer large Australian companies run by women in 2017 than were run by men named Peter. …or David! Looking at the CEOs and Chairs of the 200 largest Australian Stock Exchange (ASX) companies, there were only nine women CEOs and ten women chairing boards in those companies. The majority of these 400 leaders of our biggest companies are straight, white, able-bodied men aged 40–69 years (a group which represents only 8.4% of the population). The number of women in those key leadership positions actually fell in 2017 over 2016.

In Australia, whether we look at employment data, educational data, criminal statistics, reports about the sexualisation of women and girls in the media, film and online, or reports on family statistics and dynamics, evidence abounds that Australian society has a way to go before we could claim to have achieved gender equality. We know that women encounter misogynistic attitudes daily in small and subtle ways as well as through demonstrations that are much more overt too.

And there will be similar statistics in most countries of the world…

If we want to have a society where gender stereotypes do not constrain our young people; where both sexes have access to the full range of opportunities; where both sexes are each afforded the respect they deserve; where violence against women is eliminated; then we need to tackle this in many ways, and particularly in our schools – single sex girls' schools, single sex boys' schools and co-educational schools.

Independent schools have an important leadership role in this regard. They have the freedom to tailor their delivered curriculum in a more nuanced fashion, the independence to target their resources most appropriately in a pastoral context to affect real change in this area, and the influence to speak out, in the media and in educational circles, to demonstrate the way forward.

In Australia, there is a way to go! The challenge for us here, as leaders of independent schools, is to:

- Help young women develop the values, and the courage, to stand up for their rights; not to feel constrained by stereotypes, not to accept injustice and ill-treatment of themselves, to be empowered to overcome barriers.

- Help young men develop the values to respect women, not to objectify them, to value women in all their diversity and differences.
- Encourage young men and young women to understand good relationships, relationships based on respect and integrity and the dignity of every person, regardless of gender.
- Help young men and young women not to accept sexist or misogynistic behaviour in others when they see it, not to stand by and see girls and young women be constrained by the application of rigid gender stereotypes, wherever that occurs.
- Teach all our children to be critical consumers of an overly sexualised society. To help all our young people navigate the world of social and digital media.

Schools are crucial to addressing these issues. There are a variety of ways to address this.

1. Formally, through a variety of Curriculum Areas. For example, our New South Wales syllabus for Personal Development, Health and Physical Education covers prescribed topics such as:
    - discuss how gender stereotypes can have an impact on rights and responsibilities in relationships
    - critically analyse gender messages in popular culture and consider their impact on individual and community health, safety, wellbeing and participation in physical activity
2. Through pastoral programmes – everything from sexual harassment and consent to cyber bullying and human rights. For example, it is important to discuss how to evaluate, assess and analyse messages from advertising billboards, lyrics of popular songs, social media posts and magazine articles, etc., to note the objectification of women, the acceptance of gender-based violence and domination, and the stereotyping of gender roles.
3. Through the "informal curriculum" – what we tolerate in schools, and what we reward. How we speak. What we ignore. The development of a school ethos and culture that models respectful practices and is consistent in dealing with incidents of gender-based violence and discrimination.

As the Head of a single sex independent girls' school, I am acutely aware of the clear need to continue to promote the girls' empowerment agenda and to help girls and young women find their places, their voices and their agency in a world governed by social media messaging and expectations. And the same exists for our Heads of single sex boys' schools and co-ed schools too. Tim Winton, the great Australian author, wrote about his most recent book "The Shepherd's Hut", "*But patriarchy is bondage for boys, too…. There's a constant pressure to enlist, to pull on the uniform of misogyny and join the Shithead Army that enforces and polices sexism.*"

The challenge facing schools is clear. And I believe that our independent schools, blessed as they are with the freedom to innovate, and often with greater resources too, should lead the way until we see violence, sexual abuse, misogynistic behaviour and all forms of exploitation and constraint towards women eliminated.

Natasha Devon

In November 2017, I found myself in the eye of a media storm after extolling the virtues of gender neutral language during an address to the Girls' Schools Association annual conference in Manchester.

During my hour-long keynote speech, which covered a number of topics relating to mental health in schools, I mentioned how heteronormative and cisnormative assumptions (our tendency to presume the person in front of us is straight, cisgender, wants to get married and have babies unless they have specifically expressed sentiments to the contrary) creates an environment in which anyone who deviates from those archetypes feels excluded from their community. In particular, LGBT+ pupils (who represent 10% of the student population) are effectively bullied through unconscious exclusion.

Since a sense of belonging is a fundamental human psychological need, I went on to hypothesise that widespread use of hetero and cisnormative language has a knock-on effect on the mental health of LGBT+ young people, using the fact that gay people are four times more likely to develop depression and 45 per cent of transgender people have attempted suicide to support my claims.

Afterwards, I was taken to a press room, in which a journalist from a right-wing newspaper asked me to 'justify' my recommendation that teachers should 'not say "girl" or "boy"' because it will 'offend transgender people'. The tone of the question troubled me. It was a hugely reductive interpretation of what I had said. Also, to use the word 'offend' places transgender children in the role of aggressor, as opposed to victim. In an attempt to counteract this, I emphasised the benefits of gender neutral language for all young people when in a school environment, adding that the terms 'girl' and 'boy' come with a weight of invisible social expectation which it probably isn't helpful to be continuously reminded of when you're trying to learn. A blanket 'ban' on gender specific words is, of course, ridiculous and untenable, but it struck me as good practice for teachers to keep them to a minimum when addressing groups of pupils.

By the time I went to bed that evening, the online headlines read 'Government Advisor ORDERS teachers to BAN the word "girls" because it REMINDS pupils of their gender' (inexplicable capitalisation by tabloids, not me). The following day I was plastered somewhere within the first five pages of every best-selling newspaper in the country, the *Daily Mail*'s 'hot take' on the saga having found its way into the gleeful clutches of Piers Morgan who decreed that it was 'political correctness gone mad' and that I should 'let kids be kids'.

As I then endured the inevitable barrage of death and rape threats to which any female public figure who dares to stick her head about the ideological parapet is now routinely exposed to on social media, it occurred to me that I had made the mistake of taking for granted that everyone views gender in the same way as I do. In doing so I had 'jumped the shark' by suggesting what many perceived to be a radical change before everyone was on the same page about the basics.

What follows, therefore, is my attempt to explain gender, as I (and the scientists I regularly consult with on the matter) see it:

Gender is not the same as biological sex and is completely separate from sexuality. Your sex lies between your legs and is determined by your genitals, your gender lies between your ears and has to do with the traits assigned by both nature and nurture to each sex. Both are influenced by chromosomes and hormones.

Before puberty, there is not much physical difference between female and male children. Girls, for example, are just as strong as boys, on average, during this time. However, there are psychological differences, again on average and once again created through a combination of biology and social expectation. Children are socialised into specific roles from the moment they are born, as anyone who has ever tried to find a gender-neutral 'congratulations on the birth of your baby' greeting card will attest.

If gender is a spectrum, with masculinity falling at one end and femininity at the other, then most men will fall somewhere at the masculine end and most women at the feminine. However, this is on average – by definition the median point in a number of variables. There exist people who fall at an almost infinite number of points along the gender spectrum. Whilst it is true to say that masculine people are different from feminine people, it is by no means certain that someone who presents in a female body will be feminine or vice versa. Equally, it does not follow that someone who does not fully identify with the social expectations associated with their biological sex will necessarily be transgender.

Furthermore, feminine and masculine traits can be defined and exploited in positive and negative ways. For example, a masculine characteristic is a desire to demonstrate strength. If a masculine person lives in a culture where strength is defined as protecting others or standing up for what they believe is right, then it is likely that desire will manifest in a positive way. If, conversely, society deems that 'strong' people more readily express themselves through violence than words and that strength is interchangeable with stoicism, you have one potential explanation for the astronomical rates of male suicide in the UK.

It is (probably) true to say that if all things were equal, women would naturally be drawn to certain professions in larger numbers than men and vice versa. However, we cannot know that definitively because things aren't currently equal. In single-sex schools, where there are no such thing as 'girl' and 'boy' subjects, larger numbers of female pupils choose to study STEM at GCSE and A Level, which would suggest that, at present, gender expectations are too oppressive.

Some gender stereotypes are rooted in what might be described as broad truth. However, they become deeply problematic when used by a society which not only dictates what men and women, girls and boys 'should' be like but asks us constantly to 'prove' our masculinity and femininity in order to garner approval and acceptance.

In making our environment and language more gender neutral, it does not follow that all people must be. What it will do is give greater choice, freedom and an all-important sense of belonging to those who, for whatever reason, do not conform.

Richard Hoskins

I was a fifteen-year-old boarder when I first sent off for oestrogen to alter my birth gender. The package from Amsterdam arrived at my home, where my father swooped. In a rage he incinerated everything at the bottom of the garden. Then he picked up the phone to my housemaster and gave immediate notice of my withdrawal. When I finished at my new sixth form, I would go to Sandhurst and learn how to be a 'real man'.

Had he been away on one of his many business trips, my life might have turned out very differently. It was another 30 years before I tried again. But would Uppingham School in the late 1970s have handled my desire to transition gender any differently? Despite being the pioneering school of whole-person education, I rather doubt it.

That was then and this is now. Gender transition is all the rage. Barely a day passes without another news story relating to gender fluidity. There is much here to celebrate. There is an openness to discuss the issue. Society has made important advances. Legal amendments enshrine greater protection for transgender people. Treatments are readily available, even for primary age children. Normally this means hormone blockers until the age of sixteen, followed by gender altering medication. Transgender counsellors are seeing unprecedented requests from children. The Gender Identity Development Service (known as GIDS) in North London has seen a six-fold increase in the numbers of three-to-eighteen-year-olds being referred in five years. They saw over 2,000 in the last year alone.

Schools are attempting to adjust to this new landscape. At least 80 state schools now have gender-neutral policies. In the Independent sector, the approach is more patchy. A number, such as Brighton College and St Paul's Girls School, permit gender-neutral clothes, whilst the latter also allows pupils to be called by boys' names. Others have fared less felicitously. Highgate Head, Adam Pettit, was forced to apologise to parents for introducing gender-neutral toilets in a decision that was condemned as 'seriously misguided'. There are also distinctive dilemmas for transitioning pupils and staff in those Independent schools whose ethos is founded upon single-sex education.

It is easy to criticise anxious parents. As one myself, I can understand the concerns. We all want the best for our offspring. We want them to be happy. For gender-fluid children, life may be easier than it was 40 years ago when I wished to transition. However, the picture is not quite as rosy as we might imagine. The road ahead for a transgender child is rock-strewn.

Never before have children felt such social pressure to conform. Independent school children, perhaps even more than in the state sector, feel peer pressure not to be seen as 'different'. From fashion to makeup, hairstyles to life choices, never have children so craved peer acceptance. Cyber bullying can be instantaneous, and crushing. Today's children don't like to stand out from their peers: especially if they are seen as 'weird', 'bizarre' or 'freakish': all words I have been called both by adults and children.

Children may also be affected by gender in the lives of adults around them. Teachers who transition are liable to face considerable classroom pressure. One eagle-eyed fifth form girl spotted my naturally polished, and moderately shaped, fingernails. A barrage of questions ensued from the benign, 'Do you shape them yourself?' to, 'Oh my god, sir, do you wear dresses at home?' The pupils were more curious than aggressive, but it did hasten my desire to exit teaching.

Nor should we overlook the particular dilemma for children when a parent, or their partner, transitions. As well as destabilising their worldview, it may render them open to peer ridicule. It can feel like bereavement for such children. They need very careful and sensitive management at school.

We have come a long way in understanding gender. Simplistic binary categorisations in both nature and nurture have been undone by advancing science. Nevertheless, this is also an appropriate moment to sound a, perhaps surprising, note of caution. We need to watch that the current gender trend is not simply the latest social craze, upon which children are all-too-ready to pounce. I knew from a young age that I wasn't stereotypically male. But that doesn't mean it was right to transition. Independent schools need to be highly supportive of pupils *and* counsellors, whose role should include testing why the child feels 'born into the wrong body'. Changing gender is an incredibly painful process: emotionally, socially and physically for everyone involved. It may also mask other, deeper, factors, which necessitate careful exploration.

Fionnuala Kennedy

The *National Geographic* magazine released a special issue in December 2016 that dealt entirely with the notion of gender, and which featured seven different people on the cover, each of whom was described via their particular gender identification, so transgender female, androgynous and so on. It's a beautiful cover of some equally beautiful humans, and an issue that felt timely in its exploration of, in the editor's words, 'the degree to which the intensely personal subject of gender identity has entered the public square'. And enter it this subject has: students and young people today rail against what they deem an antiquated, restrictive and prejudicial gender binary, thinking of gender instead as existing on a continuum or spectrum of identities and expressions; 72, I think, is the current estimate of the different number of ways in which to identify one's gender.

And all of this thinking is, of course, to be applauded: the so-called 'Snowflake Generation' might in fact be one of the most open-minded, forward-thinking generations since the Swinging Sixties. But the speed with which this discussion of gender has become front and centre is leaving independent educators behind, and causing us to ask ourselves a range and number of difficult questions, some of which will inevitably cause divides and ructions. And, of course, those of us who work in and lead single-sex schools are particularly in the spotlight when it comes to examining where we are, and where we should go from here.

Interestingly, the major criticism laid at the door of the *National Geographic* at the time was that nowhere on the cover was featured a cisgender female – a woman born a girl who identifies as a woman, i.e. her sex matches her gender identity. And it is around this issue that many of our concerns – especially as educators of girls – increasingly centre. How *can* we continue to promote equality for girls and women in an unequal world – where pay is still less if you are female; where we still have a huge deficit in numbers of women in power, both politically and economically; where acts of violence against women still significantly outnumber those against men – if what we are also saying is that to assume a binary gender divide at *all* is to be discriminatory? Should we, as single-sex schools, really stop addressing our students as 'girls' because simply to define them as such is potentially to cause offence? Many of us in girls' education have worked hard in our schools to redefine the social biases (unconscious or otherwise) of the term 'girl', ensuring it connotes strength, creativity, empowerment and independence, and making sure that to run/throw/live 'like a girl' can never again be seen by those we educate as an insult; must we lose the term entirely now in the wake of a very recent and extremely complicated discussion, the result of which we may not fully understand for decades to come? Or can we simply be whole-hearted (and, dare I say it, sensible) about this, treating pupils as individuals with individual needs, whilst also recognising that the fight for women's rights is far from over?

The problem was recently summed up very neatly indeed by a co-educational grammar school in Guernsey that ditched the monikers of Head Boy and Head Girl for 'Senior Students' and left the appointment of school prefects to be completely fluid, outside of the strictures of gender. A sensitive move in many ways, and no doubt seen as such by many students. But the result of this was that two boys were given the positions of power. The students in that school may well have been delighted with the process and indeed the outcome; those two boys may well have been the 'right' choices for the roles; and no doubt the Head's decision was a sensitive move in many ways. But in a world where I would argue we still need quotas for women at CEO and cabinet level in this country (and I am aware that is a controversial standpoint), and where global inequality for women remains a significant concern, I can't comfortably accept that schools should be suggesting that equality for women is so well-established that we can now abandon the notion of girls entirely. It is our young people who will stride out and be the change we need in the world, whatever their gender identification; and part of that change must, surely, involve a fight for girls and women.

So, where does that leave educators, and single-sex schools in particular? Legally, we are in unclear territory, working with an Equality Act that seems deliberately vague, unwilling to commit where the sands still seem to be shifting. So perhaps we should, returning to that hesitant word I used earlier, be sensible, and support students as best we can. As a body of independent schools, we need to show leadership, sensitivity and intelligence, handling this difficult issue not with a sense of fear at becoming redundant if we are single-sex, but with the knowledge that we have many years of understanding how to help young people as the world around them changes and shifts. We should listen to them, ensuring pupil voices on and around gender are heard, as well as making sure they hear from older role models who have experienced questioning their own gender identity. There are excellent speakers, resources and suggestions available, as provided by such organisations as Stonewall UK, Headtalks and Gendered Intelligence, and pastoral leaders should be looking into building these into their programmes and thinking, for pupils, staff and parents. And it will of course be important for a school to be as upfront and open as possible as to their own interpretation and policy of gender identity, joining the national discussion with compassion and with vigour.

Lucy Pearson

It becomes ever clearer to me that schools as we currently know and understand them are set up all wrong. As the crucibles of development for tomorrow's adults, schools should be agile, responsive and creative; the reality is they are more likely to be cumbersome, sluggish and unimaginative. It's not the schools' fault: it's the burden of history, with its heavy hand on our biddable shoulder, which established a model for how young people should be educated that is now woefully out of date yet few feel able to challenge or change significantly.

Nowhere is this out modishness becoming more obvious than in the realm of gender, whether it's a question of definition, equality, language, culture or leadership.

As young people more commonly challenge the binary model of gender classification and see in themselves and in those around them a broad spectrum of gender identity, the schools they inhabit must seem increasingly out of touch and restrictive. It's almost laughable, if not criminal.

So much of what a young person experiences in school is based upon their classification as either 'boy' or 'girl', meaning that this classification is hugely significant for their learning, educational experience and personal development.

Take the co-educational schools: how many of us when allocating individuals to form groups work hard to 'create a balance of boys and girls'? We have it in our heads that an equal balance of 'gender' (when seen as binary) is better or more productive than an equal balance of interests or values or motivations or backgrounds. From the outset we make sweeping assumptions about a young person's behaviours, preferences and characteristics based upon whether they are 'boy' or 'girl'.

And our generalised understanding of what a 'boy' and a 'girl' is – of what they like and how they behave – affects curriculum delivery, co-curricular provision, uniform expectations and much more besides. So what happens when a boy says, 'But that's not me, I'm not like that'? Do we ignore him, and tell him to fit into the system, or do we really listen to what he is saying and look to ourselves to fit with him, because actually, that's our job?

Single-sex schools face a particular challenge when a pupil declares themselves to be non-binary, or the opposite of their biological definition. Does the pupil still belong or don't they? If they do, what does that mean for how the school can and must define itself (what about keeping those floodgates firmly locked?) And if it's decided they don't – well, no good will come of a school jettisoning a pupil because they have come to realise who or what they are. After all, isn't that a vital part of the business we are in, helping young people to figure themselves out? And if it is, and when they do, our obligation must be to accept them for who they are.

Co-educational schools will often appoint a Head Boy and Head Girl (and Deputies) to ensure parity and fairness; we still use the language of difference (Girls' Games/ Boys' Games) when we should be using a different language altogether. And please, let us not assume that all girls want to play netball, hockey and rounders and all boys want to play rugby, football and cricket, because it's simply not true. Let's give them choice from the start to pursue whichever sports interest them. If girls want to play football, let them. If the boys want to play netball, let them. (But what about our fixture lists and results!?) Helping young people be healthy is very much on us, so let's stop making it harder for ourselves because we want to set the gender agenda: let the young people make their choices – and let them play. That's our greater responsibility.

Many independent schools like to use the word 'leading' in their promotional material: so let's lead. Let's be the sector that changes the way schools are, that modernises and introduces and reinvents for the twenty-first-century child. There are changes being made in many schools around the gender agenda, but they tinker at the edges rather than galvanising a cultural shift and a different way of thinking.

Creating educational environments that *support young people to do what feels right for them* is what we must be doing. And to do this, we are going to have to look forward not backwards, lifting the heavy hand of history from our shoulder and telling society that history has had its time with education, now it's ours.

Chapter 8

The innovation challenge

Introduction to the innovation challenge

It seems axiomatic to say that unless an organisation innovates it will die. But how true is this of schools? There is a meme that floats around social media whenever a senior politician extols school leaders to be more inventive: on the one side of the image is a sepia-coloured picture of an Edwardian classroom, the children sit rigidly in serried rows behind desks, staring forlornly at the camera. The other half of the image is of a classroom from the twenty-first century and, guess what? Yes, the children are still in rows, trapped behind those restrictive desks, the expressions are the same, and only the uniforms seem to have changed.

Those who tweet this usually do so to point out how little progress has been made in over a century. The image, for those who describe themselves as 'progressive', or in favour of 'child centred learning', is damning evidence of a lasting utilitarian approach to teaching. The same people offer no workable alternative to the traditional, secondary school classroom (and many of those educational consultants who complain most loudly have never been professionally inconvenienced by having to teach). Some point out that the classroom hasn't evolved, outwardly, that much because it works better than any affordable alternative. Some models don't move beyond a certain design because they cannot be improved upon. The classroom, with one teacher, a whiteboard and desks, could be just one such example: the apogee for delivering knowledge.

For independent schools the pressure to *not* change is, in some cases, intense and even alluring. Dominic Randolph, who is one of the most creative school leaders in American schools, admits that 'there is sublime comfort in tradition', but of equal force for him is the reality that schools 'don't know how to manage change and become more innovative'. Added to this, many parents are paying a lot of money for tradition: they like the uniforms, the emphasis on knowledge-rich curriculums (or 'stuff' over 'skills'). They want Latin and Greek taught. These parents enjoy the idiosyncrasies that each school has, the microtraditions that have grown up in those sheltered quads, inured from legislation by a conscious desire to keep alive all that links the present with a valued past. In many cases these parents went to independent schools themselves, and the fact that they can afford to consider sending their children to them is the most material illustration that they worked for them, and so they want them to work for their children. If independent schools were to innovate too much they could actually risk losing the parents who are drawn to them in the first place.

But of course, *that* view is a partial misrepresentation in itself because within the sector there are thousands of different models, ranging from the very traditional to the more outré: don't like school uniforms? The independent sector would be happy to oblige. Want to call teachers by their first name? You can pay a lot of money for that particular level of informality? Want to send your child to a vegetarian school? Again, the independent sector would probably be able to meet your needs. Such is the responsiveness of a market-driven service – rather than a top-down, government controlled system – that you are more likely to find what you're looking for if you are prepared to pay for it.

But even the most conventional, formal, independent school will be innovating beneath the reassuring familiarity of boaters and bow ties. They will be the schools with the resources to invest in wellbeing lessons, or new subject offerings, or research hubs and arts centres. They will also have the funds to invest in new methods of teaching. It is independent schools, with their separation from the state, their ability to select, to have smaller class sizes, who have the luxury to explore new approaches to teaching and learning. And of course for many, both inside and outside schools, that means using technology in new and (hopefully) constructive ways.

But there's the rub. If technology is the measuring stick of innovation (and that's a big if) then a further measure will be to assess its positive impact. How will we know if it is improving student incomes?

Schools are grappling with how best to allow their students access to the internet during school time but for many teachers it is an unwanted distraction that has no proven, lasting benefits. For others the internet represents nothing less than an educational revolution which will sweep away all known models (even those imprisoning desks). Only time will tell which reality our children will inherit, but by then the damage of an irresponsible attitude to using technology could have left society with an undesirable set of issues, including emotional problems, that we are ill-equipped to deal with because they are so relatively new.

For our contributors in this chapter change has to be managed very carefully. Although schools have to be able to take risks they do so in the full knowledge that their first priority is to the wellbeing and education of the children they teach. For Sean Dagony-Clark 'The risk of failure with new methods is elevated — not because the new methods are risky, but because they are different and new. The traditional arrangement of teacher as information deliverer, and students as information receivers who will be asked to demonstrate understanding of the information they've received, is time tested and unlikely to fail'. Hence the rows of desks, like Domesday lines, stretching across all classrooms, into the past and possibly into the future, unchanging, below the initiatives of government and school leaders, as transient, but as inevitable, as the seasons.

Such stasis is enforced because almost every pound, euro or dollar independent schools spend come from parents. Eimer Page is surely correct when she writes: 'Co-curricular learning; experiential learning; makers' spaces; differentiated learning styles; flipped classrooms; project-based learning; competency-based education... whatever we decide is innovative in one period can quickly become last year's fad in the next'. Page asks important questions about what constitutes innovation: for her school something deeply embedded (in this case Harkness) is both familiar but radically different to the many visitors from other schools from around the world who come to learn about it every year. Can something so established remain new? Retaining what works for the school is as important as rejecting what will not. It is down to the individuals to renew it afresh. Ian Yorston is of the same view, and in his essay writes about the necessity of schools to resist change unless it clearly improves what is already there. Indeed, for Yorston, we should actively try to do less because 'then − and only then − will we have the capacity to achieve more'.

For Simon Walker 'too many schools expend resources mimicking fashionable trends. IT fashion trends hold a particular allure for schools, almost always promising more than they deliver and often having unintended effects on important educational skills'. For Walker we need to ask different questions of ourselves as school leaders: 'we need a different way to frame the debate. Innovation is not about embracing the future *per se:* it is about positioning your choices *now*, to *succeed* in the future'. Those choices might mean that, increasingly, independent schools have to work with outside providers, both to connect with new and deep reserves of experience and funding and, as Randolph's school has done in several different ways, to set in a real-world context the innovations they hope their students to instigate and benefit from. But, as Dagony-Clark writes, this will be expensive: 'Schools that wish to make the next jump forward in education will commit to [a] triad of time, institutional energy, and money'. Dagony-Clark is surely right when he writes that 'Independent schools…are well positioned to lead innovative educational initiatives − perhaps uniquely positioned'. And for Randolph the sector 'should use this privilege to build an innovation capacity in our schools, experiments that could be fruitfully shared be helpful to all schools'.

Schools have many complex issues to resolve, and some − but not all − can be transformed through the right use of technology; others can be solved by innovating in assessment, curriculum, teaching and learning. For Crispin Weston effective use of technology can be liberating, but it should not compromise the essential *human-ness* of teaching:

> it is not only the centrality of human relationships that limits scale of provision in education. It is also the need for assessment, feedback and remediation, all of which are labour-intensive. Yet these can largely be automated by digital systems; and there is no necessary antagonism between such automation and the maintenance of relationships with human teachers.

There is no reason for teachers to fear time-draining activities such as testing and marking being outsourced to programs if they are more reliable and give more consistent assessment points: that will free us to interact with the students still more. After all, it isn't only students who get stuck behind desks for long periods of time: it is teachers, too, lesson planning, marking books, writing reports: activities which are *not* teaching. There is much that could be 'innovated away' in our schools if we could agree between ourselves what we value and want to preserve. Examination results and university destinations could be dead weights that drag all new ideas back to the same, restrictive, but undeniably measurable outcome. We need to look beyond them, and back to teaching because if innovation does not liberate us to teach, and teach independently, then it is part of the problem, not the solution.

Sean Dagony-Clark

Whether technology should play a part in a classroom is no longer a valid question; neither is whether to adapt teaching strategies and techniques to account for brain research and future employment. Technology is present in nearly all educational settings, at nearly all ages; it is here to stay, regardless of one's belief in its efficacy. Years of brain and learning research have shown us that some educational experiences are better than others at preparing students for their unknown future. The question all educators must answer, therefore, is how innovation should be applied to improve their students' learning experiences and outcomes. If we view innovation in classroom practice as a necessary path forward, and technological tools as purpose-driven learning instruments that are employed when useful and set aside when not, we can create far more powerful and meaningful learning experiences for our students.

The educational dividends of wise innovation are incredibly high. Project-Based Learning (PBL) and Mastery Learning (ML) may sound like buzz-words to the uninitiated, but they represent years of research on motivation, student-centered learning design, and application of constructivist theory to school practice. When expertly implemented, PBL and ML can lead to higher student motivation, increased engagement, deeper conceptual understandings, greater retention and higher transfer of learnings. Technological innovation can support and extend these gains: by liberating students from the classroom's walls and materials, technology can allow for global research, connection with industry experts, expression through still or multi-media and publication to a wide audience. These gains, applied to PBL or ML experiences, can lead to student work that truly demonstrates understanding and the full scope of a student's abilities.

Innovative learning practices can be achieved through simple tweaks of the classroom dynamic. The notion of 'authentic experiences' whereby student learning is embedded within real-world scenarios, also has its roots in constructivism. Its application can appear difficult: what teacher has time to redesign a working curriculum to make it more 'authentic'? In practice, though, this can be accomplished effectively and relatively easily through partnerships with external individuals and organisations eager to provide meaningful, situated learning experiences to students. At my last school, the other Computer Science (CS) teachers and I redesigned the Upper School CS program around this notion of authentic experience. Students' first exposure to CS was building an app that solved a problem. Their final course required them to form a startup, pitch an idea to actual engineers and entrepreneurs, and build a product that met a need. Over the last five years, this redesign of the CS program resulted in higher enrolment, stronger student engagement, more meaningful and lasting learning, and gender parity in multiple CS classes — and all in a series of courses that were not required for graduation.

Independent schools like this are well positioned to lead innovative educational initiatives – perhaps uniquely positioned. US independent schools operate separately from some or all federal and state educational mandates such as Common Core, which means less emphasis on test preparation and more time for experimental learning. Whether in the US or abroad, independent schools tend to have smaller class enrolments, which means teachers have a larger portion of attention to devote to each student. Independent schools may have a higher tolerance for risk as their school funding is not directly tied to student achievement on national or state tests. And given the necessity of continually drawing students (versus the unlimited pool of students created by district zones), educational innovation can be a competitive advantage, something that appeals to multiple constituencies from board members to parents to alums.

The risk of failure with new methods is elevated — not because the new methods are risky, but because they are different and new.

The traditional arrangement of teacher as information deliverer, and students as information receivers who will be asked to demonstrate understanding of the information they've received, is time tested and unlikely to fail. It is also unlikely to produce spectacular learning results or long-lasting, transferable knowledge. New pedagogical methods combined with technology that supports and extends them carry more risk, it's true, but also allow teachers to move educational outcomes far forward.

Innovative education, therefore, must be thoughtfully planned and meticulously implemented. It must be designed around specific learning goals, ideally with specific details about student understandings, abilities and considerations of how these will be effectively assessed. (Grant Wiggins and Jay McTighe's work on Understanding by Design provides a powerful framework for this sort of planning.) Communication between planners and teachers must be thoughtful and clear so that the execution of the new methods are well matched to their purpose. Messaging to the school's constituents must be thoughtful as well, to mitigate potential scepticism about the change. And innovation should not be a linear process; initial trials should lead to quick review and iteration, with the knowledge that the first attempt won't get everything right but the second will get closer.

Furthermore, the school must choose to devote significant time, energy and money toward innovation. It must free teachers' time to work collaboratively on innovative projects. This may require revaluation and adjustment of the school's schedule to prioritise faculty collaboration and innovative changes to curriculum. The school must work hard to build appreciation in all constituencies for innovative contributions. And it must be willing to commit money to innovative work: perhaps by increasing budgets and salaries, but perhaps also by up-staffing. Schools that wish to make the next jump forward in education will commit to this triad of time, institutional energy and money.

So, which innovations are worth trying, and how do we make them work? Certainly approaches above such as PBL and ML should be considered, ideally with an eye toward scaling them across a discipline or grade level. An institutional goal of piloting a PBL approach with a few teachers, then implementing it across a number of courses, would ensure value is derived from successful experiments. On the technological front, existing adaptive learning environments are already quite good and will be dramatically improved by the emerging fields of machine learning and artificial intelligence; the majority of teachers, at least in the core academic curriculum, would benefit from using one. As examples, Lexia Core 5 builds literacy in young kids; ALEKS improves math aptitude in older ones. A teacher can utilise these or many other adaptive systems to provide differentiated and exciting learning experiences to her students, while simultaneously augmenting her own ability to assess their understandings through automated reports of their progress. However, this is only possible after investment of capital by her institution to purchase the necessary licences.

Innovation in a school can feel challenging and risky. Teachers have little free time to conceive, build and test new approaches to their curriculum; even if they do find the time, the appeal of rebuilding a lesson or unit can feel low while the associated risks of untested experiences can feel high. Students certainly feel more comfortable staying within the lines of practiced classroom approaches and parents may question educational methods that are significantly different from the ones they experienced in school. But the potential payoff is so high and the potential outcomes so compelling that educational innovation is now a necessity, not a choice. Independent schools that wish to lead will establish educational innovation as both an administrative and academic priority; build only after thoughtful planning and with an iterative mindset; and devote meaningful time, energy and money to the process. If they don't, they will discover that the actual risk was in staying the course.

Eimer Page

Co-curricular learning; experiential learning; makers' spaces; differentiated learning styles; flipped classrooms; project-based learning; competency-based education... whatever we decide is innovative in one period can quickly become last year's fad in the next. The difficulty with the challenge of innovation in independent schools is that a new idea cannot be incorporated into the curriculum without ceasing to be new. The adoption of a pedagogical development renders it mainstream. Should we, therefore, strive for innovation for its own sake? Perhaps a more productive approach to keeping our teaching fresh is to commit to continued lifelong exploration of educational experimentation as our goal, rather than expecting some particular innovation to set us up for the remainder of a career. Innovative trends may be more important to us as teachers than they are to our students as learners. We gain the exhilaration of trying something new, and that gives us a greater degree of engagement with our subject matter. Students are well served when their teachers are engaged.

In my school, Phillips Exeter Academy, we have a course in our biology department that would be considered 'innovative' under most definitions. It is a research course where students are involved in the real work of creating solutions to diabetes. Our advanced biology students work to create strains of fruit flies that contain fluorescent genetic indicators that can show how sugars are being processed. The course was established by two of our biologists with a professor at Stanford University, but our students are producing their own genetic lines and not just using the Stanford originals. The students taking the course spend their days obsessed with the births, sex lives and deaths of their flies. Researchers exploring insulin reactions throughout the world's scientific communities can access the Exeter flies. But, the funding for the microscopes and the flights for the Stanford researchers was established for 'innovation in the sciences', and there are real and pertinent questions about whether this course still qualifies now that it has been in the course catalogue for a number of years. If a graduate-level research course with real world medical application being taught at the high school level is not innovative, what is?

Last year, we added a section with five new courses to our 92-page Courses of Instruction, specifically called 'Exeter Innovation'. This is a space for experimental courses that are team taught, e.g. bioethics or advanced ceramics & chemistry, or for courses with an experiential component, such as the digital humanities history course that ends with a trip to Gettysburg to work at the Civil War Institute. In the team taught courses, students have a choice of which department grants them graduation credit, depending on their focus for final projects. Funding has been secured to cover the additional costs of team teaching and for the field trips and longer travels. There were many more course proposals than we approved for the first year, indicating that there is a hunger in our faculty for new ways of approaching material with colleagues from other disciplines, or new ways to bring the work of the classroom to the real world. But the courses themselves will not remain in the innovations section – how could they after having been successfully executed? After spending two years in the Exeter Innovations category, courses are either moved into departments or removed entirely to leave space for new designs.

Having acknowledged that innovation is an unsustainable quality, there are trends that are worth acknowledging in the field. The shift from content to skills is common to many of the most vaunted educational innovations of the past few decades. There certainly was a period of time in education when it was important to impart particular content knowledge in a discipline, but changes in technology have meant that much of that encyclopedic knowledge is available to our students at the press of a button. Certainly, no one would want their surgeon to stop mid-surgery to look up the exact pathways of the artery his scalpel is pressing against, but in many cases the need to know classifications, dates and statistics has been replaced by the need to know how to access information – content has been replaced by skill. But this skill must be developed into much more than simply manipulating online databases or 'googling' the topic. The real end and business of learning is developing the skills to judge the quality of the evidence one has found, and using those skills to approach learning across disciplines. There are cases where mastery of a subject can only be achieved through graft – playing a musical instrument; speaking a language with fluency; handling a ball or stick – and others where mastery of skills allows one to tackle new material deftly. Should we continue to teach voluminous content in a world where skills and judgement are more urgently needed?

Exeter is known worldwide for its development and use of the Harkness method. In this mode of discussion-based learning, the students direct the course of the conversation and back up their ideas with evidence in every subject, whether it is the text or primary source in a humanities classroom, or the experiment and observations in a science classroom. But we have been using this method for over eighty years. Is it innovative if it is already an octogenarian? If it is not 'innovative' to us, it certainly seems that way to the many visitors we receive from other schools. Coupled with this, we are an old (by US standards) New England boarding school with a tradition of high academic rigour. The desire to be innovative here is matched by an equally strong desire to retain our distinctive edge as a highly rigorous academic environment.

Independent schools are looking at their relevance in this age of information access, and trying to plan for a future where parents and students can choose between staying at home and completing online modules for learning, and leaving home for our campuses. Unless our schools are prepared to commit to equipping students with the relevant skills for successful navigation of twenty-first-century challenges, and to understanding that neophilia can cloud our judgement about the worth of the experiments we try, we may find ourselves innovated into obsolescence.

Dominic A. A. Randolph

Can schools be truly innovative? I am not sure. There is a lot of momentum to the traditional nature of schools and our missions that has survived the last century. I think many teachers and administrators would like to be more innovative and believe that there needs to be significant change in our schools, but there are two issues that constrain us: there is sublime comfort in tradition, and we don't know how to manage change and become more innovative.

And yet, the world is changing swiftly. My grandmother was amazed by the early airplanes flying low over the fields of Flanders. My daughter hardly understands why one would have ever used a type-writer. Of course there are schools all over the world that are starting up with different assumptions about what constitutes good learning and effective education, and that is good; however, what could be engineered in the culture of a school that has been functioning well for decades or centuries in order to allow it to begin thinking in more innovative ways about teaching and learning? What could we 'seed' in our schools that could help us innovate and change what we do?

I have been looking for and thinking about innovation in independent schools for the last 15 years or so, and I have come to believe that some of the questions we are asking about our schools and the future are wrong-headed. People talk about disruption. People talk about the end of schools. I do not think that we should be thinking in such 'violent' terms but rather proposing an educational evolution – innovating in more gradual and purposeful ways. Rather than embracing innovation wholesale in our schools, we need to be prototyping towards innovation. Here are some ideas that would allow us all to prototype innovation in our schools and create the very foundations of change.

VENTURE: We should all become venture capitalists. I think that the job of an administrator, a department chair, or a colleague is to help others experiment and try out new things. If we viewed ourselves more as venture capitalists do, we would view each teacher as a potential start up, as an entrepreneur solving problems in their classrooms. Why wouldn't we create small innovation funds in our schools and have teachers 'pitch' their ideas to decision-makers who can then fund them. Some of the ideas will be great, but what it also changes is the mindset of the teacher and how they are viewed in schools.

HACKER: 'I don't have the right room'. Instead of waiting for the forms to be submitted or for an order to be made, or to get the school to sign on to rebuilding spaces, why don't we just hack existing spaces. Change the way the furniture is placed in the classroom. Change the furniture itself. Repaint a wall. Create a blackboard or bulletin board for children at their real height in primary classrooms where they can post their own questions and answers. We tried this out in a first grade class. It made these young learners see that they were agents of their own learning. I have to believe that is a good thing, and it cost nothing to implement. How can we hack our schools to make them more innovative organisations? How can we create more dynamic learning environments for our children?

POPUP: Traditionally, when we wish to change something in a school, we form a committee, have them develop an idea over a few months and then complain when the idea is finally implemented. Why could we not take on the idea of a pop-up shop ([https://en.m.wikipedia.org/wiki/Pop-up_retail])and just implement a small-scale version of the idea in our school setting? We have done this with optional courses we call Project Knowmad that happen out in New York City after the school year has finished. The students and teachers co-opt spaces to work and visit sites all over the city. This year we are offering nine discrete pop-up learning experiences called Project Knowmad.[1] Teachers and students alike have transformed their assumptions about good learning immeasurably just by creating a more innovative format for a class.

EXPERIENCES: In our work with the design firm IDEO, I was interested in seeing how the design company has evolved from designing objects to designing experiences, like the patient experience at the Mayo Clinic.[2] Experiential education hovers at the margins of many independent schools, mainly in the co-curriculum in outdoor education, the arts and global studies. What if we considered school entirely experiential? If we looked more carefully at the student experience of a school environment and culture, we could engineer more belonging and better learning. I think it would be innovative to look more closely and acutely at the micro- and macro-moments that comprise the student experience. Daniel Kahneman has famously stated that we experience about 20,000 moments every day. In order for schools to be better for our students, we need to engineer more effectively these moments to improve learning and help students thrive.

METRICS: How do we measure what we really care about? Do we really care about test scores and are they a good measure of learning? If we care about our students learning and thriving as proposed by the global Positive Education movement[3] how can we measure learning and thriving in good ways? How can we have more formative assessments and feedback that allows students to develop the capacities they need to learn and thrive? The current movement in some independent schools in the United States, the Mastery Transcript Consortium[4] that aims to rethink the high school transcript is an interesting development that questions the current metrics and hypothesises that if they change that might help our schools to innovate since 'we are what we measure'.

As independent schools, we have flexibility that often is not afforded to schools in the public or state sectors in many countries. This flexibility is a privilege. I think we should use this privilege to build an innovation capacity in our schools, experiments that could be fruitfully shared to be helpful to all schools. We do not need to start anew, we just need to inspire sparks of new and innovative practices within our existing practices, programs and systems. We should prototype innovation in myriad and small ways to make our school communities more comfortable with change and to prepare ourselves to confront the change that is coming.

Simon Walker

Innovating is never about following trends or fads. That is mimicry and is something entirely different. Too many schools expend resources mimicking fashionable trends. IT fashion trends hold a particular allure for schools, almost always promising more than they deliver and often having unintended effects on important educational skills.

The effect of Google on education is a great example. Google has enabled us to 'outsource memory'. Google carries our cognitive load, so that our brains can deploy more resources elsewhere. This sounds like a great benefit, but there is a cost. There is evidence that outsourcing memory to the internet creates a kind of cognitive inflation, my phrase for over-estimating your cognitive abilities.

One fascinating series of 2015 studies led researchers to conclude that when using the internet, '*people mistake access to information for their own personal understanding of the information*'. The internet affects the mind, creating errors of cognitive judgement. Whilst we *feel* knowledgeable, our actual understanding is inflated and unrealistic.

Many schools have 'innovated' their education by disposing of physical libraries, going entirely paperless, refocusing on teaching skills more than content. The jury is out on whether those changes bring costs as well as benefits to the quality of learning. Such changes are often glossy, appearing progressive and forward-looking. The alternative appears to hang onto regressive, anachronistic and outdated modes of teaching and learning.

My central question is this: *Is* that the alternative? Is innovation *really* about a choice of 'embracing the future' or 'clinging to the past'?

I believe, in fact, that we need a different way to frame the debate. Innovation is not about embracing the future *per se:* it is about positioning your choices *now*, to *succeed* in the future.

Students of today will need to succeed and thrive in *this* future of tomorrow: a world which is increasingly dominated by digital technologies, machine intelligence and global competition. All of these will drive down wages.

This is the future. *Innovation is the intelligent response to it now.*

We should start our intelligent response by thinking about what *cognitive vulnerability* human beings will be exposed to in this future. What human cognitive functions will a post-robotic, digital, globalised economy easily replace, which humans are currently employed to do?

There is a function of the mind which performs tasks very similarly to a machine. It is largely what we refer to as IQ. IQ is essentially the procedural ability the mind has to perform complex calculations accurately and at speed. It is sometimes called 'algorithmic cognition' by cognitive scientists.

Machines are increasingly able to replicate this algorithmic function; indeed, as an Oxford professor of machine-learning recently put it to me, machines 'think' through algorithms.

Human algorithmic cognition is vulnerable to machine replacement; which is why medicine, law, accountancy, trading and other high-end professional services are highly vulnerable to redundancy as AI develops.

On the other hand, there is a human cognitive function that is machine *resistant*. It is a kind of processing on which machine learning is not, and cannot (for the foreseeable future), be developed. It is what is called 'associative processing'.

Associative processing is the ability of the mind to coordinate our many facets to form a coherent representation of ourselves as whole persons. The mind forms this mental self-representation in order to navigate the unfamiliar, novel and unpredictable world. For example, when we negotiate a different culture, or adapt to a new job, or work out how to tackle a novel problem, or recruit help from others, we do so using our ability to self-represent and simulate how we might act.

My Oxford professor assured me that algorithms are very poor at navigating such unpredictable landscapes. Powerful on straight routes, they become lost and broken off-road.

In my organisation, we describe this kind of thinking as the mind's ability to *steer: to steer the road in front of us*. The engine of the human mind can be replicated by machines. But the ability of the mind to steer is a function machines will not be able to replace for many, many years.

Education needs to innovate. But not with more iPads. It needs to innovate in regard to how it assesses and trains the ability of children to steer.

While government schools are under pressure to focus ever more on speed, independent schools have a tremendous opportunity to succeed by training their children to steer.

Future schools that produce pupils with highly-tuned engines, but without effective steering, will fail. Schools that innovate to produce pupils who can both drive fast *and* steer will succeed. Innovation will have happened when schools are able to tell the difference.

Crispin Weston

In 2011, Sebastian Thrun, a charismatic Stanford Computer Science professor, published a "massive open online course". "CS221: Introduction to Artificial Intelligence" attracted 160,000 subscribers, prompting Thrun to found a new MOOC platform called Udacity. His colleague, Andrew Ng, founded Coursera, while Harvard, MIT, Berkeley and Austin hedged their positions by setting up a third platform, EdX. One year later, the *New York Times* declared 2012 to be "The Year of the MOOC"[5] and many predicted the end of higher education as we know it.

The feeding frenzy was short-lived. Drop-out rates from the new MOOCs averaged more than 90 per cent,[6] even though most participants were already highly educated. With surprising frankness, Thrun admitted that "we have a lousy product" and Udacity underwent "a very hard pivot", out of higher education and into lifelong learning.[7]

The failure of MOOCs to transform HE is mirrored by a similar record of edtech disappointment in schools. Generous UK government funding in the 2000s had no significant effect on learning outcomes. The OECD has shown an inverse correlation between the amount of class-time spent working on computers and the performance of participating countries in its four-yearly PISA tests.[8] The history of computers in American classrooms has been summarised by the title of Larry Cuban's 2003 book, *Oversold and Underused*.

In spite of this disappointing record, it would be premature to dismiss the potential of digital technology in education. In retrospect, mobile and cloud computing might both be viewed as prerequisites, giving us 1:1 device ratios and sparing schools the need to hire expensive, local systems administrators. Both have only become established in the last decade.

Meanwhile, the Year of the MOOC revealed two latent appetites, neither of which has gone away: first, the appetite of the modern world for education at a scale that traditional teaching methods cannot satisfy; second, the appetite of high-status, independent schools to play in such a new, global mass market. This is despite the risk of diluting their own luxury brands, based on personal relationships and physical institutions.

It should not be assumed that scale is only a problem for the state sector. If state schools manage to use digital technology to improve productivity, fewer parents may be prepared to pay such a large proportion of their disposable income for a high-quality, high-cost model of private education. In Chapter 4, James Tooley suggests that as the state sector is liberalised, the UK independent sector may itself be missing opportunities to expand into the mid-market. Beyond domestic markets, the emergence of edtech will surely heighten both the opportunities and threats of global competition.

It is not only the centrality of human relationships that limits scale of provision in education. It is also the need for assessment, feedback and remediation, all of which are labour-intensive. Yet these can largely be automated by digital systems; and there is no necessary antagonism between such automation and the maintenance of relationships with human teachers.

Recent edtech initiatives have ducked the need for automation, instead basing their unlikely pedagogies on the use of expositive media, commercial tools and games, and independent learning online. So long as we can learn from these mistakes, past failure need not rule out future success.

Such success will require software that combines rich interactivity and clear tasking; that automates much assessment and feedback; that manages assignment and sequencing and that tracks progress. Although such systems must be controllable by human teachers and blended with traditional classroom teaching, they will be developed by edtech suppliers, not by traditional education providers.

A third appetite to be revealed by the Year of the MOOC was that of tech-innovators for the "platform play": the online monopoly providing basic infrastructure through which other suppliers are forced to operate. MOOCs might have failed because, in their hubristic aspiration to scale straight to "massive", they underestimated the importance of the student's relationship with the human teacher. Yet this will be small comfort for traditional education providers if future forms of blended learning offer them the role of impotent franchisees, operating through an educational Uber or Amazon.

The impetus towards such an outcome lies in the interdependence of instructional software and the learning management systems that are needed to control assignment and track performance. At present, every educational app must develop its own management system, creating an unsustainable multiplicity of these systems.

Plug-and-play interoperability is therefore the final prerequisite for useful edtech innovation to occur. It can be achieved in one of only two ways: by a monopolistic edtech platform; or by a framework of open data standards. It is not easy to establish such "anticipatory" standards before a mature supply industry has yet emerged and the last 20 years are littered with a history of failed attempts.

Both for the benefits that digital technology can bring to education and for the dangers of leaving this project to an unregulated market, it is time that we made the attempt again. Learning from past failures, there is no reason why we should not succeed in creating a world-leading ecosystem for edtech innovation, of a type that would work best when blended with traditional models of face-to-face education. Better data standards would not only support innovative new teaching methods, but by defining our educational objectives more clearly, would help providers develop and justify new curricula, responding to the changing requirements of the modern world.

Given prior innovation by edtech suppliers, independent schools, free from the restraints of state control, would then be well placed to lead a second wave of innovation, which would not only preserve, but which would allow for the wider dissemination of the educational traditions and virtues that such schools already embody.

Ian Yorston

Schools shouldn't innovate. Well, not in matters of technology.

Plenty of independent schools have tried to get ahead of the pack by introducing laptops, or one-to-one tablets, or a smart new eLearning platform.

Indeed it's worth noting that the leading eLearning platform in the independent sector was started by two boys at St Paul's Boys' School.[9] And the leading management information system in the independent sector was created by a student at Rugby School.[10] They were helped enormously by the invention of the computer which we can probably credit to Alan Turing, an alumnus of Sherborne Boys. And the world wide web has been a pretty important tool too, for which we can thank Tim Berners-Lee of Emanuel School. We could usefully add in Mathematica (Stephen Wolfram, Eton College) and perhaps even offer a nod of appreciation to the Hitch-Hikers' Guide to the Galaxy (Douglas Adams, Brentwood School).

All in all, there seems to be plenty of reason to think that our alumni are doing their bit for the world of innovation in and around technology.

But schools shouldn't innovate.

Schools shouldn't innovate because it invariably costs time and money whilst producing little discernible gain. It looks attractive. Of course it does. We appoint Heads of Department, Deputy Heads and Heads and we ask them to manage things. We rather hope that they'll manage things better. And they rather hope that they'll get promoted. So, something must be done. And this is something. So here we go. Again.

I remember being lectured on management many years ago. Lecture one, slide one: "Management is about making things better; if you make other things worse in the process then it doesn't count".

I took my A Levels at Wellington College in 1979. Maths, Maths, Physics, Computing[11] and General Studies. I played in the school orchestra. Appeared in the occasional play. Edited the school magazine. Played a fair amount of sport to a reasonably high level. And revelled in Debating and Politics. Of course I did. This was 1979. Everyone was arguing about Europe.

Forty years later my son is taking his A Levels at a different Independent School. Well, not that different. He's taking Maths, Maths, Physics, Chemistry and General Studies. He plays in the school orchestra. Appears in the occasional play. Edits the school magazine. Plays a fair amount of sport to a reasonably high level. And revels in Debating and Politics. Of course he does. This is 2018. Everyone is arguing about Europe.

Plus ça change as they say over in the Modern and Foreign Languages Department whilst desperately attempting to encourage the few pupils who are still committed to speaking French. As opposed to, say, Arabic. Or Japanese. Or Chinese. Or whatever the latest fad might be.

Of course that language might actually be Python. Or Javascript. Or Swift. Or even R if a particularly enthusiastic mathematician has managed to persuade the Head of the vital need to teach our pupils data science.

It's hard fitting all this stuff in nowadays. What with the need for Critical Thinking. And Philosophy. And Citizenship. All amidst Relationship Education, Leadership, First Aid and eSafety.

And all of this must done on the latest learning management system. The one we introduced to replace the one that didn't quite work on the new tablets that we introduced to replace the laptops that never quite lasted a complete morning on an overnight charge.

What is it about independent schools that we feel this deep need to innovate so much, so often, without any evidence that it produces better outcomes for anyone? We breathlessly explain to parents that we are introducing EPQ or GPE or SFA as the latestone-size-fits-all-this-will-be-better-you'll-see and then, three years later, we quietly dismantle that particular initiative in order to introduce the next new new thing that someone thinks will finally solve all of our problems. Is it any wonder that, 40 years on, my son's experience of school is really no different to mine. And what have all those Heads been doing in all those intervening years?

So much of education is a zero-sum game. We need to recognise that there are only so many hours in the timetable and that those hours are already marginally too few to deliver the existing curriculum; we add to that load at our peril.

The strange thing is that, amidst all this determination to do more, no-one much seems to be innovating in the one space that might be genuinely useful: doing less.

Doing less is hard at independent schools. We sell ourselves to parents as places where so much happens; where more happens year-on-year; where more is so obviously better.

But artificial intelligence (AI) may yet ride to our rescue.

If we feed AI large enough quantities of robust data then there is a real chance that we can start to off-load significant amounts of work-load: planning, quizzing, cajoling pupils and marking work. Perhaps more importantly, AI platforms will help us review performance, behaviours and interests across all subjects and across all time whilst sensibly accounting for health and pastoral data, perhaps even the wea-ther and the pollen count.

And, once we are doing less, then – and only then – will we have the cap-acity to achieve more.

But we need to go about it in a moderately scientific manner. We need to decide what we can reliably measure. We need to decide what we want to achieve. We need to be really clear about what success will look like – and be clear that we can measure something that will tell us that we are on track to meet that success.

That means we need to strip what we measure back to the basics of Numeracy and Literacy. Of course, we need to ensure that we use assessments that produce reliable data, but we have MidYIS and the Americans have S.A.T.s and our medical schools have UKCAT – all of which are computer-based assessments of Numeracy and Literacy. We can probably capture some data on Sleep and Mood. And our librarians could usefully tell us how much reading is actually going on. Ironically this would see the independent sector apparently reverting to the three Rs, but we've never suffered from the suggestion that we are traditionalists at heart.

Of course we need to ensure that we are drawing robust conclusions from robust data – rather than voicing personal opinions built on carefully chosen anecdotes.[12] Ask any Year 8 about scientific method and they will parrot back: "Change one thing. Measure another. Keep everything else the same".

The real challenge of innovation is buried in that last sentence. It's not about introducing the latest technology. It's about changing paradigms rather than operating systems.

So let's decide that we genuinely want to make something better. Without making anything else worse. Decide what that something actually is. And keep everything else the same.

Written in the garden. On my iPhone. Using cloud-computing. Because – yes, whisper it who dares – there are real innovations out there that are being delivered without fuss and without fanfare.

Notes

1   www.riverdale.edu/page.cfm?p=664
2   http://vol10.cases.som.yale.edu/design-mayo/introduction/mayo-clinic
3   http://ipen-network.com
4   http://mastery.org
5   Laura Papano (2012), The Year of the MOOC, *New York Times*, New York, www.nytimes.com/2012/11/04/education/edlife/massive-open-online-courses-are-multiplying-at-a-rapid-pace.html
6   Chuang, Isaac and Ho, Andrew (2016), HarvardX and MITx: Four Years of Open Online Courses – Fall 2012-Summer 2016 http://dx.doi.org/10.2139/ssrn.2889436

7   Max Chafkin (2013), *Udacity's Sebastian Thrun, Godfather of Free Online Education, Changes Course*, FastCompany, New York, www.fastcompany.com/3021473/udacity-sebastian-thrun-uphill-climb

8   OECD (2015), *Students, Computers and Learning: Making the Connection*, PISA, OECD Publishing, Paris, https://doi.org/10.1787/9789264239555-en.

9   Firefly – https://fireflylearning.com

10 iSAMS – www.isams.com/

11 I suspect there weren't many of us taking Computing A Level in 1979. We had a PDP-8F from DEC, thanks to the foresight of the Head of Maths, Dr J Tierney.

12 See the excellent work being promoted by CEM Durham: https://evidencebased.education/do-schools-know-how-reliable-their- assessments-are/

Chapter 9

The international challenge

Introduction to the international challenge

An optimistic way of viewing the future of independent schools is to believe that all challenges are simply opportunities as yet unmet. A pessimistic way of viewing the same data, with the same projections, is to conclude that the challenges outlined in this book are likely to drive some schools into receivership: the cost of fees, plus a dwindling market (especially for boarders), are insurmountable issues which no amount of creative accountancy will solve. What neither of these views account for (leaving aside the fact that numbers in the UK are still relatively buoyant) is the sector's remarkable ability to innovate and adapt. Who would have thought, even ten years ago, that one English independent school (Dulwich College) would in 2018 be educating over 7000 pupils overseas? International markets as varied as China and Dubai have enthusiastically welcomed UK schools. For schools that have the resources and willingness to take considered risks, the rewards have been significant. Over time, what was a nascent industry has become firmly established, and as those schools have grown in size they have also deepened their experience and understanding of the local contexts, allowing them to build new schools.

Schools such as Haileybury, Wellington College and Dulwich have been pioneers, and their success has convinced others – most recently Reigate Grammar and Westminster – to move into markets that show no sign of being saturated. In the current political climate, in the UK at least, it probably makes for a refreshing change for these schools to feel wanted by politicians. Inevitably, this process has not been without some difficulties but, overall, it has been a huge success. It proves, if any proof was required, that there are many who value not just a private education, but a *British* private education. To what extent a pupil attending, say, Marlborough College Malaysia, is having the same experience and quality of education that his or her peers are receiving in the original school is a moot point, but it doesn't seem to concern parents eager to send their children to that (relatively new) school.

But there are questions that need to be answered as this new sector expands: they have serious implications for all fee-paying schools, whether they are in Shanghai or London. Russell Speirs asks: how long will the rapid recruitment of boarders to overseas' schools affect numbers in the home market? His reasoning is difficult to dispute: 'In the future, more British expatriates and foreign families in Asia and the Gulf region will surely choose to send their child "up the road" to a prestigious "British" school rather than to the UK, with the additional costs of boarding fees, travel and impact on family life'. Edward Clark and Helen Wright go further when they ask what will happen if these newly established schools become more desirable destinations than their parent school: 'might we even see British parents opting to send their children to international schools rather than to UK independent schools, because they are cheaper and offer a greater value proposition in terms of access to great universities and readiness for the workplace?' Growing up – and learning about life – in Dubai might, for some parents, appear to be better preparation for the increasingly internationalised workplace than attending a boarding school in Devon. And if that becomes a trend, the original, established market not only looks too expensive but, well, too old. The tried-and-tested ways of selling a British public school – being places of tradition and heritage – could in the near future actively work against them. The rich irony is that should this happen it is – like rapid fee increases – largely a problem of their own making.

The counter argument is that as affluence spreads throughout a society – as is happening in China – new 'customers' are being created. Furthermore, there is no prospect of numbers drying up. Indeed, globally, there is the opposite problem, as Mark Steed points out: 'there is still a huge shortfall in the provision of schooling from a global perspective. Arguably, the greatest challenge facing education today is that there are an estimated 263 million children who are not in education'. Now, obviously, such children and their families are not going to access an independent school – or indeed any school – without significant assistance, at supranational, national and local levels. Having said that, and as Jamie Martin writes in his essay, low-income families in developing countries *are* opting for fee-paying schools in growing numbers. What the sector can ask itself, as it continues to debate how it can narrow the equality gap, is how it can be involved in reaching these children. The question is as pertinent overseas as it is at home in the UK; perhaps more so, given the parlous nature of education in some of the locations of international independent schools.

And it is something the sector must do, not only because it is the right thing to do, but also because it fits with the stated aims of the school. For a school to establish another school overseas, it has to be an organic development out of what they are already doing well. For Cameron Pyke, this is what will require the most focus before a school can begin to contemplate who it educates and where; for him, schools will 'require both nuance and substance in communicating: that it is seen as entirely complementary to their social mission at home and not a commercial distraction designed to shore up already wealthy institutions'. Justin Garrick argues that schools have to become truly global if they are not only to succeed but, importantly, *deserve* to succeed. For him, if internationalism is reduced to 'transactional terms as the sale of Western education abroad, then the model is eventually doomed – like the colonial paradigm before it'. New models, driven by a desire to change the societies that these schools bridge, have to be established. And if they have the inventiveness to span such wide cultural differences, then they can attempt to lessen inequalities within the societies that host them.

There are other questions relating to supply and demand that we are only beginning to ask now. The debate around student markets drying up as these schools multiply is causing concern among those schools that have no overseas branches (and they are in the majority within the independent sector). But the same applies to staffing. If, as Speirs asserts, more teachers from the UK start work in other countries than enter teacher training, then the continued success of these schools could cause real, but unintentional, damage to the profession in that country. That said, in global terms such numbers are tiny: international schools will require 400,000 teachers in the next eight years, which sounds a lot until you realise, as Mark Steed reminds us, that the world needs approximately 3.3 million primary and 5.1 million secondary teachers by 2030 to meet demand.

Put like this, the expansion of independent schools cannot come fast enough, and quibbling over whether these are for-profit or otherwise is irrelevant – a self-indulgent, first world debate conducted by an already educated elite. Jamie Martin's essay clearly shows that there is a need there, and whether it be stand-alone institutions, or chains, independent schools will no doubt have a growing role in the future of schooling in developing countries. And the truth is that we need as many schools as practicable educating as many children as possible, if we are to raise those societies and its families out of poverty. Perhaps our independent schools can play a central part in that process; and indeed, in doing so, they may once again establish the strong moral core that was so central to their founding principles.

Edward Clark and Helen Wright

Recruiting Heads and senior leaders for international schools is probably one of the best ways to gain a superb insight into the quality of education on offer at present in schools across the world. When we spend time with leaders and potential leaders in international schools and delve into their experiences, their beliefs and their mindsets, the resounding message is that something quite extraordinary is going on in international education. The question is: will UK independent schools be quick enough to catch on to this, or will they be left behind?

At their best, international school leaders (and therefore their schools) are adept at operating in different cultures, and have a nimbleness and flexibility of approach in dealing with people, which can be streets ahead of their UK counterparts. Born of the necessity of managing parental expectations and the practicalities of school life in a very different – often multi-national – context, these leaders and their schools have developed a robust international-mindedness, and gaze on the parochialism of much of the UK independent sector with some perplexity. They know that the world is shifting and moving, and that nothing can be taken for granted any more; they know that they have to prove themselves by being at the cutting edge of educational pedagogy and practice, and that if they don't, then they and their schools won't survive.

The good news for UK independent schools is that this cutting edge incorporates much of what lies at the heart of a sound British education, and has done for centuries: the development of character, of critical thinking, of service to others and of strong values. The bad news, however, is that the best international schools – and there are thousands of these – not only offer amazing educational opportunities, but have also become experts in assessing, tracking and intervening with their students in order to ensure excellent academic outcomes and access to the world's top universities, challenging the previously widely held perception that a UK independent school education is a necessary step on the route to world class higher education. Moreover, these schools benefit from being located in parts of the world with burgeoning populations who are able to afford the education on offer to them, as well as on economies of scale, and – as Sir Michael Wilshaw pointed out in 2016 – from the expertise of UK teachers, more of whom are leaving the UK to teach than are being trained here.

As the status of these international schools rises, and as they resolve the issues which have dogged them in the past (poor safeguarding, for example, in some cases, and flaky governance) the risks to the UK independent sector from international schools are potentially deeply concerning. Could we imagine a situation where UK independent schools are seen as second best to international schools running an English-medium (often British) curriculum in different parts of the world? Might we even see British parents opting to send their children to international schools rather than to UK independent schools, because they are cheaper and offer a greater value proposition in terms of access to great universities and readiness for the workplace? UK students have the advantage of being fluent in English, still (for now, at least) the world's most important language … but add into the equation the lure of more languages, as well as the cultural confidence which comes from exposure to international life, and the sum suddenly looks a lot bigger and more attractive.

UK independent schools have an enormous amount to offer their students – and the world in general. They always have done, and (hopefully) they always will do. What they can't be, however, is complacent: there is a big, wide world of young people and parents out there, hungry for outstanding education, and the sector needs to work to improve its global offering. The challenge for UK independent schools is to prove, beyond doubt, that they are preparing students to be agile global citizens, which is hard to do when great UK teachers are more difficult to find, fees are rising, and the sector is not attracting as much international interest from educators as it could. Teachers who have lived and worked overseas bring enormous experience and fresh cultural perspectives, yet only 449 teachers from outside the UK chose to come and teach in UK independent schools in 2017.

In a utopian world, schools would work in harmony and embrace the diversity that each has to offer. In reality, international schools have thrown down the gauntlet. Has the UK independent sector even realised that it is there?

Justin Garrick

There is no doubt that the globalisation of education presents enormous opportunities to independent schools with the vision and capacity to establish offshore campuses and partnerships. There are risks, of course, both reputational and financial, as some have discovered to their cost, but there would not be so many British and other independent schools proliferating around the world were there not considerable gains to be made too.

According to data from the UK's Independent Schools Council, there are now more than 60 satellites of British independent schools operating abroad, collectively educating more international students offshore than in Britain itself; a remarkable phenomenon, the rapid emergence of which is reflected in the establishment of no less than 13 new campuses between 2016 and 2017 alone. That's only British schools; there are others too.

For many, the drive to establish international offshoots is obviously commercial; a response to financial pressures at home and to the enormous market potential of emerging middle classes abroad. As domestic populations struggle in uncertain times to support the fee levels required to operate major independent schools, the expanding, aspirational and increasingly wealthy markets of China, South and East Asia and parts of the Middle East are clearly attractive sources of additional enrolments and revenue.

Why not subsidise what domestic markets want but struggle to sustain by capitalising on new markets that want the same thing and can afford it? That might not seem especially noble, but if schools get the model right, it can be a win–win arrangement, as access to high-grade educational opportunities for families at home is supported by revenue from prosperous populations given access to the same model of education abroad.

For internationally-oriented families in target countries, that is particularly attractive because it allows students to experience so-called Western styles of teaching, learning and curriculum in preparation for study at Western universities without the emotional and financial impact entailed in sending children abroad at an early age. Yet, for all parties, there are potential benefits too; for example, additional exchange opportunities for students to experience schooling in different contexts, and opportunities for teachers to refresh and broaden their horizons with stints in partner schools overseas. In addition, there is the chance for greater continuity of learning for children of expatriate parents whose careers are only likely to become more globally mobile in the decades ahead.

In fact, therein lies the real imperative to internationalise and the challenge for independent schools to take the concept beyond the current essentially colonial model of satellites serving the interests of the centre. For those suspicious of the financial rationale, there is a genuine and far greater educational cause than just propping up the home schools with funds from franchise campuses. It is to equip all children – in both the base and the offshoot schools – for what they are destined to be: the world's first truly global generation.

Despite the nativist upsurges of contemporary politics, no serious educator should doubt that the children we teach now will live, study and work abroad – both physically and virtually via technology – crossing nations, economies, political systems, cultures and languages more frequently and in a world more mobile and permeable than has ever been the case before.

In fact, precisely because the isolationist reactions of current politics are so at odds with the life trajectories of the next generation, we have even more responsibility as educators to recognise what children now in kindergarten will need if they are to flourish in the world that they will enter on leaving school more than a decade from now, in the early 2030s and beyond. They will need multi-linguistic capacity, cross-cultural sensitivity and the global literacy that comes from experiencing at least part of their education abroad.

I don't know what the future looks like from a Brexiting Britain these days, but from where I write in Australia, there is no doubt at all that the world post-2030 will be shaped by the rise of Asia – and China, in particular – as the dominant region of the planet throughout our children's lifetimes; and that rise will be fuelled, far more than most observers recognise, not just by economic power, but by a phenomenal boom in education.

When I left school in 1990, just 3 per cent of my peers in China went to university. Less than three decades later, that proportion is over 30 per cent : a third of an enormous cohort and growing. That's just in China, let alone what's happening in India and Indonesia and elsewhere across the region. In the year 2000, the number of students enrolled at universities in East Asia equalled for the first time all university students in Europe and North America combined. According to UNESCO, in the following decade that number grew by an incredible 10 per cent every year, dwarfing multiple times over the entire university population of the West in less than the lifetime of most children currently at school.

It may not get headlines like geopolitics and trade, but there is a seismic shift occurring in the world's intellectual centre of gravity; a revolution in education on a scale unprecedented in human history that is lifting the living standards of billions in Asia and elsewhere, and is injecting hundreds of millions of educated, intelligent, motivated and aspirational minds into every field of endeavour that our students could conceivably choose to enter, including into the business of education itself.

Our job as teachers is to ensure that our children are not bystanders to that, but are confident and capable participants in it. Likewise, our job as school leaders is to do the same for our schools. If we see our international opportunities merely in transactional terms as the sale of Western education abroad, then the model is eventually doomed – like the colonial paradigm before it – when the commodity is no longer wanted in nations ultimately destined by their own tremendous educational momentum to become more prosperous and educationally progressive than the West itself.

The great international challenge facing independent schools, therefore, is to reject the parochial and to become genuinely global. It is to see their international campuses and student populations not simply as financial feeders to an increasingly dependent centre, but as equal partners in a global network of prospering schools that share core modes and values that may be derived from the origin schools, but that continually evolve through the fluid exchange of students, teachers and the perspectives and practices of different cultural contexts across all schools.

Above all, the challenge is to guarantee that the children at all campuses are equally valued, equally benefiting from the resources and diversity of the full network, and equally able to experience its full range. The challenge is to make certain that all students in a school's global network are educated as genuine peers, knowing each other and ready for the world that they will lead together.

Virginia Macgregor

In October 2013, pregnant with our first daughter, my husband and I toured a handful of New England's boarding schools. As educators we were looking for a stimulating educational environment in which to raise our family and to grow as teachers, artists and human beings.

At the time, we were living in the UK and working in a co-educational boarding school. I taught English and had just published my first novel; Hugh, my husband, was teaching Drama. We had both spent the last ten years working in some of England's most selective boarding schools and although there was much we loved about the British independent system, we wanted something different. We wanted a truly free curriculum: free from the constraints of external examination boards; free from the imposition of ever-changing government policy; free from the pressure to teach to tests we did not always believe in.

One of the first schools we visited was Phillips Exeter Academy in New Hampshire. There, we sat in the office of an English teacher from Ireland who had also taught in the UK. When we asked her what the main difference was between teaching in a US independent school versus a UK independent school, she said: 'Here, we teach to our conscience'.

Besides the generic SATs which every American student has to pass as a benchmark test to get into university, US independent schools have no external examinations. There are no GCSEs or A Levels. Each department devises its own curriculum – according to its vision, the particular passions of its teachers and the needs of its pupils. Teaching to their conscience indeed.

My husband and I are now in our third year at St Paul's School in New Hampshire, one of the top ten schools in the US. Although I am not currently teaching – my commitments as a writer and mother don't allow for this – I am nevertheless an active member of the school community. I regularly interact with the students, faculty and parents, both formally and informally, through discussions and workshops. The school's inclusion of me as a writer is testimony to the open-mindedness, flexibility and independence of its academic programme.

Hugh is the Director of Theatre. Over the past couple of years he has devised a programme which includes electives such as Documentary and Political Theatre; Philosophy, Philosophy and Ethics in Theatre; Playwriting; Directing; Shakespeare and Verse. The Theatre programme is constantly shifting according to the passions of the theatre teachers, the character and needs of the students and the demands of the modern world. How astonishing it is to be able to adapt the curriculum to address the challenges of living in today's world: an America governed by Trump; the #metoo movement; questions of race, immigration, gender and the environment. Only a truly independent school can allow for such radical relevance in its curriculum.

The word 'elective' is also important. Students in American independent schools like St Paul's choose their curriculum. There are specific requirements in each of the academic disciplines (Humanities, Arts, Mathematics, Science and Languages) but in each area they have considerable freedom to make choices, and beyond these broad requirements, they are free to choose electives taught by the particular teachers who devise courses according to their passions. For example, a student might take a playwriting elective for Theatre; an elective in Fiction of the African Diaspora in Humanities; and an Introduction to Astronomy elective in Physics. In this way students craft their own timetables: they have a measure of choice over what they study within the disciplines that make up their curriculum and so, of course, the motivation to learn and the commitment to the class is all the greater.

Another interesting aspect of choosing electives is that classes are open to all year groups. Some classes will come with prerequisites, to establish the sequence in learning that helps build knowledge, but many are open across the four-year high school age span. This means that students of different ages come to study an elective together. Another enlightened way of teaching afforded by a truly independent school.

In US independent schools, assessment is continual and rigorous and carried out by the teachers who know the students best. Teachers grade students on their contribution in class, on their effort, on the process of their learning – alongside the more standard internally devised, end of term exams. A portfolio of achievement is built through a student's time at St Paul's and it is this much more thorough, rounded and intellectually honest assessment which builds them as scholars, as human beings and which prepares them to apply to the college of their dreams. Colleges which, I would also argue, are far richer in their offerings than their UK university equivalents. I recently spoke to a St Paul's student who has been accepted into Yale. I asked him what he was going to study and he said: 'I don't know yet'. How wonderful that this eighteen-year-old student has the chance to explore everything that Yale offers before deciding on his major; that the university recognised scholarship and intellectual character over a particular grade in a particular subject; and how wonderful that he comes from an independent boarding school which has prepared him for this.

Of course, no school, no institution, is perfect but a truly independent school has the scope and motivation to question itself and to adapt: to educate itself as well as its students. We feel deeply grateful to work in a school which allows us to flourish as educators and we look forward to watching our own children grow and learn in this environment too.

Jamie Martin

In the developed world, fee-paying schools focus on a small elite (financial and cognitive), while the government sector educates the remaining majority. In the developing world, things are different: the world's poorest families often send their children to private schools. This trend is increasing even as free education becomes more available.

A low cost private school revolution has occurred; with a huge impact on global education. There are advantages and challenges regarding operating these schools at scale but it seems to me that independent schools, not government schools, are the future of education in the developing world.

Though our understanding of the private sector in poorer countries is hindered by incomplete data, we know that its extent is significant. James Tooley, a pioneer of research on these schools, has argued that they are "ubiquitous", likely educating a majority of children in urban areas and a "significant minority" in rural ones. Tooley estimates there are approaching half a million such schools in India (20 times the entire UK school sector). Africa shows a similar trend: by one estimate there are 18,000 private schools educating 1.5 million children in Lagos alone. In Kampala, they are over 80 per cent of school enrolments. One forecast argues that by 2021 one in four Africans will be at private school.

Why do parents, largely in the bottom few per cent of global earnings, turn to private schooling? Because in their countries education is the only route out of poverty, and the government-provided alternative is (on the whole) awful to an extent hard to imagine for those of us fortunate enough to be born and educated in the developed world. Low cost private schools don't tempt parents with vast playing fields or staff with elite degrees. They simply offer teachers that turn up (teacher absence on a given day can be 30% or higher in government schools) and an expectation that pupils will get at least a basic education (in the government sector the majority commonly cannot read or do basic Maths well into primary or even secondary school). Parents' impression of the two sectors is born out by academic research: studies indicate that while there is significant variation between schools in both sectors, on the whole private ones offer better teaching and learning and much more efficient use of resources.

Perhaps because they underscore the failures of the government sector, low cost private schools have begun to come under political attack. This has been especially true of those that have used technology and international investment to reach significant scale, and none more than Bridge International Academies. Whereas most private schools in poorer countries are community-run one-offs, Bridge uses a tablet-powered digital curriculum and management system to deliver daily scripted lessons to over 10,000 children in 500 schools across five different countries. Their pupils are from families who live on an average of $1.60 a day, and the average Bridge school costs under $2,000 to build. Yet Bridge students consistently outperform national average benchmarks including wealthier peers. While this has won plaudits from parents (who have flocked to Bridge's rapidly expanding schools) and international investors (such as the World Bank and Gates Foundation), Bridge has become a lightning rod for political opposition to private education in the developing world. A sustained campaign by a consortia of teaching unions, certain charities and political groups (who believe all education should only be government run and free at the point of delivery) has constrained Bridge's work in Kenya and Uganda, and is indicative of the political challenge the sector will face in future as it looks to operate at scale.

A brighter political note is the increase in private public partnerships (PPPs), where governments fund private operators to run state schools that are free to attend. This has been tried in a number of countries, most notably Liberia, where the government gave control of nearly 100 schools to eight private providers (including Bridge). A randomised control trial (the gold standard of impact measurement) found attending schools run by the private operators led to pupils learning twice as much in a school year (though subsequent allegations of sexual abuse against one provider indicate the importance of not abandoning strong accountability). One of the most effective operators was another chain, Rising Academies, with a remarkable founding story based on opening (and succeeding) in neighbouring Sierra Leone as the Ebola crisis unfolded. This, alongside providers working in refugee camps, is part of a broader trend of the private sector providing schooling in the event of state failure or natural disaster. Already working with students with some of the world's lowest education levels, in the developing world the private sector is increasingly showing itself most adept when solving education's deepest problems.

As the developing world gets richer, will it mirror the mainly government run education system of its wealthier counterparts? Perhaps not.

A diverse range of for-profit providers could offer an alternative and brighter future: global chains using technology and outside capital operating alongside community run one-off institutions; pedagogies and curriculums based on results and parental demand, instead of the whims of politicians or the ideologies of false but fashionable gurus; competition on cost and quality so that the poor get the same choice in schooling currently available to the rich; PPP models ensuring there is equity of access and political accountability. Added to this argument based on quality are African governments with weak public finances and capability that are unlikely to be able to expand provision to meet their booming populations.

The only barrier to the advance of private schools in the developing world is likely to be political. If the unlikely coalition of poor parents, social entrepreneurs and international investors that have carried them this far can overcome this ideological opposition, then the future of private education may be that it flourishes most in the parts of the world least able to afford it.

Cameron Pyke

For those at school during the final years of the Cold War, the international challenge faced by the independent sector poses a relatively novel question. If these schools had already espoused a form of internationalism in their promotion of the teaching of French, German and, increasingly from the 1990s, Spanish, this was a Western-European outlook: back in the 1980s, none had established campuses overseas and the vast majority of students (and certainly staff) probably expected to spend their careers in the United Kingdom. The collapse of the Soviet Union saw the first broadening of this perspective, against the backdrop of rhetoric about the end of history and a new global order, with some schools setting up scholarships for talented students from Central and Eastern Europe in the early 1990s and, by the end of the decade, capitalising on the remarkable potential of the Hong Kong market post-handover. The last 15 years have witnessed a far more radical shift: a sustained and increasing engagement with the opportunities and challenges of international education, particularly in the context of the significant demand for a British-style education on the part of a growing middle class in the emerging economies of South East Asia and the Middle East. At its most effective, such engagement has imaginatively combined astute commercial strategy and cogent educational mission, providing funds for a long-term commitment to broadening social access on the home front, and thereby reinvigorating a school's foundational mission and ensuring that independent schools remain agents of social mobility in their local communities.

Ensuring that these two areas – commercial strategy and educational mission – are aligned is the most immediate challenge to any school choosing to engage internationally. In a world that appears to be more in flux than at any point since the 1980s, how might this best be achieved? Three related but demanding tests seem necessary. Firstly, and most obviously, a healthy dose of realism and due diligence: regarding political context, local and national regulatory frameworks and – perhaps most important in terms of the crucial alignment cited above in the long term – choice of commercial partner. Secondly, there should be clear definition of the educational core of what one is exporting and by what model of control and oversight that will be underpinned from the UK. This is with regard to academic standards and co-curricular provision (and there should be a consideration of how far these will 'fit' with any compulsory elements of the curriculum) but also potentially more volatile areas of reputational risk such as safeguarding, anti-bribery, and health and safety. And, finally, taking all these caveats into account should be coupled with a recognition that successful engagement overseas requires a sustained long-term commitment – both moral and practical – if it is to bear commercial as well as educational fruit. This might therefore include support for well-chosen charitable projects and engagement with the British Embassy in the host country, and a recognition that an overseas school has a duty to engage sensitively and in the long term with the local community and civil society – as would be expected of a privileged institution in the UK.

And herein lies perhaps the greatest long-term aspect of the international challenge for independent schools and, in the current political context, one that will require both nuance and substance in communicating: that it is seen as entirely complementary to their social mission at home and not a commercial distraction designed to shore up already wealthy institutions. The UK media is certainly unlikely to celebrate the sector's commitment to providing first-class holistic education overseas nor its assertion of the ethical values of internationalism at home post-Brexit. And in a political climate where there is growing cross-party concern regarding inequality and social cohesion, international engagement runs a greater risk of being misconstrued than it did a decade ago. In a recent Parliamentary debate on education and society, one peer responded to the news of the expansion of a major independent school overseas to support its bursary programme: 'Its social outreach should be to the poor of Bradford, not the super-rich of Beijing'. The former Chief Inspector of Schools made a similar point, implicitly, when criticising independent schools overseas for drawing away those whom the UK government has paid to train rather than seeing this as indicative of the stronger reputation of the international sector compared to the 1990s.

Engagement with the international sector cannot therefore be seen as a stand-alone enterprise, but – properly conceived – should be at the core of a school's education mission in the community of which it is a part and therefore – with its risks and opportunities – a key aspect of its strategic development plan and communications strategy. And perhaps the most creative challenge of the international challenge in the long term will be to ensure that it is soundly commercial while also seen as complementary to a school's local partnership and access strategy.

Russell Speirs

Because of the tight geography of a school's customer base, the way in which education is bound up with national culture, law and language or because it requires an interaction between human beings which cannot be mass-produced, the education sector has been slower to internationalise than many other sectors of the economy. Nonetheless, we are now starting to see the same tangible signs of globalisation:

- international chains and global brands (e.g. Cognita, Nord Anglia, GEMS and International Schools Partnership) with market power and operating efficiencies
- transnational associations of schools and forums for exchanging ideas among staff (e.g. Global Connections, World Leading Schools, Global Alliance for Innovative Learning)
- international supply chains, such as the technology firms which support the delivery of education or the management of schools themselves (e.g. GL Assessment, ISAMS, Pamoja)

- a global workforce of teachers that will move internationally, out of and into the UK, to develop their career and experience (with help from recruitment companies with names like Compass Teacher Recruitment, Teach Away and Teacher Horizons)

There is no doubt that the increasingly international perspectives and influences that are shaping schools represent a great opportunity for all of us. But they also pose some significant, even existential, challenges.

Just take the example of the globally mobile workforce. It was recently reported that more qualified teachers left the UK to work in other countries than entered teacher training programmes.[1] So one has to ask the question: where will the teachers of the future come from? It is estimated that international schools, among which native English-speakers are highly prized, will require an additional 400,000 teachers in the next eight years.[2] How will UK independent schools respond? Will they need to increase salaries further to entice and retain their staff, thus putting additional pressure on their margins or making their fees even less affordable? Or will they re-engineer themselves and become less dependent on the small-class model that has become their hallmark and an important reason for parents to choose the sector?

Another challenge, of equal significance, relates to the students themselves. At the moment, over 53,000 students attending ISC schools in the UK are foreign nationals and, of these, some 28,000 live overseas when not at school. When one adds in the British expats, this means that about half of all UK boarders are from abroad and a significant number of UK schools depend on expatriated foreigners, working in the UK, to pay the fees.[3]

As a former pupil of Sevenoaks School, and a graduate of the European School of Management – indeed, as an enthusiastic internationalist – I find these numbers exciting and positive. As a professional adviser to independent schools, however, I find them worrying. How certain can we be that, after Brexit, London and other major centres of employment in the UK will continue to attract foreign staff who pay the school fees? Our own quick tally suggests that about 20 or more British schools now operate about 50 campuses abroad, educating over 30,000 students: more than the foreign boarders in the UK. How long will it be before this affects international boarding recruitment? In the future, more British expatriates and foreign families in

Asia and the Gulf region will surely choose to send their child "up the road" to a prestigious "British" school rather than to the UK, and thus avoid the additional costs of boarding fees, travel and impact on family life.

Of course, for every British independent school that does have a campus abroad, there are about 45 that do not. Which brings me to one of the biggest challenges facing many independent schools in the UK: should they or should they not pursue an international expansion strategy?

Many British schools are eager to widen access to their schools through the provision of means-tested bursaries but cannot generate more funds without finding new income streams. Many others are concerned that, with a rising cost base, their catchment may not have enough families who can afford the fees. So, primarily for these reasons, a very large number of schools are now considering the opportunities that China and other markets may offer.

There are a lot of stories about long-haul trips and signed MOUs leading to disappointment or, even worse, deceit. How can one be certain of the integrity of the international partner or the project? Should a deal be concluded, how can a school be sure that the venture will bring the promised financial returns? Information is sketchy and some schools' published accounts suggest international expansion is not the panacea it is sometimes made out to be. Is it a question of the emperor's new clothes? And what about the risk to the home school's reputation, should things go wrong? What about the drain on the most valuable resource of all, the focus and attention of the Head? These are all legitimate challenges but ones which an increasing number of schools are successfully addressing.

In contrast with the country that is leaving the EU and is re-thinking its international relations, we are getting to the stage where our UK schools are becoming more open to international markets and exchange. The independent sector in the UK is proudly inter-national: perhaps the time has come for it to be more openly so.

Mark Steed

The past ten years have seen a rapid expansion in British curriculum education overseas. According to International Schools Consultancy

(ISC Research), there are 5.15 million pupils studying at more than 9,854 English medium international schools around the world, of these more than 3,586 are British schools.[4] In this time, UK Independent schools have begun to establish overseas campuses,[5] which have focused on educating the rising middle classes.

Despite this rapid growth, there is still a huge shortfall in the provision of schooling from a global perspective. Arguably, the greatest challenge facing education today is that there are an estimated 263 million children who are not in education (UNESCO Institute of Statistics Fact Sheet October 2016, No.39). Furthermore, the same report estimates that the world will need 3.3 million more primary school teachers and 5.1 million more secondary teachers by 2030 to meet future demand.

Two important conclusions can be drawn from these projections. First, that the not-for-profit sector is not equipped to meet this level of demand; and, second, the traditional model of one teacher taking a class of 20–30 pupils is unsustainable – it is a luxury form of education which most developing societies cannot afford or achieve.

Education in the West has traditionally been provided on a not-for-profit basis, either by governments for state education; or, as in the case of most of the UK independent sector, by charitable organisations. State education provided by profit-making commercial companies is not common or popular in the West and is alien to the British psyche: a recent survey of parents by the Varkey Foundation found that UK parents are the least likely of parents surveyed in 29 countries to approve of private companies providing state-funded schools. Conversely, for-profit education is the norm in the aspirational developing world, so it is no surprise that Indian parents are the most likely to approve of private company involvement in education.[6]

Experience in Dubai has shown that the not-for-profit sector was not equipped to cope with the rapid increase in demand for expatriate school places as the city grew in population. Consequently, the for-profit sector stepped in, adopting a segmented approach to the Dubai market place. The larger for-profit schools' groups offer parents a choice of price points ranging from 'premium' to 'budget'. The level of provision, which equates with the fees payable, are differentiated by class size, the provision of on-site facilities, the amount of contact time, and the calibre and experience of the teachers. The Dubai for-profit sector has developed scalable models, which benefit from economies of scale and from centralised administrative and training functions.

For-profit schools' groups, such as GEMS education, already see the developing world as a potential market and have begun to transfer the expertise gained from establishing schools in the Middle East to building and running schools on an 'affordable model' in India, South Asia and Africa.[7] These firms have real potential to have a significant impact on the global demand for education over the coming years.

The sheer scale of the challenge of educating the hundreds of millions of children presently not in school, combined with the likely acute teacher shortage, means that we need to find alternative models that extend the impact of a single teacher beyond the 20–30 students who are in their physical classroom. It is clear that digital technologies have the potential to play an important role in alleviating this pressure.

Global education is very big business – it was a $5 trillion industry in 2014 and is growing by about $600 billion a year.[8] It is no surprise that commercial investors are lining up to step in to offer solutions that will harness technologies to drive the education system of the mid-twenty-first century. The investment by these firms means that online learning programmes are becoming increasingly sophisticated. They promise to do tasks currently performed by teachers by offering personalised learning experiences at a fraction of the present cost. Typically, the program 'teaches' a topic (through online videos and interactive exercises) then uses low-stakes testing to assess the student's knowledge and understanding, highlighting areas of strengths and weakness;, before recommending which courses or units to do next.

One of the great advantages of digital technologies over traditional industrial models is that they provide a cost-effective model for making education available on a huge scale. Once a digital lesson has been produced, the marginal cost of distributing it around the world approaches zero.

Ten years ago, it was unthinkable that mobile phones would transform local economies in Africa,[9] yet today it is a reality. Is it unreasonable to suggest that in ten years' time a large proportion of those hundreds of millions of children who currently are not in school, would have access to a basic education through the internet?

Notes

1   Wilshaw, Michael (2016), HMCI's monthly commentary February 2016. Ofsted [online]. Available at: www.gov.uk/government/speeches/hmcis-monthly-commentary-february-2016

2   ISC *Research Limited, Developing a British Brand Overseas, "Global forecast – International school teacher numbers to 2026"*, May 2016

3   Independent Schools Council Census and Annual report 2018 Available at www.isc.co.uk/media/4890/isc_census_2018_report.pdf

4   ISC Research, *International School Market Data Infographic*, September 2018

5   According to the Independent Schools Council, there are 47 overseas campuses educating some 32,330 and there are many more in the pipeline. Independent Schools Council ISC Census and Annual Report 2018 p.17.

6   Twenty-three per cent of UK parents and 73 per cent of Indian parents approved of private companies providing state-funded schools. Varkey Foundation *Global Parents' Survey* 2018, p.4.

7   'Gems Education to expand in India and South East Asia' *The [UAE] National* 18 January 2017

8   IBIS Capital Global EdTech Industry Report 2016

9   'Continent disconnect – Mobile phones are transforming Africa. *The Economist* 10 December 2016

Chapter 10

The political challenge

Introduction to the political challenge

Most of the chapters in this book contain five essays, but two chapters – on the international and political challenges facing independent schools – have, respectively, eight and seven. The reason for this is simply that both areas are particularly complex, and are evolving rapidly – we have attempted to capture this sense of flux by bringing in more voices. But no doubt at some point in the future lengthier books than this will be written about a period of global tumultuous change, and education will feature in there. Independent schools will appear as well, possibly, as John Blake writes here, as powerful symbols of societal change (or lack of change), or, hopefully, as more active participants in bringing about greater equality.

The political challenges facing independent schools are serious. Independent schools were first founded in England (Winchester College accepted its first pupils in 1382) and it is here that they still feel both part of the establishment, and also, increasingly, distant from significant sections of the population. Worse (for the schools in England), as Tom Richmond states in his essay, 'we have now reached a situation, unprecedented in recent times, where neither of the main political parties in England are showing any great affection for private schools'. The politicisation of the school system is not unique to the United Kingdom, but it is perhaps uniquely divisive. The media seem preoccupied with which schools leading politicians have attended, as if attending one such institution for a relatively short time forms one's views on everything, whether it is Brexit or British foreign policy in the Middle East. They do not make the same claims for politicians who have attended a school in the maintained sector.

Such arguments can be self-serving, but they do contribute to an impression that English public schools are central to the Establishment, which, in turn, is seen as inherently conservative (and also self-serving). And so if one wants to radically change society it makes sense – mainly to those on the left – to seek to change, or abolish, independent schools. They are the source from which much inequality flows. For Julie Robinson, such a view is an 'outmoded stereotype'. For her, the challenge in the future is 'to cut through prejudiced assumptions to demonstrate our great value to society'. That won't be easy, and when the political climate is as hostile as it is now, there a strong temptation for schools to turn inwards, do less, and hope they go unnoticed. But even that, for Richmond, is a risk: 'by doing less now, private schools might be forced to do even more in future, and for that they will only have themselves to blame'.

In the United Kingdom, there has never been much of an appetite for closing down all independent schools from government. But, as the former Secretary of State for Education, Estelle Morris, writes here, 'given the political unpredictability of the times, it would be foolhardy to think that this will always be the case'. However, for Morris, the threat to our schools' survival will not come from a reforming government; for her 'the greatest challenge comes... from the rapid shift in the social, political and economic context... Now the demand both politically and publicly is for wider opportunity and greater social equality'. And as Ed Dorrell points out in his essay, the old political allegiances, born out of familiarity, are evaporating: 'in this brutal political climate...what isn't experienced personally, isn't understood. And what isn't understood can be used as political football'.

That football may rapidly descend into something more tribal, and with fewer rules (a sort of political Eton wall game) when the economy struggles. And it has to be the same in every democratic country that has independent schools, because it is when money is tight that politicians look for new revenue streams. Robinson argues that in England, 'ministers need to recognise the economic benefit of our sector (£9.4 billion GDP) and value as an export'. But that could result in higher taxes being imposed, or tax incentives being removed. In other words, the more successful (and lucrative) the sector becomes, the more likely it is to attract unwanted political attention.

Perhaps those who work in independent schools need to consider things from a politician's perspective. In the United Kingdom there is a feeling that these are extraordinary times: Brexit, plus a government with no overall majority, plus the increasingly shortened news cycle and constant demands for more funding at every level, are all factors that have made political discourse increasingly hysterical and shortermist. We are not alone. Mark Scott has worked in both the media and in politics, and in Australia, the picture, for different reasons, is also changing. Scott writes that when it comes to government policy and schools, 'nobody is happy'. But somehow, changes that benefit all have to be made, and often in the face of Twitter storms and flak from the media. For him, the challenges are many, and he asks: 'through all that noise, how do we get good decisions made to shape the learning of the young people in our care, as they face a world ever-more complex and a lifetime of incessant change?' It is our duty as teachers to insist on such questions being repeatedly asked.

For Scott, experience has shown that 'governments back winners'. This sounds obvious, but is often overlooked by the winners who feel that because they have always succeeded, approval and support is no longer something they should actively pursue. But it is important – because if our sector is to avoid being singled out by politicians who want a quick and easy return from the electorate on gratuitous but highly visible attacks on perceived bastions of privilege, then we have to show that we make a valuable contribution to society. We must have the evidence – the data – that such political manoeuvring is unjustified, and could even damage the interests of the increasingly egalitarian society we all want to build. But that evidence should be a result of effective, socially responsible programmes driven by independent schools. Even complaining about such attacks could be counterproductive because, relative to the underfunded state sector (not to mention other sectors that receive government funding), private schools are clearly privileged and, crucially, are seen to be so by most people. Roger Scruton goes further when he writes about that perception in the current conditions: 'the education provided by such schools is not merely a privilege, but a privilege that disadvantages those who do not possess it'. And from that comes the sense of class envy that proves so destructive to all rational and well-founded debate. Too often, the arguments around independent schools descend into highly emotional name-calling.

But abolishing independent schools for political ends is a chimera: it does not address social inequality any more than imposing quotas on university entry or boardrooms does. If a government decided to tax us out of existence, they will have to address a number of difficult questions: what would they do about the jobs lost? What about the impact on the local economies? What about the loss of influence forged by links across many different societies and sectors? How would the state sector absorb the number of pupils who have to be taught? Scruton states that

> parents still have the duty to use their money and their influence to do what is best for their children. And that might mean paying for extra education. You could prevent this from happening, but only by making it a crime to associate for an educational purpose unless in an institution controlled by the state. To go this route is to move towards a totalitarian conception of the relation between the citizen and the state.

At what point does a free society stop from interfering with how a family chooses to spend its money? Would, for instance, the same government outlaw private tuition? What proof would they have that pursuing such a policy would have the outcomes they want?

Mark Scott is surely right when he writes that for independent schools to win over politicians, we must prove our worth, and do so in increasingly resourceful and effective ways:

> demonstrate the great return you are now showing with what you already have. Show how carefully you have assessed the lessons of the past. Give evidence for confident investment by highlighting current achievements. Show how far you have come already with current funding and a licence to reform. Ensure delivery helps those in greatest need. Indicate your restless ambition to achieve more if you are backed to do so.

The political challenge is a long game: we have to understand the pressures that policy-makers are under, and we have to work with them for the greater good of all. We have to speak in a language that is understood by each major political party, but we should go further than that. We will win the political debate, and ensure our sector is not attacked every time a politician wants a good headline, if we make ourselves more accessible, more diverse, and even more socially responsible. Politics is not an end in itself, even though some of its most effective operators might act as if it is; no, it is often the response to deep and complex changes in society. Moments such as the fire in Grenfell Tower can illuminate deep-seated issues, but it is the duty of us as educators to teach ourselves, and others, why we need to respond with rigour and, crucially, with a sincere commitment to reform.

John Blake

It is testament to the enduring symbolism of independent schools in British public life that the Russian Embassy to the United Kingdom recently chose to highlight on its social media channels that the numbers of Russian pupils in independent schools was declining.

The clear implication of the embassy's communication – delivered with all the quiet menace of a shady-looking character informing you that you had a nice car there, wouldn't it be a shame if something happened to it – is that British diplomatic responses to recent Russian government action (in Crimea, in Syria, on our own soil in Salisbury) has harmed a crucial area of the British economic and wider society by discouraging Russian parents from educating their children in our independent schools.

It might seem odd for a sector of British education to be included in the course of an ongoing and frankly bizarre tit-for-tat Twitter battle between an embassy and its host government, but then the independent school sector often finds itself cast in the role of political tool. For the Russian Embassy, they clearly imagine there is a politically powerful segment of British society that will be angered that the potential fees of Russian students are being lost to the system and accordingly pressure the government to change its attitudes.

While the faith of the Russian diplomatic service in the lobbying power of the independent sector might be of comfort to them, in the context of British politics in recent years, it actually seems rather quaint. This is because the reality of independent schools' 'symbolism' in British political discourse is not a strength, but a weakness. They are not in a position of political influence, but rather can be targeted by government action precisely because their lobbying power has waned. Indeed, for a period of time in the early days of the May ministry, the independent sector faced a grave challenge from this most Conservative of PMs, which it was saved from not by its own powers of persuasion, but the collapse of that early agenda in the wake of the 2017 general election result.

Theresa May's uniquely powerful joint Chiefs of Staff, Nick Timothy and Fiona Hill, had independent schools in their sights: for Timothy, the grammar-school educated, Joseph Chamberlain-inspired policy wonk, independent schools were bastions of excellence, but also of inactive and therefore unacceptable privilege. Like the university sector, they were rich, highly experienced in achieving academic success, but not nearly sufficiently involved in improving the schooling of the average young person in England, especially outside of the major cities.

Now, reading that summary, a great many folk involved in the independent sector will throw their hands up in horror and angrily point to the many bursaries they offer and the many interactions with their local state schools that they have. That is as maybe, and as someone who worked for a time in a free school – a state funded school, set up outside the control of local government bureaucracy – established by a coalition of independent schools, I am more aware than most of what the independent sector can and does do.

However, we should be honest that not every independent school can point to a long list of well-thought-out, targeted and useful interventions it has made in the state sector, and independent schools should be wary of becoming like the university sector, in which any criticism is met by the cry that someone, somewhere in the sector is doing something on any given issue, even if it isn't this university or that, and even if it isn't very effective.

But more than that, there has been an undeniable shift in the demographic of English society served by independent schools, and bursaries and a few high-profile schools building networks with some state schools is not going to be enough to return independent schools to a status where British politicians do not wish to interfere directly with their independence. The days are over in which GPs, teachers and county solicitors could afford to send their children to private school without the need for substantial bursaries or painful conversations about which of their children should get the one fee-paying education the re-mortgaging of the house will pay for.

Consider that Nick Timothy tells of how he became a Tory upon discovering that Labour wanted to close down the grammar school he had just won a place at. Where is that kind of loyalty to independent schooling across a sufficiently broad swathe of the voting public that could preserve the sector from hostile interactions with government? Clearly, the May government's plans to force independent schools to run academy chains were insufficiently compelling to cause people to vote for it, but equally, they were certainly not so troubling that they wished to vote against it. Had wider issues of message and organisation not undermined the Tory campaign, a bill instructing private schools what to do would already be through Parliament, at risk of losing their charitable status.

As someone who has spent a career working in state schools and writing about how they can be reformed and improved, I am not going to die in the ditch for independent schooling – in London, especially, many of those parents who once would have sent their children to private school now have genuinely excellent local state school options, and that is something to be celebrated. However, independent schools are a major part of England's educational heritage and they do contain troves of subject expertise, extra-curricular brilliance and administrative know-how that, if it could be shared on a mutually-acceptable basis with all schools, would be beneficial.

The challenge for the independent sector is to firmly embed such sharing as already exists and to enormously expand it so that, even if the average family no longer thinks it likely their child will attend a private school, they can at least see a tangible benefit in their own child's education for the continued existence of the sector.

If that challenge is failed, then the sector may well look back on the abortive attempts of the May government as a missed opportunity to fortify their position. As the Russian Embassy's tweet shows, the independent sector cannot escape its symbolic status – and in the current political climate, that may make it a target for action by governments much less forgiving than that of Theresa May.

Ed Dorrell

It is a lesser known fact that it was the middle classes that brought down the grammar school system.

This is a big statement, and one that's hard to prove. But it is without doubt that many in the middle classes were, by the early 1970s, happy to wave goodbye to the 11-plus because they perceived – correctly – that their kids stood a good chance of failing and being sent to a secondary modern. They were no longer willing to roll the dice.

For their kids to be excluded from elite education and condemned to what was often second-class schooling meant that they were willing to accept what was memorably described by right-wing journalist Stephen Pollard as the "single greatest act of educational vandalism": the abolition of grammar school education through most of the country.

In 1965, when Circular 10/65 was issued by the Labour government (when the education secretary Tony Crosland was reported by his wife to have vowed to "destroy every fucking grammar school in England"), there were more than 1,200 selective grammars – 15 years later there were fewer than 170.

Herein lies both a warning from history and a profound contemporary challenge to the independent sector: if the affluent middle classes – the readers of the *Daily Mail* and the *Telegraph* – perceive that a public school education may no longer be available to their children and grandchildren then they will not hesitate to support a politician who promises educational corrective surgery.

The reason the middle classes might feel alienated or even excluded from the independent education? A perception of rocketing school fees, of course, and the widespread idea that these schools are backfilling with rich kids from Southeast Asia and Russia.

So far, so well trammelled. But there is a further danger for the independent sector as yet not really explored: it is a lesson from the world of further education. What isn't experienced by the political or media classes is likely to be ignored, undermined and killed by a thousand cuts. It is often observed that the reason the vocational college sector is treated so poorly by the government is because no cabinet minister or newspaper editor has ever sent their son or daughter to college. I would suggest that we are close to reaching the same situation for much of the independent school sector. Most MPs and journalists cannot afford the fees of a London day school or an HMC boarding school.

It is a truth near universally understood in this brutal political climate that what isn't experienced personally, isn't understood. And what isn't understood can be used as political football.

We are at that point.

Two years ago Michael Gove, a former (privately educated) education secretary who educates his kids in the state sector, used a *Times* column to ruthlessly kick the independent sector in a way that would have been unthinkable by a Conservative politician even a decade ago. And then Justine Greening, when education secretary, used a green paper to threaten private schools if they didn't play ball with her agenda.

In short, the independent sector is losing (has lost?) the battle for hearts and minds among both the ruling classes and the aspirant middle classes. But I'm not sure many in the sector truly understand the extent of their predicament.

The political wind is changing – and not just amongst the Tories. Tony Blair's New Labour was prepared to hold the indie sector close, even making it a cornerstone of its academies strategy – but a Jeremy Corbyn-led Labour is a very different proposition. What is more, even without winning an election, Corbyn is clearly changing the terms of the debate (by moving what is sometimes called the Overton Window) and making hitherto unthinkable policy ideas more mainstream. Abolition of independent education is openly discussed in Westminster.

Attend any contemporary gathering of independent schools and their heads and representatives will explain away fee rises – insisting that it's not just because of the gratuitous construction arms race – as a consequence of other costs rising such as pension contributions. They will then go on – with a degree of inevitability – to discuss the enormous lengths they are going to to increase bursaries (without mentioning that many of these bursaries will not be for the genuinely poor, but will instead go to subsidising the middle classes who can no longer afford their schools). In some, limited, cases, this twin-track approach might have some success in winning round critics, but for many it will be way too little, way too late. And that is before we even start discussing the challenge of improved results in many comprehensives.

The scale of the PR and political challenge faced by the independent sector is Leviathan. Something radical needs to be done to avert disaster.

Estelle Morris

The independent sector embraces a very diverse group of schools. Many schools are genuinely innovative; others have highly regarded expertise in areas like special education needs. However, most independent schools compete with state schools in the same exams for the same jobs and the same university places.

Enthusiasm for the independent sector has always been one of the political divides between the right and the left. Despite this, successive Labour governments have offered little real threat and even with the present left wing Labour leadership, abolishing private education hasn't yet appeared in a policy document. However, given the political unpredictability of the times, it would be foolhardy to think that this will always be the case. At the very least, falling real income in the middle classes and possible future tax rises under a Labour government do pose a threat to the independent schools market. We are already seeing some schools increasingly concentrating on recruiting overseas – a move which takes them further away from the mainstream education system and certainly ought to threaten their charitable status.

I would argue, however, that the greatest challenge comes not from any political philosophy but from the rapid shift in the social, political and economic context in which schools exist. The long heritage of many independent schools roots them in an era when the purpose of education was to maintain the existing social and economic order. Now the demand both politically and publicly is for wider opportunity and greater social equality.

Private education is not the only divide in our school system. However, it is the one that has the strongest impact on life chances. When we look around the world to learn from other successful school systems, the international evidence shows that the highest overall performers are nations which are the least socially divided.

Government brings about change not only through its own actions but the power it has to influence the behaviour of others. Currently, the Conservative government, as part of its social mobility agenda, has its sights firmly set on weakening the link between independent schools and access to Russell Group Universities and therefore top jobs. An example of this is in Higher Education, where greater diversity in admissions is increasingly becoming a measure of success. This is reflected in that the only area where the Regulator – The Office for Students – has the power to intervene in the freedom of universities is in the area of admissions policy.

The same trend can be seen in many top companies. It is increasingly the case that their selection procedures are 'background blind' or actively seek to recruit from non-traditional backgrounds. Both these trends will have a real impact on independent schools and eventually could undermine one of their selling points.

One can hardly argue, however, that these moves have so far brought about revolutionary change. Independent school students still have a better chance of gaining entry to a top university than others with the same grades and the 7 per cent of privately educated adults who still have a disproportionate number of the top jobs. However, in the near future, regardless of whether the government is hard left or hard right, I believe there is a growing desire within society to challenge inequality wherever it is perceived; be it the #MeToo campaign, pay equality or the questioning of traditional authority.

I understand the dilemma facing independent schools, in that most want to be part of the wider education family. However, the very exclusivity that they sell to parents is a major barrier if progress is to be made. It will no longer be sufficient to offer bursaries to the brightest and most motivated children from the state sector who are the most likely to succeed wherever they are educated. These children are not the challenge. The challenge for the independent sector lies in how much they can contribute to the lives of low achievers from troubled backgrounds, how they can work with the state sector to make a real contribution to the lives of all their pupils.

I personally cannot see in the immediate future the circumstances whereby any government of any colour would prohibit parents from paying for education. However, if change doesn't happen, I can see a government withdrawing charitable status – especially during a period of extended austerity. Perhaps just as importantly, unless schools can adapt to the changes, they run the risk of being seen as irrelevant to solving the major problems facing society – and I don't believe that is where they want to be.

Tom Richmond

Having just been appointed Prime Minister, Theresa May stood on the steps of 10 Downing Street in July 2016 to outline her vision of the country that she would like to lead and the problems it currently faced. She decried the 'burning injustice' still visible in our society, noting that "if you're at a state school, you're less likely to reach the top professions than if you're educated privately". She wanted to reassure parents who "worry about the cost of living and getting your kids into a good school" that she was on their side, ending with the bold declaration that she would "make Britain a country that works not for a privileged few, but for every one of us". Inevitably, such a speech was heavy on rhetoric and light on detail, leaving the education community wondering what this might mean for them.

Two months later, the government abruptly announced radical plans to force independent schools to offer more bursaries to those from less wealthy backgrounds and contribute more to the state sector if they wanted to keep their charitable status (which brings significant tax advantages). Larger private schools would have to either sponsor existing state schools or set up new ones, while smaller institutions would be required to provide direct support for teaching and leadership in state schools. What's more, Theresa May drew attention to private school fees rising above inflation, as well as claiming that they had "become more and more divorced from normal life". While it remained a consultation at this stage, it was clear that the Prime Minister had private schools firmly in her sights. The 2017 Conservative Party election manifesto offered no respite, emphasising that the government were "keeping open the option of changing the tax status of independent schools if progress is not made".

It is fair to say that the 2017 election did not work out as the government had hoped, diminishing their capacity and hunger for bold reform. By the time that they eventually published a response to their consultation in May 2018, the wind in their sails had noticeably weakened. The strident initiatives that had been floated in the original consultation were replaced with a 'joint understanding' between the Department for Education and independent schools about how the state and independent sector could work together in future. This consisted of little more than state schools being 'encouraged' to partner with independent schools, who were themselves merely 'encouraged' to build on existing partnerships and to target their bursaries at those from the poorest households. Alongside these timid proposals came a quiet acknowledgement from the government that "partnerships only flourish effectively if they are voluntarily entered into by both partners".

Are private schools out of the woods just yet? Perhaps not. Their finances remain a source of considerable political consternation. In the run-up to the 2017 election, the Labour Party announced plans to charge VAT on private school fees to fund free school meals for primary school pupils. Even former Conservative Education Secretary Michael Gove recently branded private schools as "welfare junkies" and called for them to be stripped of their charitable status and forced to pay business rates. Furthermore, the Scottish Government has recently announced plans to strip charitable tax relief from most independent schools by April 2020, potentially leading to the loss of their 80 per cent reduction in business rates.

Deciding how to respond in this political climate is far from straightforward. Some private schools in England have decided not to wait until the axe falls and have instead voluntarily foregone their charitable status, despite the detrimental impact on their finances. Others are happy to dance to the government's tune by promoting more partnership activities and trying to draw attention to their bursary schemes. Whether either of these strategies guarantees their survival remains to be seen. It is unlikely that Theresa May will launch a second offensive against private schools when she has rather more pressing and significant matters to deal with elsewhere in government. However, a new Prime Minister, regardless of their political affiliation, may still see the contribution that private schools make to society (and the contributions they demand from parents) as an opportunity to criticise these institutions and make greater demands of them.

We have now reached a situation, unprecedented in recent times, where neither of the main political parties in England are showing any great affection for private schools. For many years, these institutions enjoyed a relatively easy ride as successive Prime Ministers and Education Secretaries chose revamping state education as the centrepiece of their education policies, most notably through the rollout of 'academy schools'. This led to a tacit agreement between politicians and private schools, through which they could largely ignore each other, particularly when the financial climate was benign for the early part of the twenty-first century. The government's subsequent struggles to balance the books plus the sheen wearing off the academies programme has brought this uneasy standoff to an abrupt end. Private schools are perfectly entitled to play the waiting game and hope that they can fend off any revived attempts to recast their role in our education system. The risk is that by doing less now, private schools might be forced to do even more in future, and for that they will only have themselves to blame.

Julie Robinson

The independent education sector receives mixed messages from politicians. Some wish to close us, some want to raise our taxes, some wish to remove charitable status or at least the associated rates relief. Some appreciate the work we do and are happy that we continue, independently. However, independent schools have been told to provide more bursaries for the disadvantaged, to set up more academies and free schools, to provide more academic outreach supporting state schools, to share facilities more, to engage in more partnership working of all kinds… It seems that whatever the independent sector is doing, it can never be enough.

A perceived increase in social inequality (real or imagined) has driven policy towards improving social mobility and independent schooling is an easy focus for attack, characterised as "the privileged few".

The government is more involved in education than ever. Since 2012, central government has been responsible for the performance of most secondary schools as they left local authority control to become academies, which are directly accountable to the Department for Education. Ironically, since 2010, the government has lauded increasing autonomy for schools at the same time as intervening in the work of independent schools.

Many of the country's policy-makers have been educated independently – but this does not help. The media attacks privately educated ministers for their privilege and perpetuates an image of the independent sector based on an outmoded stereotype. Publicly, we are portrayed as a luxury for wealthy elites rather than a world of opportunity for the aspirational.

The sector is far more diverse than many realise. An important part is played by specialist independent schools, particularly in SEND (almost half the independent schools in the highest fees bracket are special schools).

The sector adds capacity to the state system. In addition to a long track record of academic success, these schools value extra-curricular activities and provide flexibility and resources to train future Olympians.

We are small but effective. A typical ISC association school has under 200 pupils.[1] Very few independent schools are large and supported by wealthy foundations.

The parents exercising freedom of choice include international business leaders as well as corner-shop owners; there are wealthy families but also disadvantaged and edge-of-care children receiving life-changing educational experiences through 110 per cent bursaries. This range is rarely visible to the general public. We expect to pay for nursery education, tutors and university tuition fees. Surely, parents have a right to pay for independent school fees if they feel that is right for their children? Some pay enormous premiums for homes within the catchment area of top state schools. The metaphorical playing field is not level in a range of ways.

The challenge for our sector is to cut through prejudiced assumptions to demonstrate our great value to society. Ministers need to recognise the economic benefit of our sector (£13.7 billion GDP[2] and value as an export. Let's not forget the positive ripple-effects of transformational bursaries, cross-sector university entrance support and careers advice, specialist teachers sharing best practice and the many other benefits of working together as part of a diverse national education system. Independent schools should be a source of pride.

We are a small but important sector; we have helped lift standards and led successful reforms such as those of GCSE (based on IGCSE) and A-level (based on Pre-U). Nick Gibb's pedagogical reforms were modelled on independent school practices. The concept of independence inspired academies, free schools and grant-maintained schools. Without independent schools, there is no alternative to a government-run system, no high benchmark, no demonstration of what can be achieved.

Labour's manifesto pledge to tax school fees would price children out, forcing them into an already-stretched state-maintained sector; the Conservatives' 2016 document "Schools that work for everyone" demands that all independents do more to support state schools; Scotland has already ruled to rescind mandatory non-domestic rates relief for Scottish independent schools that are charities. Wherever we look, we find political challenge.

The country is demonstrably better off if independent schools are allowed the freedom to flourish and accept increasing numbers of children from a broad variety of backgrounds. Secretaries of State change so frequently that it is a challenge for them to master their brief and see through the anti-establishment bias playing out against us. Our challenge is to help schools make their good works seen so that politicians join those who understand that the sector is a positive force in education nationally, rather than undermine our effectiveness through attack.

Mark Scott

Who would be a politician? Well, many people, I guess. Not too many elections have been called off for lack of candidates.

For more than 30 years, I have had a box seat from which to observe the political beast. As a political advisor, a journalist and editor, running Australia's public broadcaster and now Australia's largest education system, there has barely been a day where I have not been engaged with the political process.

I would simply observe that, despite the march of candidates for the jobs, it has never been a more difficult time to be a politician. And the politicians I know have never felt more insecure. Every political seat, district or constituency feels marginal. The voters seem unimpressed everywhere. Incumbency is a curse. Even if you feel you are doing a good job in elected office, can you communicate your achievements in a way that gets recognition and your tenure renewed?

No policy area demands more long-run thinking than education, but reforms need to be delivered in a political era when short-run thinking dominates. What do these times mean for the political challenge of education policy-making?

Through all that noise, how do we get good decisions made to shape the learning of the young people in our care, as they face a world ever-more complex and a lifetime of incessant change?

In an Australian context, it is clear the political debate around education and, in particular, education funding is at its most intense level for decades. It is education's moment. After a quarter of a century of economic growth, Australians understand the nation's future prosperity will depend not on the resources we dig out of the ground, but on the people who walk the land. How equipped are Australia's future generations to compete in an economy transformed by globalisation and technology?

In Australia, debates around how to best fund schools have been a feature of the political landscape for more than 50 years. The Gonski reforms of 2012 proposed to put to rest debates about Australian schools funding. It recommended significant additional funding for education to meet the policy challenge, but allocated to schools based on the needs of students, irrespective of the school they attended. The hopes for reform were thwarted by some states being reluctant to sign up to the plan, and then the Federal Government baulking at full implementation costs, finally reshaping it.

The new model has most funding for independent schools coming from the Federal Government and has seen an eruption of complaints from public education advocates at the relative priority of giving any government funding to wealthy independent schools. The twist in reform, back to a model based around sector funding, was particularly disappointing: all school systems had supported a policy in which additional funding targeted students in greatest need. Now the sector debates are back with venom. Wealthy independent schools in particular are being challenged about their ambitious capital works programmes. Not so wealthy independent schools fear they are all seen equally as well-off as their deep-pocketed counterparts. Some Catholic school systems shout their needy students risk being overlooked and neglected.

Nobody is very happy. Least of all education ministers, attempting to chart a course through the policy morass. A consequence of the policy changes will be more focus on the impact of government expenditure on education everywhere. Independent schools can expect continued scrutiny that government funding is finding its way to improving teaching and learning outcomes.

While educators argue how an increased school funding pie should be allocated, there are many elsewhere in government who question whether an increase in education funding will bring any further benefit at all. They argue that the problem isn't the funding, it is the schools themselves: a failure of leadership and reform, an inability to innovate and drive higher standards.

Independent school educators, like their public education counterparts, need to be ever better in developing the case for investment of public funds with evidence. All will need data to show additional funding is making a real difference to teaching and learning outcomes. They will need to show the public funding attracted by independent schools, which helps underpin the long established diversity in the Australian education system, is not a high opportunity cost, denying funding to other schools and students with greater educational need.

All school systems will need to demonstrate that they have learned from experience, and that the way we are investing now, using global evidence and sharing outstanding practice, is turning aspiration into evidence of improvement.

Thirty years of politician-watching has reinforced my view that governments back winners. Don't be in the queue for funding crying poor, blaming your current performance on inadequate resourcing. Don't try and make a case that you are more deserving that all those others in the queue seeking funding.

Instead, demonstrate the great return you are now showing with what you already have. Show how carefully you have assessed the lessons of the past. Give evidence for confident investment by highlighting current achievements. Show how far you have come with current funding and a licence to reform. Ensure delivery helps those in greatest need. Indicate your restless ambition to achieve more if you are backed to do so.

Why should a harried politician back our schools? Why prioritise the investment in schooling?

Because the case is clear, the evidence is strong and the confidence is contagious. Because the compelling connection has been made between investment in our schools and demonstrable increases in teaching and learning outcomes for students.

Roger Scruton

In the conditions in which we in Britain now live, it is undeniable that education at an independent school is a privilege, secured as a rule by those who can pay for it, and not available to all. And our prevailing culture is one in which privileges are frowned upon, especially if they are earned by wealth rather than by hard work or talent. Moreover, education has been absorbed into national policy, to be regarded as a right of the child, rather than a duty of the parent; the assumption is therefore that education should be available to all in the same way and to the same effect, and that the one provider is the state.

Undeniably, the existence of independent schools, enjoying substantial budgets delivered by parents who can afford the fees, able to employ the best teachers in conditions that attach them to the school and which make teaching and learning a shared joy, is going to offend the egalitarian temper of our times. The education provided by such schools is not merely a privilege, but a privilege that disadvantages those who do not possess it. It ensures that pupils graduating from independent schools confront opportunities that are open to them, but not to the remainder.

Whatever we think of those arguments, they are now deeply embedded in the political culture, and cannot be shrugged off. As a result, the real case for independent initiatives in education is seldom made. There are those who defend independent education on the grounds of freedom. To prevent people from associating for an educational purpose, they argue, merely because the result is to confer an advantage on the people involved, is to strike a blow at the heart of society. The freedom to associate for purposes of our own is fundamental to our civil liberties, was guaranteed as such by the US Constitution, and is deeply rooted in the jurisprudence of the common law. To withdraw that freedom merely because it confers a privilege is to rely on an argument that might be applied to virtually all the advantages of society. The result would be an intolerable tyranny.

Powerful though that argument is, it does not, to my mind, get to the heart of the matter. It does not consider what is so special about education: we should be both wary of forbidding it and anxious to make it available as widely as we can. Those who worry about the unequal benefit think only of the benefit to the child. The argument that education is a child's right focuses on this feature, so emphasising equality. Focusing instead on the interests of the parent opens the way to another conception, and one that distinguishes children from each other, as much as the argument from rights assimilates them. My duty towards my children is a duty to them as individuals. They are my responsibility, and I am obliged to do what is best for them. If this means spending money on their education, then that is what I must do. The fact that some parents can spend more than others surely cannot affect the moral argument, which assumes that we are all under a duty to do what we can for those who depend on us.

From this point of view, independent education arises from a natural duty. Even if the schools are all in the hands of the state and devoted to treating their pupils equally, parents still have the duty to use their money and their influence to do what is best for their children. And that might mean paying for extra education. You could prevent this from happening, but only by making it a crime to associate for an educational purpose unless in an institution controlled by the state. To go this route is to move towards a totalitarian conception of the relation between the citizen and the state.

But even that argument does not, in my view, get to the heart of the matter. Children have an interest in education, yes; parents have an interest in education, yes. But there are two other interests that we must consider: the interest of society and the interest of knowledge. Society needs an educated elite, and there is a question how best to produce such a thing. It could be that, in our efforts to give every child an equal chance, we impede the flow of talent to the top. But society depends on that flow. It needs the bar, the judiciary, the civil service, the diplomatic corps, the teaching profession, and all those professions must recruit the people who have the most to offer. How do the people whom we need at the top get there? That is an extremely complex question, which can be answered only by exploring the motives and the social circumstances that impede or advance the desire of children to learn and the desire of adults to teach them.

Independent schools, with an ethos of their own, have evolved in response to those desires. They embody knowledge of the learning process that cannot be easily taught from scratch. Over the last two centuries, they have proved themselves able to produce the educated elite that saw us through bad times. In those bad times, we were challenged to compete in all fields – intellectual, military, ethical and economic. And the elite that we produced has proved decisive for our national survival.

Finally, and most importantly, there is the interest of knowledge, which is the one most important thing at risk in all our educational experiments. Knowledge is an intrinsic value, which cannot be weighed in terms of cost and benefit. It is the value on which civilisations are built and to which, as Aristotle said, our faculties naturally aspire. Education involves the transmission of knowledge, and knowledge is often lost in the attempt. Educationists influenced by Rousseau and Dewey have insisted in recent times on the rights of the child, emphasising 'child-centred' teaching – that is, teaching that engages with the interests and abilities of those who as yet have no education. But there is precious little evidence that such a method of teaching succeeds in the main goal, which is not about the interests of the child at all, but about the transmission of knowledge. Knowledge not transmitted is knowledge lost. And regardless of whether the knowledge transmitted is – or is thought to be – useful, it creates a duty that lies on all of us to see that it is preserved and if possible amplified.

In any case, we cannot know in advance which bits of knowledge will be the most useful in the on-going march of history. Latin, Greek and Ancient History, condemned for their futility by all the progressives of the Victorian period, turned out to be exactly what was needed in the task of governing an empire acquired in a 'fit of absence of mind'. How else do you prepare yourself to govern countries with competing gods, strange languages and a tribal conception of obligations, than by studying the only civilisations that have been able to write the matter down?

Conversely, the crazy mathematicians of the time, like Boole in England and Frege and Cantor in Germany, seemed to their classicist contemporaries to be lost in futile problems about nothing: what hangs on knowing the contours of the empty set or the sequence of transfinite cardinals? In fact, this wonderful store of knowledge turned out to be exactly what was needed by the science of computation.

It is not necessary to labour the point. But it is important, nevertheless, to insist on the conditions in which new knowledge is acquired and old knowledge conserved. Cooperation, free enquiry and the right to choose the students and assistants with which to collaborate, are all necessary, and when it comes to teaching, the natural right of knowledge is to choose the brain that can contain it, rather than the brains provided by the state. It is surely one of the advantages of independent education that it can make the space for that brain, through scholarships, subsidies and the facilities provided by people who realise that knowledge is more important, in the end, than politics. The interest of knowledge might sometimes require setting aside the demand for equality in favour of the right of teachers to decide who their pupils should be.

In conclusion, let me say this: I am a teacher. I have acquired much knowledge, and I long to impart that knowledge. But, after a lifetime of struggling against egalitarian prejudice, I have decided that I can impart my knowledge only to volunteers. Conscripts are a total waste of time. Whether I make a sacrifice by offering my knowledge *gratis*, or they make one in paying for it, the important thing is that the deal between us is a free transaction, in which the state plays no part. My duty is to impart the stuff in my head; the privilege of my pupils is to absorb it. And so should it be. But the thing that benefits most is neither me nor my students; it is the stuff in my head.

Notes

1 www.isc.co.uk/media/4890/isc_census_2018_report.pdf
2 www.isc.co.uk/media/5364/isc_impact_of_independent_schools_on_the_uk_economy.pdf

Conclusion

David James and Jane Lunnon

Since the sixth century, great independent schools have been part of the history of Britain and, for the last few hundred years, of the world. Many, founded 500, 600, even 700 years ago, have (like Larkin's *Arundel Tomb*) persisted, "through centuries of change" as generations of children (almost exclusively boys of course) have walked across their courtyards, corridors and playing fields. The Duke of Wellington's nineteenth century assertion that "the Battle of Waterloo was won on the playing fields of Eton" may well be apocryphal, but it speaks to the profound impact which independent schools have had on the history and development of societies far beyond those pitches in Berkshire. Schools, originally founded to educate the deserving poor, have become over time, the province of the wealthy, aspirational and powerful. The nineteenth-century golden age of the British boarding school, powered (and sometimes funded) by the industrial revolution, reflected this. Hundreds of Victorian boarding schools were established in countries ruled by the British Empire, to educate those boys who would go on to ensure that this Empire survived. At roughly the same time, in the mid nineteenth century, independent girls' schools started to appear. The revolutionary work of pioneers like Miss Beale and Miss Bus, or educational charities like the Girls' Public Day School Trust, saw modest but valiant replicas of the boys' senior schools.

Even their sternest critics would agree that Independent schools have real historical significance. Perhaps that is reason enough to want to celebrate them. But this book is not primarily concerned with the past but with the present and the future of these schools and with the very concept of independent education itself. Our aim here has been in part to explore what place these great educational institutions have in our thrusting, thriving, technologically connected world? To consider the value of schools established for empire builders when the empire they were educating children to build is long gone? To ask what moral justification can be offered for such institutions that only the super rich can afford. Questions which feel as pertinent to independent prep schools, many of whom are on the frontline for survival in shrinking and increasingly competitive markets. These questions and many more have been asked in a variety of ways, in this book.

And they are being asked in the face of increasing political headwinds. Our private schools may have been originally founded to educate the poor and dispossessed but survey after survey in the last 50 years, suggests that social mobility in many developed societies has stagnated. There are plenty of reasons for this but at the very least, private education has not demonstrably helped the progression of the oppressed or vulnerable in society and with fee increases in the UK pricing out 99 per cent of the population, it does not, on the face of it, look likely to do so in the immediate future. No wonder charitable status and business rates relief for independent schools are under pressure like never before in the UK.

In addition to this difficult climate, our contributors have explored the intense academic and pastoral challenges confronting anyone involved in education today. Independent schools may be free from the often suffocating restrictions of government curricula but they are still preparing children for government assessments which largely dictate the next stage in a student's educational journey. In a world that ranks and reviews almost everything, and where grade based success is a key measure of the value and performance of a school, our contributors have asked whether it is possible for independent schools to be truly independent. If education is measured and monetised, how free are schools to really educate the whole person? Or, as Jane Cameron puts in her piece, if the generation of alpha grades is the starting point for those paying the piper, what place is there for the encouragement of "dream-catching and star-gazing", whatever the age or stage of the child?

The pastoral challenges are almost more daunting. Our writers have referenced the astonishing educational potential of technology, whilst simultaneously articulating the risks for adolescents whose identities are increasingly inextricably entangled with their online brand and with relentless sexualized messaging. At a time of dizzying technological development, it is hard for schools, for the staff, for those supposedly in charge, to keep track, let alone find solutions. Self-harm, anxiety, depression even, tragically, suicide rates in teens, are all on the rise across the western world. Adults and educators are desperate to help but as Chapter 1 suggests, to some extent schools (and government medical facilities too) are struggling to cope with rising levels of the mental health concerns. Independent schools may have freedom and resource, but there is uncertainty about where to start in a technologically driven world and when they are confronting pastoral issues which many have never encountered before. The gender discussion in Chapter 6 reflects this. How can century-old schools (often single-sex) best support children who no longer define themselves by one gender over another, or who feel trapped in the wrong body? How can you empower girls to be strong, vibrant, ambitious women and at the same time, accommodate those who refute the very notion of binary gender definitions. It is not impossible, but it is a new challenge, in which, single sex independent schools and boarding schools often find themselves on the front line.

So there is a cold wind blowing and independent schools are being buffeted from all sides. The big question is whether there really is an answer blowing in that wind, or is the threat, as some of our contributors predict, rather more existential.

Thankfully, the answer is a resounding yes and that's not just because of the burgeoning overseas' markets, which are explored comprehensively in Chapter 9. In each chapter, our contributors have celebrated what already works well in schools, sharing practical solutions from around the world, offering new ideas, new approaches and new models for schools to explore. Independent schools are built on hope, dynamism and innovation as well as tradition, convention and centuries of experience. The sense of energy and a real enthusiasm for re-defining independent education for a new world, pervades these chapters and suggests that a quiet revolution is not only possible but upon us. To conclude, we have sought to synthesise the most powerful recommendations in each section and we present this as a manifesto for independent education in the twenty-first century.

Access and diversity

Do the handfuls of life-changing bursaries (referenced so movingly by David Ejim-McCubbin) really justify the charitable status most independent schools enjoy? Can we do anything to ensure that minority groups are truly represented in our schools? And can anything be done to dramatically improve access to such schools for the children who need it most now?

The answer to each of these questions is: yes. Hope is offered powerfully in this chapter. Ian Davenport and Patrick Derham remind us that bursaries are not simply life-changing for those fortunate enough to receive one; the ripple effect in the home communities of bursary students is significant, as is the subsequent desire to continue to make a difference, as Patrick Derham has so manifestly demonstrated in his own career. The message is about increasing aspiration in all, especially ethnic minority groups and making it abundantly clear that independent schools are not remote, unattainable, gated communities, inaccessible to "the likes of us". A shift in mindset is already underway. And encouragingly, the increasing confidence amongst possible recipients is reinforced by the now widespread and whole-hearted recognition from schools of their own responsibility in this regard, expressed through bursary fund-raising campaigns and in the establishment of sponsored academies and free schools. Independent schools across the country are exploring ways to open up, to share their educational vision and to reach more pupils from more diverse backgrounds than ever before. The moral purpose which drove the foundation of so many of our schools, has been reignited and reinvigorated for the twenty first century and we hear in these chapters about the vivid, impactful and unforgettable partnership work in which independent schools are engaged, supported by dedicated charities like SpringBoard and Into University. The imagination, energy and sense of purpose which independent schools have brought to the challenge of delivering outstanding education over hundreds of years, is now being brought to bear to increase social mobility and diversity – it feels likely that the impact will, indeed, be life-changing, long-lasting and revolutionary.

Political

Unsurprisingly, the message from most contributors in this section is of the deeply unsympathetic political climate in which UK independent schools are currently operating. The message is of a sector that failed to read the runes, that blindly continued to enjoy its privileges untouched by economic downturns. Apart from the robust defence offered by Julie Robinson and the critical points she makes about choice, cost and the practicalities of the obliteration of an entire sector, there is something perversely energising about all the messages here. They are a call to arms and, as many of the other chapters suggest, good things will come of this. The combined determination and vision of leaders and educators in our independent schools to prove the validity and moral purpose of their communities by widening access and increasing diversity can only be a good thing. Perhaps most striking here is Roger Scruton's contribution with its transatlantic, unapologetic argument for intellectual elitism. An elitism, he argues, primarily focused on the preservation and transference of knowledge; knowledge which is beautiful and rare and difficult and which simply cannot be accessed by all; knowledge which needs protecting and which may be historic but is also vital for the present and future development of society. For that, he argues, you need the right conditions and these are the independent schools in America, which have, for two centuries, fostered a culture of scholarship and intellectual exploration within their august walls.

Innovation

The great freedom which independent schools have to design their own routes to knowledge and understanding and steer their own paths through learning, also means unprecedented potential to play, to explore, to innovate. Of course, that innovation is now entwined with the power of technology: virtual reality (VR), augmented reality (AR) and artificial intelligence (AI) are transforming learning and teaching. But it is not just about technology. As Simon Walker powerfully points out, computer "brains can collect and hold information, they can power the engine, but only the human mind can steer a course to the future". And that is where the innovation in our schools needs to focus. The best schools, be they government or privately funded, are places of innovation. Free to contextualize learning and bring meaning and purpose to the curriculum above and beyond government assessment or curriculum stipulations. This chapter joyfully reminds us that schools are educational workshops. Places where pedagogical experiment can be rigorously tested and then disseminated. Places where real-world partnerships can be leveraged to contextualise and reinforce learning. Places where we can design courses that bring subjects and disciplines together in energising, enchanting ways. And above all perhaps, places where we can model the play, try, take a risk, fail, fail again, fail better approach with our children, thus readying them for a world and a workplace which we know not only values but desperately needs these skills.

International

One key area of innovation in recent years has been the independent sector's expansion overseas. It is hard to read this chapter and not feel excited by the energy, ambition and inspiration associated with the growth of international independent education. The challenges are acknowledged: the risk of a talent drain from the UK as trained teachers head to often short-term but lucrative postings overseas, the possibility of diverting international boarders in UK schools to increasingly compelling local versions and, of course, the ever-present threat of political antagonism in countries opposed to non-government educational provision. These are all fair enough but the case for enthusiastically embracing international growth is also made robustly by all our contributors here. Aside from the undeniable need to add to the number of good schools around the world (as James Martin points out there are 263 million [LJ(S1)] children still not benefitting from any kind of formal education), there is also the sense that our newly connected world requires us to think differently about the whole business of education. It is not simply a matter of independent schools cashing in; although if the profits from international expansion help to increase social mobility at home as well as overseas, it is hard to see international education as anything other than a win/win. But it is about much more than this. It is about a complete ideological shift. The technological revolution has broken down national borders in an entirely unprecedented way; should our schools, the way we educate, the way we think about what education is, reflect and celebrate this? That is precisely what the best independent schools overseas are doing. Justin Garrick makes the point resoundingly: "our job is to equip our children for what they are destined to be: the world's first truly global generation". This is a challenge, and an opportunity, that needs to be taken seriously.

Junior

The challenges being faced across the piece are not simply the province of the senior schools. Indeed, as this chapter makes abundantly clear, to some extent, the independent prep schools are feeling the contraction in the sector most acutely. In our economically and politically uncertain times, it seems many parents are husbanding resources to pay for senior schooling – prioritising small classes and expert coaching through their child's critical public exam years, over the joy of a prep school experience in the early years. Prep schools, by virtue of their size tend to be much more vulnerable to the exigencies of the marketplace and to excellent state provision in the primary sector. One pupil choosing not to attend a prep school of 200, is proportionately much more significant, of course, than a senior school student (more likely to be one of 700 or 800), re-thinking their decision. This has led to the demise of several prep schools in the last five years. And on top of these concerns, prep school staff experience the pressure of parental expectation more strongly than their colleagues in senior schools; not least because parents tend to be in their schools, every day, at drop-off and pick up time. The relationships are more immediate, personal and therefore (at times) demanding. Prep schools are feeling increasingly friendless and exposed and that is conveyed strongly in this chapter. Nevertheless, there is hope and it lies in Ben Thomas' articulation of the inspiring breadth of the prep school curriculum bursting "with innovation, imagination and creativity". The reminder that our prep schools are places of outstanding education, where the great adventure of learning and the fun of being a child is nurtured and fostered. And where, as Jane Cameron points out, there can be a powerful sense of belonging and mutual purpose in the creation of dynamic and exciting communities in which all stakeholders take ownership and work collaboratively for the greater good and happiness of all. Idealistic perhaps, but a point worth asserting and asserting all the more strongly in dark times. The building of a community in which people believe costs nothing. It is about shared values and a shared sense of purpose. And independent prep schools know how to do that extremely well.

Pastoral

Revolutionary zeal and the courage to think (and act) differently is what our contributors advocate in Chapter 1. Emma Robertson and Rachel Kelly both invite schools to leverage pupil power and to create powerful partnerships between students and staff to navigate the pastoral challenges ahead of them. Effective, palatable and realistic responses to the compelling but dizzyingly protean technological landscape can only really be arrived at with teen and adult collaboration, they suggest. And the same applies to the wider pastoral challenges: peer mentoring programmes can offer support not only to individuals in need of it, but to staff and management as they develop policies, curricula and co-curricular programmes. Perhaps Anthony Seldon's call to arms is the best summary of the need here though: the solution to our pastoral problems lies where it has always lain, with people. By prioritising human beings over success metrics and by ensuring that the needs of children and staff are placed at the heart of all school decisions, schools create a culture of safety, trust and, it is hoped, joy. Of course, this can't solve everything, because people are still people with all the fragilities and fallibilities that that implies, but focusing on the growth, wellbeing and fulfillment of staff and students is key.

Gender

This feels, in some ways, like the most problematic of the issues which our book (and indeed, our schools) are tackling. As our contributors suggest, there are no easy or straightforward solutions to an issue which is being looked at across a profound generational divide. The proposal that gender is fluid and non-binary, that it exists on a spectrum, is not just radical, it is ground-breaking. It shifts the ground from beneath our feet. And responding to this notion requires, as Lucy Pearson suggests, an entire and revolutionary re-think in our schools, most of which were established (and therefore reflect) the historically prevalent view that boys are boys, girls are girls and that defining people and indeed demarcating society in this way, makes absolute sense. What to do then, when more and more individuals in our care, feel things profoundly differently, when the so-called snowflake generation have the chutzpah to challenge this most inherent of assumptions and are increasingly demanding both individually and collectively to be heard. And how to square this with the need to ensure gender equality for girls and young women? Of course, these are not questions exclusive to independent schools but because so many were set up as single-sex schools and because so many around the world are boarding schools, there is no doubt that the issue is being thrown into sharp and immediate focus in our sector. And the answers? Well, there is much more thinking and discussion needed. School leaders, staff, pupils and parents need to find their way here: sensitively and with compassion and care. Fionnuala Kennedy advocates a "sensible, individually focused" approach and for the moment, that feels like pretty good advice. As Richard Hoskins' article movingly suggests, there is encouragement and hope to be found in the open discussion and exploration of this issue by our schools. Whilst there is dialogue and discussion, there is progress and that must and surely will continue.

Academic

The origin and nucleus of most schools, the primary point of any school is the learning that happens in it. The academic life of a school is its raison d'etre. It is still the primary way in which a school measures its performance and assesses the success of its children. Kevin Stannard channels William Blake, inviting us to "cast off the mind-forged manacles" of government assessment and traditional curriculum choices. And he is not alone in this. All our contributors here speak with one voice. What is the point of independent education they ask, if it is not to encourage our children to think differently: to stop, reflect, think for themselves and to embrace the struggle as they do so; "the moments that jar" as Ian Warwick puts it. And equally, all our contributors agree, this cannot just be about what we expect our children to do. As schools, as teachers, as leaders, as governors of independent schools, we have a moral obligation to think differently ourselves. To truly smash those manacles and to remind ourselves what scholarship is, what intellectual freedom should look like and how it should manifest itself. Like many of the other challenges in this book, it requires courage, imagination and vision to do. But Briony Scott evokes the spirit of Plato's akademiea. The pursuit of wisdom is sacred and solemn and something that needs freedom of thought and resource, courage and imagination. Thankfully, these are all available in independent schools and now, perhaps, more than ever, is the time to take up the challenge. Because, if we don't, who will?

So, we have sought to offer here a series of provocations, challenges and important discussions focusing on some of the key issues for independent educators around the world in the twenty-first century. It is not intended to be a comprehensive exploration, far from it, it is, perhaps, just the start of the discussion, but the hope is that this collection of expertise and insight demonstrates not only the difficulties but also the great resourcefulness and energy of private education. In the end, of course, it is not about politics, or finance, or technology or even about curricula, or learning approaches. Ultimately, schools, of any sort, are about children – and of the great reservoir of energy, potential and talent, they represent individually and collectively. Schools are, as Jane Cameron reminds us, "custodians of the joy of childhood" and at the heart of that joy is love. Love for the children, love for our staff and love for the knowledge which it is our privilege and our pleasure to pass on – in one way or another, to the next generation. If we can remember that and guard it, in our decision-making and planning, then surely independent schools can hold on to what they have learnt from their long history, withstand whatever pressures are brought to bear on them today and move confidently into the twenty-second century, secure in the knowledge which Larkin only slightly undercuts: "what will survive of us is love".

Index

Note: **bold** page numbers denote tables.

#metoo 153, 175

abolition of independent schools 166, 168, 173, 174
academic challenges 21–36, 195–196; and pastoral concerns 5–6, 7, 8, 14, 19; *see also* assessment
academies 59, 60, 85–86, 171, 173, 177, 178, 179, 190
access challenges 70–89, 168–169, 190; *see also* bursaries
Action for Happiness 20
Adams, Douglas 138–139
affordability 49–50, 51, 55, 58, **65**, 70, 98; *see also* fees; financial challenges
Africa 1, 62, 65, 155, 156, 157, 163
AI (artificial intelligence) 17, 41, 73, 128–129, 136, 137, 141, 191
Akpan-Inwang, Emmanuel 91, 92–95
ALEKS 129
algorithmic cognition 135–136
Allum, Jenny 109, 110–112
alumni 50, 63, 127, 139–140
anxiety 6, 11, 189
Apple 12
AR (augmented reality) 191
Aristotle 184

Arnold Foundation at Rugby School 75
Asia 70, 145, 149, 151, 157, 160–161, 163, 172; *see also* China/Chinese students
assessment 14, 15, 19, 32–33, 134, 163, 188, 195; and digital technology 125–126, 129, 138, 142; in US 32, 142, 154; *see also* exams, stranglehold of
Association of Governing Bodies of Independent Schools (AGBIS) 67, 100
associative processing 136
Austin, University of Texas at 137
Australia 2, 56, 109, 110–112, 151, 167, 180–182
authentic experiences 127

Baker, Kenneth 31
Barclay Review of Business Rates 60–61
Barot, Jaideep 91, 92, 95–97
Berkeley 137
Berners-Lee, Tim 139
Blair, Tony 173
Blake, John 165, 169–171
Blake, William 31, 195
Blanquer, Jean-Michel 12

BME (Black and Minority Ethnic)
pupils and staff 91, 92, 93,
95–97, 98
Boarding School Partnerships 87
boarding schools 44, 49–50,
73, 81, 187; and bursaries 63,
71, 84, 86; for disadvantaged
households 75–76, 77–78, 84,
86–88, 95; ethnic diversity at
93, 98; and gender issues 109,
189, 195; junior schools 43, 44,
45, 47, 48, 49–50; overseas pupils
50, 93, 98, 145, 160–161; and
parental expectations 43, 45, 47;
pastoral challenges in 6–7, 19; in
Scotland 60; in US 132, 152–154;
see also SpringBoard
bond market 64
Boole, George 184
Brentwood School 138–139
Brexit 44, 94, 151, 158, 160,
165, 167
Bridewell Royal Hospital (King
Edward's, Witley) 86, 87–88
Bridge International Academies 56,
65, 155–156
Brighton College 85–86, 115
Brown, Jenny 90, 91, 97–99
bullying 11; online 12, 17, 19,
111, 116; and unconscious
exclusion 112
bursaries 73–79, 82–86, 94, 98, 159,
161, 170, 177, 190; award criteria
63, 72, 75, 82, 84, 86, 88, 173, 175,
176, 178, 179; funding 47, 50, 55,
63, 68, 71, 83, 84–85, 100–101,
159, 190; for middle-income
households 85, 98, 173; *see also*
SpringBoard
Buttle UK 87

Cambridge, University of 21–22, 26,
32, 82, 100
Cameron, David 82

Cameron, Jane 37, 40–42, 188,
193, 196
Canford School 48
Cantor, Georg 184
Capability Scotland 60
charitable status of independent
schools 63, 67, 83, 84, 162,
171, 174, 175, 176, 177, 178,
188, 190; in Scotland 56,
60–61, 177, 179
Charities and Trustee Investment
(Scotland) Act 2005 60
Charity Commission 47, 63
Child and Adolescent Mental Health
Services 14
China/Chinese students 90,
93, 94, 144, 145, 149, 151,
159, 161
Christ's Hospital 63
Churchill, Winston 81
Circular 10/65 172
City of London School 24
Clark, Edward 145, 147–149
class sizes 22, 25, 43–44, 58,
67, 70, 79, 85, 123, 127, 160,
162–163, 193
cloud computing 137, 142
Cognita 159
cognitive functions 135–136
Compass Teacher Recruitment 160
comprehensive schools *see* state
schools
constructivism 126, 127
Corbyn, Jeremy 173
costs 39, 43–44, 48, 66, 67, 68,
70–71, 72, 85, 98, 173
Coursera 137
Crosland, Tony 172
Crouch, Stephen 55, 57–59
Croxteth 73
CS (Computer Science) 127,
137, 140
Cuban, Larry 137
curling parents 8, 9, 10

curricula: and the academic challenge 22, 23, 25, 29, 30, 31, 32–33, 52, 188, 195; in developing world 155–156, 158; and diversity 92, 102, 104, 105; and gender 108, 110, 111, 120; and innovation 123, 127, 128, 129, 139, 191, 193; in international schools 148, 150, 156–157; in junior schools 40, 41, 42, 49, 52, 193; and the pastoral challenge 12–13, 15, 18, 42, 62–63, 194; in Scotland 60; in US 153
Curriculum 2000 reforms 32
cyber bullying 12, 17, 19, 111, 116

Dagony-Clark, Sean 124, 125, 126–129
Daily Mail 113, 172
Dalai Lama 102
Davenport, Ian 72–75, 190
debt, managing 63–64
Dennis, Nick 90, 92, 99–102
depression 6, 11, 112, 189
Derham, Patrick 71, 75–77, 79, 81, 190
developing world 54, 62, 64–65, 66, 146, 147, 154–157, 162, 163; *see also* international challenges
Devon, Natasha 108, 112–115
Dewey, John 184
DfE (Department for Education) 25, 87, 176, 178
Digital Awareness UK 17
digital technology 16–18, 30, 42, 111, 123–143, 191; in developing world 155–156, 163; and pastoral challenges 8, 10, 12, 13, 15, 16–18, 19, 41, 42, 188–189; and teachers 12, 16–17, 30, 124, 125–126, 128–129, 138, 163; *see also* IT (information technology); mobile phones; social media

Direct Grant schools 83
diversity 4, 83, 86, 87, 90–106, 168–169, 174–175, 182, 190; teachers from minority ethnic backgrounds 90, 91, 92, 95, 96–97, 98–99, 100
Dorrell, Ed 166, 171–173
Dubai 144, 145, 162–163
Dukes Coffee 105
Dulwich College 2, 144
Dunnett, Mungo 43
Dweck, Carol 5

Eastbourne 46
eating disorders 11, 19
EBacc 32–33
edtech 137–139
Education Act (1944) 81, 102
Education: The Engagement and Its Frustration (Oakeshott) 30–31
Edward, John 56, 59–61
EdX 137
Ejim-Cubbins, David 72, 77–81, 190
eLearning 139
Emanuel School 139
emotional intelligence 5, 10, 15, 41
empathy 41, 42, 93
equality 72, 73, 86, 165, 166, 167, 174, 183, 184, 185; and the developing world 146; gender 109, 110–112, 117–118, 127, 175, 195; *see also* social mobility
Equality Act 118
Eton 63, 83, 138–139, 187
European School of Management 160
Evitt, Phillip 37, 39, 42–44
exams, stranglehold of 8, 22, 31–33; in junior schools 37, 40, 41, 47–48, 52
Exeter Innovations 130–131
experiences, designing 133–134
experiential learning 124, 129, 130, 134
EYLA (Eastside Young Leaders Academy) 79, 81

Facebook 19
facilities 54, 55, 58, 62, 68, 70, 94
fees 2, 54, 56–57, 60, 61, 64, **65**, 66,
    82, 85, 94; rise of 1, 2, 7, 39, 43,
    44, 47, 50, 51, 55, 56, 60, 61, 66,
    85, 94, 172, 176; *see also* bursaries
financial challenges 54–69;
    affordability 49–50, 51, 55, 58, **65**,
    70, 98; *see also* costs; fees
Financial Times 94
Foster, Richard 37, 39
France 12
franchise schools 50, 85, 150; *see also*
    international challenges
free school meals 72, 74–75, 84
free schools 59, 62, 85–86, 170, 178,
    179, 190
Frege, Gottlob 184
Freud, Sigmund 11
further education 15, 172; *see also*
    university

Gardiner, Howard 5
Garrick, Justin 146, 149–152,
    192–193
Gates Foundation 156
GDP of independent schools
    166, 179
GEMS 56, 159, 163
gender 91, 92, 96, 99, 107–121, 189,
    194–195; and biological sex 108,
    113–114
gender equality 109, 110–112,
    117–118, 127, 175, 195
gender identity 107, 108–109,
    117–120
gender neutral language 112, 113,
    114–115, 120
gender stereotypes 91, 110–111, 114,
    115, 116
Gendered Intelligence 119
Ghana 65
Ghandi, Indira 98
Gibb, Nick 179

GIDS (Gender Identity
    Development Service) 115
Girls' Public Day School Trust 187
Girls' Schools Association 112
GL Assessment 159
Global Alliance for Innovative
    Learning 159
Global Connections 159
globalisation 159–161
Gonski reforms of 2012 181
Google 12, 135
Gove, Michael 172–173, 177
government *see* political challenges
grammar schools 47, 59, 170,
    171–172
grant-maintained schools 179
Greening, Justine 173
Grenfell Tower fire 71, 75, 169
Guernsey 118

hacking classrooms 133
Haileybury 144
Harkness method 124, 131
Harrow School 97
Harvard Business Review 101
Harvard University 6, 137
Hattie, John 70
Headtalks 119
helicopter parents 8, 9, 10
Heriot-Watt University 64
Highgate School 115
Hill, Fiona 170
Hillman, Nick 71–72, 81–83
History of Art 30
HMC (Headmasters' and
    Headmistresses' Conference) 11,
    17, 96, 100
Hong Kong 157
Hoskins, Richard 108, 115–116, 195
humanities 29–30, 32–33, 104, 130

IDEO (design firm) 133–134
India 62, 65, 151, 155, 162, 163
Indonesia 151

inequality 73, 75, 76, 77, 86–87, 92, 93, 99, 158–159, 166, 168, 175, 178; *see also* diversity; equality
Informatics 30
innovation 22, 32, 33, 41, 49, 55, 76, 94, 122–143, 191–192
Instagram 19
Institute of Fiscal Studies 85
international challenges 68, 144–164; digital technology and 163, 192; diversion of students from UK schools 48, 60–61, 145, 148, 192; and junior schools 44, 45, 46, 47, 48; overseas branches of UK schools 2–3, 39, 48, 50, 144–145, 146, 147, 149–150, 152, 157–159, 160–162, 192–193; overseas pupils 44, 45, 46, 47, 50, 68, 80, 90, 98, 157, 160, 174; teachers, impact on numbers of 146–147, 148, 160, 192; *see also* developing world
International Schools Partnership 159
internationalism 145, 146, 150, 157, 158, 159–160
IntoUniversity 91–92, 99, 190
IQ 135–136
ISAMS 159
ISBA (Independent Schools' Bursars Association) 67
ISC (Independent Schools Council) 66, 83, 84, 85, 91, 93, 100, 149, 160, 179
IT (information technology) 30, 125, 135; *see also* CS (Computer Science); digital technology

James, David 1–4, 187–196
Johnson, Julie 7, 8–11
junior schools 37–53, 193; boarding at 43, 44, 45, 47, 48, 49–50; curricula in 40, 41, 42, 49, 52, 193; exams, stranglehold of 37, 40, 41, 47–48, 52; and international challenges 44, 45, 46, 47, 48; and parents 37, 38, 39, 41, 43, 44, 45, 46–47, 48, 51–52, 193

Kahneman, Daniel 134
Kampala 155
Keats, John 12
Kelly, Rachel 6, 11–13, 194
Kennedy, Fionnuala 108–109, 117–119, 195
Kenya 65, 156
King Edward's School Birmingham 76, 83, 84
King Edward's School, Witley (Bridewell) 86, 87–88
King's School for Mathematics 62–63
knowledge 25, 28, 34, 122, 128, 184–186, 191, 196; and skills 14, 24, 131

Lady Margaret Hall, Oxford University 99
Lagos 155
language: gender neutral 112, 113, 114–115, 120; and meaning 107
languages 29–30, 32–33, 140, 157
Larkin, Philip 187, 196
Leadership, Equality and Diversity Fund 97
Lenon, Barnaby 71, 83–86
Lexia Core 5 129
LGBT+ pupils 112–115
Liberia 65, 156
libraries 135, 142
Lloyds Bank 100
loans for parents 62
local authorities 59–60, 62, 81, 84, 87, 178

London 24, 34, 41, 45–46, 48, 50, 51–52, 64, 73, 77–79, 85–86, 160, 171
London Business School 63
looked-after children 72, 74–75, 84, 95
love 20, 196
low-cost independent schools 56, 65–66, **65**; in developing world 54, 62, 64–65, 154–157
low-income households 63, 72, 83, 84, 92, 94–95, 98
Lucas, Ralph 1, 39, 44, 45, 46–48
Lunnon, Jane 1–4, 187–196

MacGregor, Heather 55
Macron, Emmanuel 12
Manchester Grammar School 76, 83, 84
Mandela, Nelson 13
Marlborough College Malaysia 144
Martin, Jamie 1, 146, 147, 154–157, 192
Mastery Transcript Consortium 134
Mathematica 138–139
maths 104, 129, 184
May, Theresa 169–170, 171, 175–176, 177
Mayo Clinic 133–134
McGregor, Heather 61–64
McGregor, Virginia 152–154
McKinsey 100
McTighe, Jay 128
means-testing 60, 63, 67, 75, 82, 84, 86, 161
mental health 5, 6, 8, 10, 11, 12–13, 15, 41, 189; of LGBT+ pupils 112; self-harm 11, 189; of staff 7, 8; suicide 12, 13, 19, 114, 189; *see also* pastoral challenges
Mental Health Foundation 13
mentoring 13, 18, 30, 194

Middle East 13, 144, 145, 149, 157, 162–163
middle-income/middle class households 70, 71, 83, 85, 98, 149, 157, 162, 171–172, 173, 174
MidYIS 142
Millfield School 73
mindfulness 9, 10, 12, 20
MIT (Massachusetts Institute of Technology) 137
ML (Mastery Learning) 126–127, 128
mobile phones 12, 142, 163
MOOCs (massive open online courses) 137, 138
Moore, Dick 6, 13–16
Morgan, Piers 113
Moritz, Michael 83
Morris, Estelle 166, 173–175
Myatt, Mary 92, 102–106

National Autistic Society 60
National Education Union's Equal Access to Promotion 97
National Foundation for Educational Research 74
National Geographic 117
National Insurance contributions 43
neuroscience 15
New South Wales 111
New York City 133
New York Times 137
Newcastle 50, 55, 65
Ng, Andrew 137
NHS (National Health Service) 11–12
Nigeria 65, 155
Nord Anglia 159
North East of England 50, 64
Norwich, Diocese of 105
Nuffield Foundation 40

Oakeshott, Michael 30–31
OECD (Organisation for Economic Co-operation and Development) 137
Ofsted 14, 33
Omega Schools 65
Open University 24
'optimisation' of children 37, 43
Our Kids: The American Dream in Crisis (Putnam) 76
overseas schools and pupils *see* international challenges
Oversold and Underused (Cuban) 137
Overton Window 173
Oxford Internet Institute 11
Oxford, University of 21–22, 26, 82, 83, 99, 100

Page, Eimer 124, 129–132
Pamoja 159
parents 1, 3, 7, 8, 9–10, 20, 38, 39, 42–43, 44, 46, 49, 51–52, 59, 65–66, 179; academic expectations 14, 19, 21–22, 23, 33–34, 35, 37, 39, 41, 43, 44, 46, 51–52, 55; curling 8, 9, 10; duty towards children 168, 182, 183–184; and gender issues 108–109, 115–116; helicopter 8, 9, 10; and innovation 123, 124, 127, 129; and junior schools 37, 38, 39, 41, 43, 44, 45, 46–47, 48, 51–52, 193; pastoral concerns 7, 9, 35, 39; preference for small class sizes 70, 160, 193; *see also* financial challenges
Parker, Sir John 100
partnerships 73, 91–92, 99, 127, 158, 176, 177, 178, 190, 192; between independent and state sector 76, 91, 101, 176, 177; international 149, 156–157, 159; PPPs (private public partnerships) 156–157

passion, encouraging 41
pastoral challenges 5–20, 39, 41, 49, 107, 188–189, 194; and academic concerns 5–6, 7, 8, 14, 19; and digital technology 13, 15, 16, 17, 18; and gender 110, 111, 119; *see also* wellbeing
PBL (Project- Based Learning) 126–127, 128
Pearson, Lucy 109, 119–121, 194
pedagogy 46, 101, 102
Peer Education Project 13
peer support 13, 18, 194
pensions 43, 67, 173
Pettit, Adam 115
Phillips Exeter Academy 130–131, 153
physics teachers 25
Pike, Helen 22–23, 24–26
PISA (Programme for International Student Assessment) tests 137
Plato 27, 195
political challenges 15–16, 39, 47, 48, 54, 58, 67, 71–72, 81–82, 158–159, 165–186, 188, 190–191; and access 71–72, 81–82, 83, 84, 85–86, 174; overseas 3, 39, 144, 155–156, 157, 158, 192; *see also* charitable status of independent schools
Pollard, Stephen 172
pop-up learning 133
Positive Education 134
PPPs (private public partnerships) 156–157
prep schools *see* junior schools
Priory Group 60
Project Knowmad 133
Przybylski, Andrew 11
Putnam, Robert 76
Pyke, Cameron 146, 157–159

Randolph, Dominic A. A. 122–123, 125, 132–134
Reedham Children's Trust 87
refugee families 91, 97, 156
Reigate Grammar 144
relevance 49, 50–51, 71, 73
ResearchEd 24
resilience 7, 9, 10, 12, 14, 17, 38, 41
Richmond, Tom 165, 175–178
Rising Academies 156
Robertson, Emma 16–18, 194
Robinson, Julie 166, 178–180, 191
Rousseau, Jean-Jacques 184
Royal National Children's SpringBoard Foundation see SpringBoard
Rugby School 77, 79–80, 105, 139
Russell Group Universities 21–22, 174
Russia 1, 90, 93, 94, 169, 172

safeguarding 6–7, 8, 14, 17, 45; in international schools 148, 158; see also pastoral challenges
SATs (US) 142, 153
scholarships 67–68, 84, 97
Scotland 56, 59–61, 177, 179
Scott, Briony 23, 26–29, 195
Scott, Mark 167, 168, 180–182
Scruton, Roger 167, 168, 182–186, 191
Seldon, Anthony 5, 18–20, 194
self-harm 11, 189; see also suicide
Seligman, Martin 5, 19
Sevenoaks School 160
Sherborne Boys' School 139
Sierra Leone 156
'signalling effect' of university 32
single-sex schools 45, 67, 91, 187, 195; and gender 109, 115, 117–119, 120, 189; and STEM (science, technology, engineering and maths) subjects 108, 114

Sir John Cass's Foundation 87, 88
SMSC (spiritual, moral, social and cultural education) 102–106
social media 3, 14, 16–18, 19, 41, 80–81, 111, 112, 113, 122, 167, 169, 178; see also digital technology
social mobility 72, 73, 74–75, 82–83, 84, 87–88, 99, 174, 188, 190, 192; see also bursaries; equality
South East of England 44, 50
South West of England 96
SPC (Social media, Pressure, Copycat) 19
special needs 60, 66, 178
Speirs, Russell 145, 146, 159–161
Spence, Joseph 23, 29–31
SpringBoard 72–74, 75–76, 84, 87, 88, 91–92, 190
St Paul's Boys' School 139
St Paul's Girls' School 115
St Paul's School (New Hampshire) 153–154
Stanford University 130, 137
Stannard, Kevin 22, 31–33, 195
state schools 3, 17, 24, 33, 44, 46, 62, 66, 77–79, 80, 84, 175–176; cost per pupil 66, 82, 85; and digital technology 138; gender neutral policies in 115; quality of 44, 47, 85, 171, 173; teachers in 25–26
Steed, Mark 145, 146–147, 161–163
STEER mental well-being tracking process 74
steering 136, 191
STEM (science, technology, engineering and maths) subjects 25, 29, 30, 62; and gender 108, 114
stereotypes 91, 96, 116, 166, 178; about independent schools 166, 178; gender 91, 110–111, 114, 115, 116

Stonewall UK 119
suicide 12, 13, 19, 114, 189
support staff 68, 70, 91
Sutton Trust 26
Swinnerton-Dyer, Peter 32

Tait, Peter 101
taxes 57, 58, 60, 67, 166, 168, 174,
    176–177, 178, 179
Teach Away 160
Teacher Horizons 160
teachers 22, 25–26, 58, 66,
    68, 116, 185; and academic
    challenges 11, 14, 23, 24, 26, 34;
    at boarding schools 45; and
    digital technology 12, 16–17,
    30, 124, 125–126, 128–129,
    138, 163; and the gender
    challenge 108–109, 112–113;
    and innovation 127, 128, 129,
    130, 133, 138; international
    challenges and opportunities
    146–147, 148, 149, 150, 152,
    155, 160, 162, 192; mental
    health of 7, 8; from minority
    ethnic backgrounds 90, 91,
    92, 95, 96–97, 98–99, 100;
    and pastoral challenges 5, 9,
    11, 12, 13, 14, 16–17; pay and
    pensions of 50, 67, 68; subject
    knowledge of 23, 25, 34
Teachers' Pension Scheme 67
technology *see* digital technology
teen pregnancies 11
Thatcher, Margaret 81
The City of London
    Corporation 87
The Royal National Children's
    SpringBoard Foundation *see*
    SpringBoard
Thomas, Ben 38–39, 49–53, 193
Thomas's Academy (Fulham) 51
Thrun, Sebastian 137

The Times 172–173
Timothy, Nick 170–171
Tooley, James 54, 55, 56, 64–66,
    138, 155
Tottenham 73
transgender people 112–116,
    117, 189
transitioning and schools 108–109
Turing, Alan 139
tutoring 14, 37, 41, 47, 48, 52, 168
Twain, Mark 28
Twitter 24, 167, 169

Udacity 137
Uganda 65, 155, 156
UKCAT 142
Understanding by Design 128
UNESCO 151, 162
university 21–22, 23, 31–32, 33–34,
    52, 54–55, 61, 81, 82, 95, 99,
    148, 151, 174, 175; in US 32,
    63, 82–83, 137, 153, 154
Uppingham School 115
US (United States) 2, 12, 56,
    70, 152–154, 183, 191; and
    innovation 127, 130–131,
    133–134, 137; university 32,
    63, 82–83, 137, 153, 154

values 49, 51, 52, 75, 92, 101, 102,
    103–104, 110–111, 148, 152,
    158, 193
Varkey Foundation 162
VAT on fees 67, 176–177
vocational education 31, 76, 172
Voisin, Justine 86–88
VR (virtual reality) 191

Waldorf School (Silicon Valley) 12
Wales 59, 60, 61
Walker, Simon 125, 134–136, 191
Warwick, Ian 23, 33–35, 195
Watson, David 83

wellbeing 5, 7, 8, 9, 10, 14, 22, 42, 46, 111, 124, 194
Wellington College 2, 105, 140, 144
Wellington, Duke of 187
Westminster 76, 144
Weston, Crispin 125, 137–139
Wiggins, Grant 128
Willetts, David 32
Williams, Shirley 81
Willis, Judy 41
Wilshaw, Sir Michael 148
Wilson, Harold 81
Wimbledon High School for Girls 109
Winchester College 165

Windlesham House School 44–45
Winton, Tim 112
wisdom 26–29, 195–196
Wisdom, Norman 59
Wolf, Alison 32
Wolfram, Stephen 138–139
WomenEd 24
Woodgate, David 56, 66–69
World Bank 156
World Leading Schools 159
Wright, Helen 145, 147–149

Yale 154
Yorston, Ian 124–125, 139–142